John Baldock, is an experienced teacher and art historian. His interest in medieval Christian art, its symbolism and mythology, led to the writing of his first book, *The Elements of Christian Symbolism. The Alternative Gospel* is the outcome of a further questioning of our literal understanding of the gospel story, and a personal exploration of what it means to be a human being. He lives in rural Dorset with his partner, three cats, two dogs and a house-trained computer.

by the same author

The Elements of Christian Symbolism
The Little Book of the Bible
The Little Book of Love
The Little Book of Sufi Wisdom
The Little Book of Zen Wisdom

THE
ALTERNATIVE
GOSPEL

The Hidden Teaching of Jesus

JOHN BALDOCK

ELEMENT

Shaftesbury, Dorset • Boston, Massachusetts • Melbourne, Victoria

First published in the UK in 1997 by
Element Books Limited
Shaftesbury, Dorset SP7 8BP

Published in the USA in 1997 by
Element Books, Inc.
160 North Washington St, Boston MA 02114

Published in Australia in 1997 by
Element Books and distributed
by Penguin Books Australia Limited
487 Maroondah Highway, Ringwood,
Victoria 3134

Cover design by Mark Slader
Page design by Roger Lightfoot
Typeset by Footnote Graphics, Warminster, Wilts
Printed and bound in Great Britain by
J. W. Arrowsmiths, Bristol

British Library Cataloguing in Publication
data available

Library of Congress Cataloging in Publication
data available

ISBN 1-86204-165-2

Our life is a faint tracing on the surface of mystery.

Annie Dillard, *Pilgrim at Tinker Creek*

CONTENTS

ILLUSTRATIONS

For Margaret

ACKNOWLEDGEMENTS

The interpretation of the gospel message presented in these pages evolved from a series of illustrated talks given over a number of years in England, Germany, Switzerland and the USA. The two principal themes explored in those talks – the gospel story as an allegory of our own inner life or spiritual journey, and the medieval cathedral as a multi-dimensional model of the Way – were the subject of an earlier book, *The Elements of Christian Symbolism*, published by Element Books in 1990. Since then comments made by audiences and readers alike have confirmed that conventional interpretations of the gospel story are unable to satisfy completely the deep-seated yearning for spiritual understanding and fulfilment currently felt by many in the West. The writing of this alternative, spiritual interpretation of the gospel story has taken several years and I am indebted to the many friends and acquaintances who have provided encouragement, inspiration and support during that time.

I am especially grateful to Maryann Madden for her inspirational guidance, wisdom and profound insights into the nature of human being; to Jutta Carless and Peter Cunz for the constancy of their friendship and for the many fruitful discussions during which the central theme of this book gradually took shape; to Babette Barthelmess for introducing me to the work of Julian Jaynes, for her joyful encouragement over the years, and, together with Helga Ehlert, for the generous support they gave during the early stages of writing; to Mariam Al-Khalil for the timely gift of the computer on which this book was written. I am particularly grateful to Ann Edwards and Rosemary Cox for their supportive encouragement during the latter stages of writing, and to Annabel Lubikowski, Juliet Salaman, Elizabeth Stewart and Brenda Woodward for their comments on the unedited manuscript. I am also grateful to fellow authors Scilla Elworthy and Barry Gardner for their comments, and to the following for the part they each played in bringing this book into being: Nicoli Bailey, Richard Carless, Anne Cunz, Daniel Ellis, Jim Engel, Christa Grasser, Hunter and Mary Ingalls, Ron Lemire, Bruce and Karen Miller, Hajo Noll, Maggie Quinn, Michael and Kathleen Sandrin, Werner Schmidt, Miles and Alima Silverman, Chris and Penny Webster, and Tony Stanton.

I am indebted to Michael Mann, Chairman and Publisher of Element Books, for his friendship and encouragement, and his patience with a sometimes reluctant author; to Paul Cash for his perceptive editorial comments which helped to make this a better book; to Matthew Cory of Element's editorial department for his sensitive handling of both book and author, and to Juliet Standing for her copy editing.

Special thanks are due to Dr Philip Ward-Jackson and Janet Balmforth of the Conway Library at the Courtauld Institute of Art, London, for their assistance with the illustrations of the statues of the Church and Synagogue from Strasbourg Cathedral.

Finally, my heartfelt thanks go to Margaret Irvine for sharing the agonies and ecstasies that seem be an intrinsic part of this particular author's writing process.

INTRODUCTION

Centuries of theological emphasis on the inherent sinfulness of humankind and the total otherness of God have brought us progressive alienation from Nature, from our fellow beings, and from ourselves. Similar emphasis on a literal interpretation of the gospel narratives, with its accompanying concern for the historical Jesus, has diverted our attention from the profound message – the *evangelion*, or 'good news' – that lies at the heart of the gospels.[1]

In seeking to recapture something of the spirit of that original message *The Alternative Gospel* proposes that the 'good news' at the heart of the gospels does not concern itself with whether or not we believe in God. Nor did those who compiled the gospel narratives intend them to be understood as biographical accounts of the life of an historical Jesus. Probably the last thing they intended to do was start a new religion. On the contrary, the gospels were written in response to our apparent lack of the most fundamental self-knowledge – of who we are, where we come from and our purpose in being here. They are a combination of sacred myth and allegorical teaching stories. As such, the characters and events portrayed in the gospels are intended to provide us with timeless insights into human psychology, spirituality, and the profound nature and experience of human *being*. The underlying message is simple. *In essence we are spiritual beings. Our purpose in being here is to become fully human.*

As the word 'myth' is now little more than a synonym for 'fiction' the term 'sacred myth' requires some explanation. Sacred myths are encountered in the founding scriptures of all the great world religions. They present us with two contrasting views of reality simultaneously, portraying as one our outer (human) and inner (spiritual) experience of the mystery we call Life. Generally speaking, the words 'myth' and 'mythical' are used in this book to denote the coexistence of these two levels of meaning – the human or literal, and the spiritual.

Our deeper understanding of the gospels (or any other sacred myths) is governed by our ability to transcend the literal sense of the words so as to discover their intended spiritual meaning. The first part of the book therefore takes us on an exploratory journey into the spiritual dimension and meaning of myth. As well as investigating the possible origins of myth we shall examine the underlying meaning of a number of traditional mythical themes. We shall consider various mythological devices such as personification and the use of events as metaphors for abstract concepts and ideas, or as insights into human nature and the workings of the human psyche. Our exploration will also take us into the oral tradition and the collective wisdom, or *sophia perennis*, that tradition passed on from one generation to the next through the language of myth.

This same collective wisdom lies at the very heart of the Judaeo-Christian myth. But the nature of myth is such that the underlying meaning of a particular myth or mythical theme is frequently lost in transmission through successive generations. Eventually there comes a time when it is understood solely in literal or historical terms – as evidenced in the archaeological quest for Noah's ark, for example, or the belief in the historical fact of the virgin birth of Jesus. It is then extremely difficult to re-mythologize the story, for what was once myth has taken the appearance of fact in the minds of many.

It is easy for us to overlook the fact that the roots of the gospel message are firmly embedded in ancient Hebrew and Jewish myth. In Part Two we shall see how the authors of the gospel narratives wove together a number of traditional mythical themes to extend the Jewish myth so that it encompassed the appearance of the Messiah (the mythical saviour of Israel) on the world stage. Their intention was to demonstrate that the salvation of Israel – and of all people – lies within us. In effect, the particular path our life takes is governed by our relationship with the Source of our being – the universal life-force or Spirit within us – and our openness to its guidance. Like the Hebrew prophets before them, the authors of the gospels advocated a 'new' nondualistic relationship – a 'new' covenant' – based on *direct knowledge of God* or *spiritual consciousness.*

But what was acceptable practice at the time the gospels were first compiled has long since ceased to be so. Since then the good news concerning our innate 'covenant' in the Spirit has tended to be interpreted literally, thereby reinforcing the dualism of our dominant Man-and-God mode of consciousness. Moreover, the continuing quest for a Jesus who is the historical counterpart of the 'Jesus' of the gospels has largely ignored the gospels' mythical dimension. With the passage of time our understanding of the gospels as allegory has been further eclipsed by the propagation of a moral or theological interpretation of their message. As a consequence the message the gospel writers originally sought to convey has become considerably distorted, if not totally obscured. Our potential to regain our original, nondualistic spiritual mode of consciousness is therefore in need of constant restatement.

Ultimately our understanding of the gospels and their message depends on our personal state of consciousness – be it dualistic or nondualistic. Yet however we interpret them, the spiritually inspired nature of the gospels causes them to be a constant and timeless source of revelation. It would therefore be both arrogant and naïve to suggest that the interpretation afforded the gospels in these pages is in any sense the only true or definitive meaning. Beyond definitive interpretation, the subtle nature of the gospel message allows it to be presented in an infinite number of ways, each of which has the potential to awaken us to the knowledge of who we are and our purpose in being here. And the deeper we journey into the gospels the closer we come to that knowledge, for their words constantly offer us fresh insights into the true nature of human *being*. Some of the events the gospel writers describe – for example, the Feeding of the Five Thousand – offer us expansive images of a cosmic process. Others, more intimate, take us into our own inner space enabling us to see ourselves as though in a mirror.

In the course of our exploration of the gospels we shall discover that the anticipated coming of the Messiah, the Son of man, does not refer to the advent in human history of a specific individual who was, is, or will be some kind of 'saviour of humankind'. Like many other mythical biblical expressions, the coming of the Messiah – from the Hebrew *mashiah*, meaning 'Anointed One', the Greek translation of which is *khristos*, from which comes our word 'Christ' – is an allegorical allusion to an 'inner' spiritual experience. It is not the prophecy of an 'outer' historical event. In portraying it as the latter those who compiled the gospel narratives were not simply adding a new dimension to the Jewish myth. They were seeking to reaffirm the inherent nonduality and inter-connectedness of our humanity and our spirituality.

How did they do this? Using a device that had been used many times before to represent invisible forces at work in the universe, the authors of the gospels *personified* the Spirit – the mysterious element, energy, or life-force which is the interconnectedness that permeates all things visible and invisible, and which thus binds the Many inseparably to the One. With the skill of consummate storytellers, they wove this personification together with the myth of the Messiah or Christ and the life of Jesus to such a degree that the three elements – the Spirit, the mythical Messiah/Christ, and the historical Jesus – have become inseparable.

In effect, the authors of the gospels created a powerful new myth in which the central figure of Jesus fulfils the Hebrew/Jewish prophecies about the Messiah. But more significant than this, the gospel narratives of his life – from his miraculous Incarnation to the mystery of his Ascension – provide a powerful allegory for the mysterious workings of the Spirit as well as for the potential spiritual journey, or inner life, of every human being. Indeed, the authors of the gospels wedded together the spiritual and human dimensions of our being so effectively that from the very beginnings of Christian history theologians have argued the degree to which Jesus was/is human and/or divine. The deliberations of the three great councils of the early Church – Nicaea, Ephesus and Chalcedon – demonstrate the extent to which the focus had soon shifted from the nature of the message to the nature of the messenger.[2]

By focusing their attention on the person and nature of Jesus, the influential declarations pronounced by these councils have had the long-term effect of distancing us from the original gospel message concerning our own human/spiritual nature and the mystery of our relationship with what we call 'God' or 'the Divine'. With the passage of time the development of a whole new dualistic man-and-God theology around the expanded figure of a cosmic Christ has obscured the simple message the gospel writers originally sought to convey. In its sheer simplicity that message is of potentially far greater consequence for a universal community of the Spirit than the theological interpretation normally accorded it by the Church.

The empowering message that *in essence* we are all spiritual beings is as meaningful now as it was some two thousand years ago. But such a message was understandably anathema to the religious authorities of the time. Its implicit declaration that the Spirit is the supreme authority and guiding light in human affairs threatened to undermine their powerful hold over the hearts and minds of the people.

Unless we periodically remind ourselves of the true function and nature of myth, our tendency is forever to be turning myth into history and allegory into fact. It is therefore inevitable that the gospel myth would itself be turned into religious history. The emergence of a new religion, which gradually formulated its own doctrine and teachings, was eventually to obscure the truly universal nature of the gospel message. Once again, religious leaders – whom the Jesus of the gospels castigates as 'hypocrites' and 'the blind leading the blind' – assumed a position of power. It was not long before they regained possession of the keys to the kingdom of heaven, and with that control over the hearts and minds of the common people.

But religion is *not* the same as spirituality. As we shall see, the ever-present potential for conflict between religious and spiritual authority is an integral part of the gospel narratives. For those who compiled the gospels this same conflict illustrates the mental chasm that separates human understanding from spiritual consciousness.

In striking contrast to the message of spiritual empowerment the authors of the gospels seek to convey, an unquestioning belief in the literal meaning of the gospel myth is disempowering. Indeed, it has disempowered us to such an extent that we have now handed over responsibility for our lives to a plethora of external 'saviours' in the form of politicians, scientists, religious leaders, employers, doctors, bankers, lawyers, teachers . . . Of course, there is one advantage to be gained from handing over responsibility for our lives in this way: when things appear to go wrong it is these saviours who are conveniently to blame for our misfortune; or we can blame unforeseen circumstances, even the occasional 'act of God', because these things can equally be said to be beyond our control. But there is also a disadvantage in assuming that our lives are ultimately governed by the whims of others, or even by forces alien to us, and that is the profound sense of powerlessness we may experience with regard to our own direction and purpose in life.

The genuine sense of powerlessness experienced by many people today, and the all-too-real suffering that often accompanies it, is partly due to our predominantly dualistic mode of thinking – a mode of thinking that in recent centuries has led us to separate body from mind and soul, matter from spirit, Man from God, God from Reality, and, finally, our spirituality from our humanity. And yet it was through such mythical themes as the Incarnation, Mary's impregnation by the Spirit, the Word made flesh, the Resurrection and Ascension, that the gospel writers sought to reconcile us to our own original spiritual nature. In that context the gospel references to repentance, conversion and rebirth have little to do with the traditional moral or religious connotations of these words. Instead they signify the process referred to variously as spiritual empowerment, transformation, enlightenment or spiritual consciousness – a process that profoundly alters our perception and understanding of life on earth through the harmonious integration of our individual human personality and our eternal spiritual essence.

The process of spiritual empowerment can also be described as the metamorphosis from 'I am' to 'I AM'. It is the transformation of our narrow, egocentric 'this-worldly' experience of life into one in which, through the realization of our original nature as physical manifestations of the life-giving Spirit, we experience life as spiritual beings, beings who are truly 'born of the Spirit'. It is in that context that the authors of the gospels sought to provide us with profound insights into what it really means to be *fully* human. In seeking to remind us that our spirituality is not separate from our humanity and that our spiritual life is not separate from our everyday life, they give voice to the timeless and universal Myth of Being which is the real subject of this book.

PART ONE

THROUGH MYTH TO MEANING

The whole meaning, importance and value of life are determined by the mystery behind it, by an infinity which cannot be rationalised but can only be expressed in myths and symbols.

Nicolas Berdyaeff

1

Myth: A Forgotten Language

A few years ago I attended an Easter Morning service in a small country church in a village not far from my home. When the time came for the priest to deliver his sermon he took his place in the pulpit and immediately declaimed to the congregation words to the effect that the Virgin Birth of Jesus was an historical fact, and that those who dared to question it were guilty of heresy.

The priest's outburst had been provoked by some comments recently made by the then Bishop of Durham, the Right Reverend David Jenkins, concerning the Virgin Birth. Seized upon by the popular press, the Bishop's comments had been widely reported as denying one of the basic tenets of the Christian religion. Yet I am sure that such a denial had been far from the Bishop's mind, and heresy even further. Instead of querying the 'truth' or otherwise of the Virgin Birth, he had been questioning the adequacy of our literal understanding of it. In taking what he had said at face value, both the priest and the popular press seem to have missed the very essence of the point the Bishop was making.

The same issue of understanding had been expressed perhaps less controversially by the anonymous fourteenth-century author of *The Cloud of Unknowing*, who warned: 'Take care not to interpret physically what is intended spiritually, even though material expressions are used . . . The most spiritual thing imaginable, if we are to speak of it at all . . . must always be spoken of in physical words. But what of it? Are we to understand it physically? Indeed not, but spiritually.'[1]

The Cloud of Unknowing dates from a time when it was

possibly easier to understand things spiritually, for the medieval mind enjoyed a perception that was less dualistic than our own. To the people of the Middle Ages the material and spiritual worlds were one. True knowledge and understanding came not from 'the study of things in themselves – the outward forms – but in penetrating to the inner meaning.'[2] The linguistic imagery of the gospel narratives was thus able to impregnate the everyday lives of what was still a predominantly agrarian population with a deeper, spiritual meaning. By contrast, gospel references to sheep and shepherds, fish and fishermen, vineyards and wildernesses, which were initially intended for an audience to whom these things were part of daily life, are far removed from the day-to-day life of the modern Western city dweller. The original gospel message must at times seem equally far removed from everyday reality. Yet for those willing to penetrate the outer form of the words the message is still there.

In fact the distance provided by changes in time and circumstance can be used fruitfully, for it enables us to stand back from the historical context of the events described in the gospels. Their underlying meaning can then be given a revitalized significance more appropriate to our own time and place. And yet, as the incident that opened this chapter demonstrates, we tend to focus our attention on the physical *fact* – the outer form – of the gospel narratives rather than on their inner meaning or message. This message, which concerns itself with human experience – or, rather, with *potential* human experience – transcends the conventional barriers of time and place. Contrary to popular belief, the message at the heart of the gospels is not confined to the domain of religion. Nor is it exclusively Christian, since it was in existence long before the gospels recounting the life of Jesus were compiled.

The essence of this universal message is that we *each* have the capacity to learn and evolve, and to experience for ourselves something of the profound spiritual mystery of what it really means to be a *human being*. Others may act as our role models, or even attempt to mould us as they would wish us to be, but our own individual experience of being human will always be unique.

This learning process is reciprocal because as humankind evolves it too is learning what it means to be human. What each of us learns individually contributes to the learning process of humankind as a whole. What humankind as a whole has learnt in the course of its evolution forms an ever-expanding pool of collective wisdom. Also known as the perennial wisdom, or *sophia perennis*, this collective wisdom is freely available to us all. But as the seemingly never-ending cycle of human suffering and conflict would appear to show, it is ignored by most.

Where is this collective wisdom stored? In the layer of consciousness the psychologist Carl Jung dubbed the *collective unconscious*, from where it emerges to express itself in the allegorical language of myths, symbols, and dreams. As its name implies, the collective unconscious is a layer of universal consciousness. Consisting of patterns of thoughts, memories, and experiences common to all humankind, it exists in each and every one of us conjointly with our layers of individual consciousness – ie our immediate, subjective or *personal consciousness*, and our *personal unconscious*. But due to the unique nature of human experience, the extent to which we are aware of its existence varies from one person to the next.

This collective or perennial wisdom is also the foundation stone of all religious and spiritual traditions, through which it expresses itself in the form of universal truths. Yet whenever a religious tradition focuses on its own truths rather than on the universal truths on which it is founded, that tradition almost invariably ends up transforming its sacred myths into historical fact and its symbols into signs.[3] Instead of remaining a vehicle for the collective wisdom it turns to cultivating its own belief systems and doctrines. In the process the universal truths it once taught end up as little more than a code of moral or social behaviour. But the collective wisdom is passed on in other ways too, most notably by what is commonly known as the oral tradition.

The oral tradition

We live in the age of communications technology. With our phones, fax machines, the Internet, satellite links and information superhighways giving us instant access to an ever-expanding global library of information, it is hard for us to imagine what life must have been like before the advent of the written word, when the only means of passing on information from one person to another was by word of mouth.

In the broadest sense the oral tradition is just that: the passing on of information orally, by the spoken word. More specifically it refers to the art of storytelling from memory, without a written script, but in practice it is more than either of these. The oral tradition is the means by which communal groups transmit their history and their collective wisdom from one generation to the next. In the process the two frequently blend together in the creation of what we now call myths and legends – stories in which the *sophia perennis* has become inseparable from history.

What we generally refer to as 'history' begins with the advent of the written word, the keeping of documentary records and the recording of historical facts. As such it is the antithesis of myth and legend, which are not 'fact' in any historical sense. But what may appear to us to be little more than a product of the human imagination *was* history for our ancestors. In the same way that our own study of history enables us to understand how past events have had a formative influence on the present, so the types of myth known as Creation Myths and Myths of Origin provided our ancestors with an explanation of how their present was inextricably linked to the past. Whereas we interpret the events of history as the end-product of various human social, economic, or political endeavours, they saw them as the unfolding work of an intelligence far greater than their own.

Aided by intuitive insights from the collective wisdom, an active oral tradition narrates 'history' in such a way as to give both form and meaning to the mysterious workings of an intelligent universe. It is thus able to pass on to successive generations a knowledge of the universal laws that give pattern and purpose to human existence. We find an example of this in the Old Testament books of Genesis and Exodus, where we see the two streams of wisdom and 'history' merging to provide succeeding generations of the tribes of Israel with a sense of universal purpose and destiny.

Occasionally the epic 'historical' myths of the oral tradition were broken up into shorter episodes to become pithy teaching stories. In turn, these stories were either inserted into existing myths or joined together to form new ones. This kind of exchange was not restricted by geographical, religious, or linguistic boundaries. The cultural intercourse provided by the movement of people from one country to another for reasons of trade, migration, or invasion afforded ample opportunity for a given myth, or group of myths, to cross from one culture to another.

Myths evolve in other ways too, for the oral tradition is essentially an organic process in which their retelling from one generation to the next plays an important part in their development. As they pass through successive re-tellings they are adapted and moulded to incorporate the additional insights and wisdom gained from an ever-expanding totality of human experience. But when myths take on a more or less definitive form – when, for example, they are either written down or treated as historical fact in the modern sense – they undergo a significant change. The organic process comes to a halt as the myths become fixed in time and space, historically and geographically, as Babylonian, Greek, or Roman. As a consequence, something of their essence, their timeless wisdom and truth is lost.

Something else is lost when a myth is written down – the energy given it by the human voice. If you have ever told a story to a young child, you will know what a difference the voice, the spoken word, can make. If children read a story for themselves, their concentration focuses on reading the words. If the same story is told to them, they are free to respond with their imagination. How many of us, I wonder, have cherished memories of our own childhood when we were transported by tales of magic carpets to make-believe castles in strange lands? Or, hand-in-hand with Peter Pan or the Snowman, flew away through the dark night skies into the world of dreams?

Yes, the spoken word is both magical and powerful. As children we respond to it equally with our emotions and our imagination; when we lose our child-like innocence we tend to respond from our emotions alone. And the power of our emotions can be awesome. Just how awesome can be felt in the emotionally charged atmosphere of a major football game or pop music concert. All the more so when the crowd's emotions are released in a unisonant chant. The emotions of a crowd can also be fed, even manipulated, by a speaker who knows how to exploit emotional energy. We can see this being done at any large political or electoral rally – which poses the incidental question: how many politicians are elected by our emotions rather than for the wisdom of their policies? When it comes to religious emotion, cult leaders, fundamentalist preachers, and televangelists are also formidable exponents. They know how to work their audiences through a whole range of emotions, from fear and guilt to the feel-good factor, tuning them up and playing them with the dexterity of virtuoso violinists. Emotional energy can also be manipulated perniciously, when the power of the spoken word is used to incite an audience to aggressive or violent action. Hitler and Mussolini knew well how to play their audiences, as newsreels of their huge rallies show; and we know what forces their skilfully delivered words unleashed.

In practice the oral tradition has the potential to work with much more subtle levels of energy than the simple power of oratory, and with much deeper levels of human consciousness than our easily manipulable emotions. How effectively it does this depends on the speaker. In tribal and other communities where the oral tradition is strong, this function is delegated to an appointed storyteller, whose role is to learn, retain, and pass on the collective wisdom of the community. The same role can also be assumed by one of the community's elders, or a particular individual who is respected for his or her wisdom.

But the function of the speaker is not simply to tell stories. Through the telling of stories, through using the spoken word, the speaker fulfils his or her true function as the collective voice for his or her intended audience. By putting into physical words the collective wisdom that lies unspoken in the deeper levels of human consciousness, the speaker expresses the inner wisdom we already know, but which we have not yet managed to put into words for ourselves.

Sometimes this process provokes a sense of *déjà entendu*, or a profound feeling of insight and understanding, as though we at last understood something we already knew in our heart of hearts. The process is described in Proverbs, where we are told: 'The words of a whisperer are like delicious morsels; they go down into the inner parts of the body.'[4] A whisperer, or wise speaker, enables the members of his or her audience to listen to and hear the sound of their own inner voice directly, without any interference from the conscious, analytical mind or the emotions. They take us back to our original nature, to that point of innocence within ourselves which is personified in Adam and Eve's state of primal innocence before they were expelled from the Garden of Eden. From there we can both know and experience directly the reality of who we are, before that same self-knowledge becomes veiled from us by the strength of our emotions, our belief systems, and the incessant chatter of thoughts in our subjective conscious mind.

I suggest that it was in this same spirit of self-discovery that the parables and stories that make up the longer gospel narratives were first recounted, and that this is the way in which they are intended to be heard. That this is the case would appear to be borne out by the enigmatic parables about the nature of the kingdom of heaven which find their resolution in the simple statement 'the kingdom of heaven is within you'. What we are looking for lies within us. Or, as spiritual tradition tells us: 'What you are looking for is what is looking.'

Although outwardly the oral tradition appears to bear little relation to modern communications technology, the two do have something in common. Both are in the business of passing on information, or in the case of the oral tradition what is properly called knowledge or wisdom. Yet communication is a two-way process. We now have at our disposal the most sophisticated communications technology ever made available to humankind, but sophisticated technology is no guarantee that we understand what is being communicated to us. The same applies to the collective wisdom passed on by the oral tradition because the reality portrayed in its myths and teaching stories is so very different to the reality we normally perceive through our physical senses.

Myth: Language of the gods?

The most ancient myths present us with an upside-down world in which celestial deities – who frequently exhibit the most basic of human foibles – consort with mere mortals while ordinary humans are transformed into extraordinary heroes and heroines through the acquisition of supernatural powers. It is this enigmatic aspect of myth, this interweaving of the celestial and human realms, which offers us a potential key to a deeper understanding of myth. For the interaction of gods and mortals not only mirrors the way in which we actually 'hear' myths, it also provides us with a clue to the way in which myths possibly first came into being. But when *did* human beings first become aware of the existence of the gods?

One possible explanation is that our early ancestors 'invented' the gods, using them to personify the powerful forces at work in the universe. The reduction of these unseen forces to a form that could be more easily handled by the human mind enabled our ancestors to relate to them in human terms. An additional element seems to have come into play when, at an unspecifiable stage in the course of our evolving experience of the universe, we became aware of its interconnectedness and wholeness. This numinous sense of the underlying unity of all things likewise found its expression through the medium of personification, giving rise in some cultures to the concept of a supreme god or goddess, or, in the case of Middle Eastern culture, to the One God of the three monotheistic religions to which it gave birth: Judaism, Christianity, and Islam.

Somewhere along the line, however, a widespread popular belief in the literal existence of a Supreme Being began to take over from the numinous experience it had originally sought to personify. But more important than how the belief arose in a God made literally 'in the image of Man' – a God referred to as 'He' or 'Father' – is the lasting influence this belief has had on the psychospiritual evolution of the Westernized world. For in spite of the considerable intellectual advances we have made in arts, sciences and technology since European civilization first emerged from the Dark Ages, Western religious beliefs appear to be more firmly rooted in the sort of primitive superstitions that Christianity sought to stamp out than in either the teachings expounded in the gospels or the reality of human experience. We need only call to mind artistic representations of God as a bearded old man on a cloud, or medieval images of Satan and the torments of Hell, to realize the extent to which these extremely fanciful, frequently fearsome, images have become embedded in our collective psyche. So much so that they still seem to hold us in some kind of superstitious thrall.

An alternative explanation for the existence of the gods is put forward by the psychologist Julian Jaynes, who connects the appearance of the gods to our ongoing evolution as human beings. More specifically, he links it with the evolution of language and the development of human consciousness. While space prevents doing justice to the whole of Jaynes' theory on the origin of human consciousness,[5] some aspects of it are extremely relevant to our present exploration of the language of myth. To put them in context, however, we need to make a brief detour to look at significant differences in the way in which the left and right hemispheres of the human brain function, as this forms an essential part of Jaynes' theory.

The right hemisphere processes information in a *synthetic* manner, dealing with objects, ideas, and experiential situations in such a way that it looks at and grasps the whole picture all at once. The left hemisphere, which is more *analytic* and verbal, tends to 'narratize', to think things through in a linear, logical fashion.[6] The latter is the mental activity of which we are normally aware, and which we generally refer to as our *conscious* mind. By comparison, the activity of the right hemisphere generally passes unnoticed and could therefore be said to be part of our *unconscious* or *nonconscious* mind.

Both cerebral hemispheres hear and understand language, but normally it is only the left hemisphere – where the areas of the brain that govern speech and mental function are located – that has the ability to 'speak'. Clinical research has shown that the hearing of hallucinatory voices is linked to the stimulation of an area of the right hemisphere of the brain. Although these mental voices could be said to originate at the point of stimulation on the right hemisphere, they are actually 'spoken' or 'heard' by the auditory areas of the left hemisphere.[7] Commenting on this research, Jaynes adds that 'the important thing about all these stimulation-caused experiences is their *otherness*, their opposition from the self, rather than the self's own actions or own words.'[8]

We now come to the heart of Jaynes' theory, which is the proposition that there was a time when we experienced a different mentality in which auditory hallucinations played a crucial role. Prior to the evolution of consciousness 'human nature was split in two, an executive part called a god, and a follower part called a man. Neither part was conscious.'[9]

Jaynes refers to this nonconscious mentality as the 'bicameral mind', presumably because the functions assumed by its gods and mortals reflect those of the two hemispheres or 'chambers' of the human brain. On the one hand, we have the right hemisphere, the god-side. Its function is one of synthesis, of sizing up problems and organizing action 'according to an ongoing pattern or purpose . . . fitting all the disparate parts together . . . sorting out the experiences of a civilization and fitting them together into a pattern that could "tell" the individual what to do.' On the other hand, we have the left hemisphere where we find man 'in his verbal analytical sanctuary' which dutifully obeys the 'voices of the gods'.[10] The functioning of the left and right hemispheres – our 'man-side' and our 'god-side' – would therefore seem to correspond to the two motivating forces or 'wills' that govern us: the human, and the spiritual or 'divine'.

Describing the gods as 'the most remarkable feature of the evolution of life since the development of *Homo sapiens* himself', Jaynes goes on to say that they were 'in no sense "figments of the imagination" of anyone. They *were* man's volition. They occupied his nervous system, probably his right hemisphere, and from stores of admonitory and preceptive experience, transmuted this experience into articulated speech which then "told" the man what to do.'[11] These hallucinatory 'voices of the gods' provided bicameral beings with a point of certainty on which they could rely in an ever-changing world. But with no clinician's electrode to stimulate the right hemisphere of the brain, what was it that triggered these mental voices that told the individual what to do?

The answer would seem to be the stress caused by any brand-new situation.

> During the eras of the bicameral mind, we may suppose that the stress threshold for hallucinations was much, much lower than in either normal people or schizophrenics today. The only stress necessary was that which occurs when a change of behaviour is necessary because of some novelty in a situation. Anything that could not be dealt with on the basis of habit . . . anything that required any decision at all was sufficient to cause an auditory hallucination.[12]

In the Middle East, which is where we consider the roots of our own civilization to lie, Jaynes dates the decline of the bicameral era and the disappearance of the hallucinatory voices of the gods to the latter part of the second millennium BCE. It was, he suggests, precipitated by a chaotic period in which natural catastrophes, wars, invasions and mass migrations were probably enough to leave even the gods speechless, or to cause the bicameral mind so much stress that it triggered a confusion of voices. This period also saw the development of writing, which inevitably diminished the auditory authority of the gods, and the evolution of consciousness that coincided with the breakdown of the bicameral mind.[13]

Eventually the gods seem to have disappeared completely, withdrawing into their heavens and leaving us to lament their departure. With the demise of the voices of the gods we acquired another voice, the 'I' of subjective consciousness. We were able to ask ourselves what we had done to cause the gods to go away, and in so doing we gave voice for the first time to the now familiar themes of the world's religions: 'Why have the gods left us? Like friends who depart from us, they must be offended. Our misfortunes are our punishments for our offences. We go down on our knees, begging to be forgiven.' Even our redemption is seen to lie 'in some return of the word of a god'.[14]

From these seeds of lament grew the notions of divine judgement and retribution, of human sinfulness and guilt, that have since become an integral part of our collective psyche. They also gave birth to the fearsome concepts of hellfire and eternal damnation, and the belief that at some point in time we will be held to account for our godless state. But are we really godless?

If Julian Jaynes' theory is correct, we only became aware of the existence of the gods *after* they had left us to face the world on our own. At least, it may have appeared at the time as though the gods left us, yet perhaps we can now see that in reality they did not leave us at all. At a particular stage of our evolution we simply stopped hearing their voices. Ever since then, or so it would seem, we have been trying to find our way back to them in an attempt to recapture something of the authoritative wisdom and guidance they once offered us. But with the passing of time the way back to them has become overgrown with all sorts of belief systems setting out who or what the gods – or the One God – are, or are not. So much so that we can see neither the wood for the trees, nor the gods for our concepts of them.

If we go looking for the gods in their heavenly hideaway, we will not find them. They do not exist. They were auditory hallucinations. The paradox is that we may find ourselves. Or rather that part of ourselves which gave birth to the hallucinatory voices, which in turn gave birth to the gods and their myths. Once we find that part we may perhaps begin to understand that myths are not really about gods. They are not *about* anything. They are the *sophia perennis* that was communicated to the 'man-part' of our mind (our left-brain) by the hallucinatory voices of the gods, and when the gods had departed by the wise men and women, the 'whisperers' of the oral tradition.

I suggested earlier that the enigmatic quality of myth, the interaction of the celestial and human realms, was a key to a deeper understanding of myth. When we listen to a myth we hear it with two minds. Our conscious, verbal and analytical mind (our left-brain) hears the physical words, which it processes in a linear fashion, one at a time, as it hears them. Our unconscious, synthesizing mind (our right-brain) hears far more than the physical words. Making its way beyond the literal, allegorical or moral connotations of the myth, it becomes one with the collective wisdom the words seek to express. It then endeavours to communicate this 'wisdom of the gods' to the conscious mind, in the form of insight, understanding and profound self-knowledge.

Parables, teaching stories, and the wisdom of the gods

The process described above also applies to the way we hear the teaching stories of the oral tradition, of which the parables contained in the gospel narratives are an example. The familiar words 'He who has ears, let him hear,' which are frequently used to begin or end a parable, are addressed to our unconscious mind, calling it to order so that it hears what it is intended to hear. If we take this to mean that we should concentrate our efforts on listening to the physical words, we will simply hear the literal meaning rather than the meaning *behind* the words. Jesus refers to our capacity for two levels of hearing when he explains to his disciples why he speaks to the crowds in parables:

> '. . . I speak to them in parables, because seeing they do not see, and hearing they do not hear, nor do they understand. With them indeed is fulfilled the prophecy of Isaiah which says: "You shall indeed hear but never understand, and you shall indeed see but never perceive. For this people's heart has grown dull, and their ears are heavy of hearing, and their eyes they have closed . . ."'[15]

On another occasion he tells his followers:

> 'To you has been given the secret of the kingdom of God, but for those outside everything is in parables . . . Take heed what you hear; the measure you give will be the measure you get, and still more will be given you. For to him who has will more be given; and from him who has not, even what he has will be taken away . . .' With many such parables he spoke *the word* to them, as they were able to hear it; he did not speak to them without a parable, but privately to his own disciples he explained everything.[16]

In the light of what has been said thus far about the workings of the human mind, we can say that Jesus only *appears* to teach in parables. If we hear the meaning we are intended to hear, they are not parables at all. As the first quotation implies, if we are accustomed to hearing solely with our physical ears (our left-brain) as opposed to our inner ears (our right-brain), we lose our innate capacity to understand what is really being communicated to us. This point is expanded upon in the second quotation, where it is revealed that if we are able to hear with our inner ears we will hear more than just the physical words. We will hear *the word*, the collective wisdom, or 'word of God' as it became known following the demise of the hallucinatory voices of the gods. Nevertheless, for some people the parables will always remain as parables, as physical words. For others they will not be parables at all, they will be the unalloyed *sophia perennis*, pure wisdom. The gospel writers spell out this physical words/wisdom duality very clearly:

> All this Jesus said to the crowds in parables; indeed he said nothing to them without a parable. This was to fulfil what was spoken by the prophet Isaiah:
> 'I will open my mouth in parables, I will utter what has been hidden since the foundation of the world.'[17]

Are we to understand from this last sentence that the parables contain a secret or hidden teaching, which, as the earlier quotation implies, Jesus gave to his disciples in private? A secret teaching which, to this day, is reserved for an élite few? I think not. What we have here is a further reminder of our dualistic, left-brain/right-brain understanding. Our left-brain hears the physical words of the parable; our right-brain hears the 'hidden' teaching, which consists of the wisdom *behind* the words. In reality, the parables are simultaneously parables and not parables. It all depends on how we hear them.

Maybe this last point can be illustrated more effectively by referring to a painting by the Belgian surrealist, René Magritte. The painting I have in mind is of an apple, a very realistic apple, underneath which the artist has painted the words '*Ceci n'est pas une pomme*' (This is not an apple.). By presenting us with something that is simultaneously an apple and not an apple Magritte confronts us with a mirror image of our own duality-creating thought processes. It is only when we try to take a bite out

of the painting that the truth of the artist's words is revealed. *This
is not an apple.*

The parables and teaching stories of the oral tradition need to be
approached in a similar way, by taking a metaphorical bite out of
them in order get at the truth *inside* them and thus hear the hidden
wisdom being communicated through the physical words. But is
this wisdom really *hidden*? It would appear not. Nothing is hidden
from us. At least, not if we are prepared to open our ears. 'For
nothing is hid that shall not be made manifest, nor anything secret
that shall not be known and come to light. Take heed then how
you hear . . .'[18]

Ultimately 'hearing' concerns itself with more than the way we
hear and understand the words of parables and teaching stories. It
also applies to our own everyday life – whether we take life at its
face value, for what it appears to be, or endeavour to understand
the profound mystery beneath its surface.

Understanding the mystery of life means more than simply
comprehending it in purely physical or material terms. It means
penetrating life to its very Source, so that we are able both to know
and experience the reality of who we are and where we come from.
This idea is not a new one. It was eloquently expressed well over
two thousand years ago in Proverbs, where true wisdom – that is,
understanding and insight – was perceived to come from the
Source of Life itself:

> The Lord created me [Wisdom] at the beginning of his work,
>   the first of his acts of old.
> Ages ago I was set up,
>   at the first, before the beginning of the earth.
> When there were no depths I was brought forth,
>   when there were no springs abounding with water.
> Before the mountains had been shaped,
>   before the hills, I was brought forth;
> before he had made the earth with its fields,
>   or the first of the dust of the world.
> When he established the heavens, I was there . . . [19]

Furthermore, the perception that wisdom and understanding
emanates from the Source of Life leads to these qualities being
sought after above all else, for they are seen as the key to life itself:

> Wisdom is the principal thing; therefore get wisdom, and whatever
> you get, get insight.[20]

Learn where there is wisdom, where there is strength, where there is understanding, that you may at the same time discern where there is length of days, and life, where there is light for the eyes, and peace.[21]

Wisdom is a fountain of life to him who has it . . . .[22]

A new point of certainty

For bicameral human beings the wisdom spoken by the voices of the gods provided an immutable point of certainty in an ever changing world. When the voices fell silent human folly led us to turn our backs on the ultimate Source of wisdom within ourselves. Our need for a point of certainty was transferred to a literal belief in external gods who gave both meaning and purpose to human life.

If we now look back through time from our current state of subjective consciousness, with its prodigious capacity for introspection, it is virtually inconceivable to us that there could ever have been a time when human beings had no consciousness, no awareness of their awareness of the world. A time when there was no 'I' or 'me'; no 'I' to be conscious of what I was busy doing, to think about it, or to decide what I would do next; no 'I' to talk things over with myself. A time when there was even no 'I' to think about and analyse my thoughts. As far as we are concerned our capacity for conscious thought has now become the new point of certainty in an ever-changing world, our very *raison d'être*, enabling us to affirm with Descartes, *'Je pense, donc je suis'*. 'I think, therefore I am.' Where would we now be *without* thought? Without thought how would we even know we exist?

If Jaynes' theory is correct, our present state of subjective consciousness evolved as a result of the breakdown of the bicameral mind. This breakdown was caused partly by the stress of living in a time of violent change and considerable uncertainty. We are currently passing through a very similar time, and, could we but see it, we are also in the middle of a further developmental stage in the evolution of human consciousness. The trigger of stress is present, not only in the way in which we live our individual lives, but also on the collective human scale. Two world wars and the long-term fear of a third, the outbreaks of genocide, the increase in both violent crime and the violence in our cities, are only the more obvious examples from recent decades of the effects of our inhumanity towards our fellow human beings. The effects of our violence on the natural world, of which we ourselves are an integral part, are also becoming visible, bringing us to a point at which, deep in our collective psyche, we are now questioning our very ability to survive at all. *We have been brought face to face with our own human frailty*, and once again we are looking for a new point of certainty.

It would seem that since the dawn of consciousness the ascendancy of our conscious, analytical mind has gradually pushed our intuitive, synthesizing mind into the shadows, but this particular wheel has almost come full cycle. Our belief in purely external gods – whatever form we have given them – is waning. Once again we are learning to place our trust in our own innate wisdom: the Wisdom or higher intelligence that permeates the entire universe, including ourselves.

A further sign of the continuing evolution of human con- sciousness is the re-emergence of our synthesizing mind from the shadows and our growing awareness of 'wholes' – not only in our increasing realization of the underlying interconnectedness of all things, but even in the endeavours of our conscious, analytical mind to find the ultimate Theory of Everything.

The wheel has also moved forward. Language has evolved and names have changed. The numinous experience that came to be called God is being referred to by different names, both old and new, that reflect more directly the nature of our own numinous experience of the world in which we live: enlightenment, higher or spiritual consciousness, the Light, Spirit, love, peace, and many more. But whatever name we use to refer to it, in essence the experience remains the same. It is the experience of our original undivided nature, the experience of pure *being*.

2

MYTH AND THE ORIGIN
OF LIFE

When our attention becomes focused exclusively on the most obvious aspect of the universe, its physical or material aspect, we lose sight of the meaning and purpose that lie hidden beneath the surface busy-ness of our everyday lives. We also lose contact with that part of our mind where things are perceived in terms of 'wholes' – the god-part – which is the seat of our innate capacity for true wisdom and insight.

This is the situation in which Western civilization as a whole finds itself today. Our extreme materialism, our fascination with our own scientific and technological achievements, and our pre-occupation with the supremacy of analytical and intellectual thought have all served to stultify our ability to use and trust our own intuitive wisdom and understanding. As a result the word 'myth' has itself become an antonym for reality, though myths are neither real nor unreal in any normally accepted sense of these words. For thousands of years they have been a universal language for expressing that which cannot be expressed in any other way. Their seemingly unreal tales of a world or worlds inhabited equally by mortals and immortals may be regarded as a simple but effective device for taking us beyond the seemingly finite world of ordinary everyday reality. In the process myths give form to the wisdom and insights of the collective unconscious which, on emerging into the light of day, become our own inner wisdom reflected in the mirror of our conscious mind.

For our ancestors the myth-makers, the mythical process did not end there. They frequently mythologized actual historical events in order to portray their deeper significance within an ever-expanding totality of human experience. In doing so they not only placed these events firmly within the unfolding design of an intelligent universe, they also created a potential bridge to a higher order of reality. This process has a direct relevance for us in relation to our own lives. Once we begin to understand the workings of mythical language – the language of the collective wisdom – we can begin to use that same understanding to connect with the deeper significance and purpose that lie beneath the apparently mundane events of our everyday lives.

Myth and the creation of the universe

One important cultural function of myths, especially *creation myths*, is that they provide a rich cosmology for the society within which they evolve. At the same time as presenting a coherent explanation for the creation of the universe, they also explain the origins of a particular civilization or culture, thus defining its place within the overall scheme of things. Creation myths are the mythical equivalent of the elusive Theory of Everything, and have much in common with similar theories proposed by philosophers, scientists, and historians. They determine the meaning and purpose of existence in such a way that both the individual and the society as a whole can relate to them with certainty.

It is probably fair to say that we normally understand the phrase the 'creation of the universe' as referring to the initial physical manifestation of the universe, to the moment the universe came into being, the Big Bang, a finite historical event that only happened once, somewhere at the beginning of time. Science and history have tended to treat the creation of the universe in terms of an observable fact, from the point of view of observers of the event, rather than as participants in it. Myth advances a very different account of the origins of the universe.

Broadly speaking, beneath their seemingly fictitious accounts of how the universe came into being, creation myths portray *a continuously-occurring procreative event* – the Creation – in relation to which the physical universe and the chronological sequencing of historical events are merely the most tangible effects. In this respect myth has little to do with the dimension of time as we use it when setting events into the linear framework of history. It concerns itself with the *subjective experiential reality of the Creation*, rather than with the phenomenon of its objective factual reality.

Myths from a range of different cultures express the Creation as being the manifestation of a single cosmic Source, a numen or monad. An obvious symbol for this Source was the Sun, but human experience has combined with insightful imagination to furnish a number of other universal symbols to signify the vitality and inherent unity (or nonduality) of the Creation: the Cosmic Tree, the Cosmic Egg or Womb of Life, the Cosmic Axis, and the Wheel of Life/the Universe. The procreative nature of the Creation has also been represented as the sexual union of a supreme god and goddess, whose intercourse symbolizes the primordial act of love, the intimate coupling of heaven and earth, which is the eternal begetting of the universe.

Other myths associate the Creation with the sacrificial death, sometimes self-inflicted, of a god or goddess, thus combining the idea that there can be no creation without sacrifice – no life without death – with a belief in the essential nonduality of the universe. But like all symbolic representations, the personification of the ever-unfolding, ever-evolving nature of the universe as an act of creative sacrifice is open to misinterpretation. Whereas the idea of 'no life without death' had originally sought to express the *cyclical* demise and renewal, the ever-changing nature of Life itself, it eventually became a *linear* concept with an unnerving ring of finality to it. From being little more than a comma in time, death has become the full stop at the end of it.

However we may attempt to explain it, the Creation would indeed seem to be the ultimate mystery – a mystery which creation myths do *not* attempt to solve. Drawing their imagery from the realms of ordinary, everyday life, creation Myths express the *extra*-ordinary human experience of our participation in this mystery. It is therefore important not to confuse the means they use to express this experience with the experience itself. Our analytical mind can easily be distracted by the outer words of the myths. The purpose of our present exploration is to get behind the words in order to catch a glimpse of what it is the myths are really trying to communicate. In the process what we learn may also provide us with a renewed sense of meaning and purpose in our everyday lives.

The ultimate mystery and our relationship with it have also been expressed in other, more abstract ways, which similarly seek to convey something of the mysterious workings of the universe as well as defining our own place and function within these workings. In many religious and spiritual traditions we find the nonduality of the universe expressed in terms of a single cosmic power, which is both the origin and infinite totality of the universe. Whether we choose to call this totality God, the One, the All or the Absolute, the enigma of this particular mythical cosmogony, or theory of the origins of the universe, is that the causal force manifests itself without in any way compromising its essential nonduality. It simply is what it is, and we are part of it.

Having said that, it seems to be a characteristic of modern Western thinking that the more elaborate the concept or theory we are able to formulate with our conscious mind, the more we feel we have understood. For our Westernized intellect, with its prodigious capacity for formulating complex concepts, it is perhaps something of an insult to suggest that in essence life is simple and that it is we who have made it complicated. The same can be said of the message that lies at the heart of the gospels. In reality, it too is very simple. It is we who have turned it into something complicated by trying to understand it with our conscious, analytical mind.

This last point is illustrated by the biblical myth of the Tower of Babel,[1] in which the tower serves as a powerful metaphor for the complex belief systems we have evolved about God and how to get to him. Built by the 'men of the plains', the tower is intended to have its top 'in the heavens'. But when God sees what they are doing he decides to put an end to their project. The ensuing chaos, in which the people are scattered to the four corners of the earth, parallels our own confusion when our belief systems fail to take us any nearer to God. The essential point of the myth is that it is the belief that we somehow have to *get to* God which is itself the primary cause of our dualistic sense of separation from him.

Belief systems are a poor substitute for the wisdom and understanding that come from within us, from the Source of life itself. As we saw towards the end of the previous chapter, for the writers of Proverbs it is wisdom (Greek: *sophia*), the creative power of God, that gives form and life to the intelligent universe. Our own references to the Universal Mind, or Mind of God, are themselves echoes of this same tradition, transformed to reflect our preoccupation with the human mind and the seemingly infinite power of thought. Similarly, the metaphors we use, such as 'a thought in the Mind of God' and 'cosmic consciousness', are our attempts to describe our own profound experience of life from the inside, looking out, rather than from the outside, looking in.

For our ancestors, the use of expressions like 'the Will', 'the Presence', or 'the Spirit' of God was their way of conveying to others the numinous experience of what they felt to be the life-force of the Creation, alive and living within the physical human body. In that sense, perhaps they even felt that the physical words they used to express this experience *were* the self-expression of God, the One, the All or the Absolute – quite literally, they were 'the word of God'.

The 'good news' of this numinous experience – the experience of being one with the infinite totality of the All, of being *fully* human, of pure *being* – was passed on to other generations, first through the oral tradition, and later the scriptures. It became the very heart of the collective wisdom, the *sophia perennis*. In its narrative form it gave rise to the sacred myths of the various religious and spiritual traditions – myths that present us with two realities simultaneously, portraying as one our outer and inner experience of the mystery we call Life.

Myth and the source of life

In the beginning God created the heavens and the earth. The earth was without form and void, and darkness was upon the face of the deep; and the Spirit of God was moving over the face of the waters. And God said, 'Let there be light'; and there was light . . . [2]

So begins the biblical creation Myth. The universal mythical vocabulary we frequently encounter in other mythological traditions is present here in the primaeval formlessness of matter (the Void), and in the primordial 'waters of the deep' (the Womb of Life), out of which all things emerge, as well as in the apparent dualism of darkness and light, and 'the heavens and the earth'. Also present is the idea of a Creator and a creative act (the Creation), brought about by a creative force (the Spirit).

Another version of the biblical myth of the Creation, the second in Genesis, takes us into the minds of our ancestors to see how they perceived the numinous origins of human life. The description of the first human being formed, moulded from the dust of the ground and given the gift of life by the Breath or Spirit of God introduces the notion of our own seemingly dual nature – part-matter, part-spirit; part-earthly, part-heavenly. The play on words of the original Hebrew – by which 'man' or 'Adam', *adham*, is formed from the 'dust of the ground', *adhamah* – is missed in translation.

> In the day that the Lord God made the earth and the heavens, when no plant of the field was yet in the earth and no herb of the field had yet sprung up – for the Lord God had not caused it to rain upon the earth, and there was no man to till the ground; but a flood went up from the earth and watered the whole face of the ground – then the Lord God formed man of dust from the ground, and breathed into his nostrils the breath of life [the Spirit]; and man became a living being.[3]

The passage also mentions an all-important third constituent of our human form. The flood that wells 'up from the earth' to dampen the dust of the ground expresses the traditional mythical idea of the 'waters under the earth'. These waters, which are related to the primordial Chaos from which all life emerges, represent the initial formlessness of existence as well as the ever-changing nature of the manifest world, which is itself the flux and flow of the Creation.[4] In depicting the creation of human beings from a combination of these three elements – unformed 'potential' or formlessness (water), physical matter or form (dust), and an ethereal life-force (the Breath or Spirit) – the writer describes what is commonly perceived to be the essential triunity of the Creation. The appearance here of this fundamental Law of Three, which is common to many ancient mythical traditions, reveals that we too have a triple nature by which we are part-unformed, part-formed, part-beyond form. Our triple nature is also reflected in current idiom as *mind-body-spirit*, and the mysterious way in which these three aspects of our being interact with each other is part of our potential experience of being fully human.

The idea that we are formed, moulded out of physical matter by a Creator/God is reiterated later on by Isaiah and Jeremiah. Inspired by an observation from everyday life – the potter at his wheel – the verbal image contains the same elements of earth and water used in the creation of Adam. Although water is not mentioned by name in the following quotations, it is an all-important ingredient in the potter's art; it keeps the clay moist and pliable, thereby assisting the potter to mould the clay into the form of pot he or she has in mind.

> O Lord, thou art our Father; we are the clay, and thou art our potter; and we all are the work of thy hand.[5]

> The word of God said to Jeremiah, 'Arise and go down to the potter's house, and there I will let you hear my words.' So I went down to the potter's house, and there he was working at his wheel. And the vessel he was making of clay was spoiled in the potter's hand, and he reworked it into another vessel, as it seemed good to the potter to do.
>
> Then the word of the Lord came to me: 'O house of Israel, can I not do with you as this potter has done?' says the Lord 'Behold, like the clay in the potter's hand, so are you in my hand . . .'[6]

Whilst these references to the potter and the clay provide us with an image of the human form being mysteriously moulded by a divine hand, this same image has a strong element of dualism in its implication that we are moulded from the outside. Seeing the creation of our human form through different eyes, the author of Psalm 139 depicts the process as taking place from the inside – the 'inward parts' – from an 'unformed substance', even before our manifestation as physical form. As the psalm reveals, we cannot separate ourselves from the creative power of the Spirit. Whatever we do, wherever we go, the Spirit is there within us.

> Whither shall I go from thy Spirit?
>   Or whither shall I flee from thy presence?
> If I ascend to heaven, thou art there!
>   If I make my bed in Sheol,* thou art there!
> If I take the wings of the morning
>   and dwell in the uttermost parts of the sea,
> even there thy hand shall lead me . . .

> For thou didst form my inward parts,
>   thou didst knit me together in my mother's womb . . .
> Thou knowest me right well;
>   my frame was not hidden from thee,

---

* *Sheol*, the Pit or underworld, synonymous with Hell

when I was being made in secret,
    intricately wrought in the depths of the earth.
Thy eyes beheld my unformed substance;
    in thy book were written, every one of them,
the days that were formed for me,
    when as yet there was none of them.[7]

Whereas the last three lines may be understood as meaning that our lives follow a predetermined course, I suggest that they refer to our *potential* path through life. Like our essential spiritual nature, the existence of this potential path is there for us to realize – in both senses of the word – for ourselves, first by becoming aware of it, and then by making it a reality.

The way in which we go about this is what really determines the course of our lives, because there is the ever-present probability that our personality will wish to follow a different path from that of our spiritual essence. When this happens our spiritual essence will endeavour to communicate to our conscious mind the wisdom and insights we need in order for us to regain our true path in life. This wisdom is generally communicated in one of two ways – either internally, through thought, words, images, or dreams; or externally, through the apparently mundane events of our daily lives, the oral tradition, sacred texts, wise men or women, or spiritual teachers and advisors. Yet the dominant nature of our subjective conscious mind is such that it frequently prevents us from understanding the insights we are given.

The fact that our egocentric 'I' may even close our mind to the more profound aspects of our being is a recurring theme in the sacred texts of the world's religions, including both the Old and New Testaments. In the Old Testament our numinous relationship with the One Reality is frequently expressed in terms of a covenant, or bond, between God and man – itself a reminder of our original nondual nature – which we in our ignorance are forever breaking. The call to listen to the wisdom emanating from our spiritual essence is generally expressed as a call for us to turn to God, or to return to the way of the Lord. But as the following passage from Deuteronomy reveals, this is no purely external God.

The commandment which I command you this day is not too hard for you, neither is it far off. It is not in heaven, that you should say, 'Who will go up for us to heaven, and bring it to us, that we may hear it and do it?' Neither is it beyond the sea, that you should say,

'Who will go over the sea for us, and bring it to us, that we may hear it and do it?' But the word is very near you; it is in your mouth and in your heart, so that you can do it.[8]

The idea implied here, that the Will of God seeks to accomplish itself through our human will, can also be understood as the self-expression of our essence, as the need for our original spiritual nature to express itself through our acquired physical nature. This does not necessarily mean that we have to become 'religious', for it applies to all human beings. It is simply a call for us to turn inwards, into our 'innermost parts', to the Source of Life within the deeper recesses of our being. In doing so we may realize who we are, where we come from and where we are going. As we are reminded in the New Testament: 'Do you not know that your body is a temple of the Holy Spirit within you . . . ?'[9] Or again: 'The kingdom of God is within you.'[10]

When taken together, these two quotations provide us with a verbal image of our spiritual nature – an ethereal realm within a physical body – which finds its visual equivalent in the imposing Gothic cathedrals and churches of northern Europe. Built during the twelfth and thirteenth centuries, these edifices were inspired by what has come to be known as the 'Gothic spirit', a deep-seated desire to see through the outer reality of the material world to the ethereal world that lies both within and beyond it.

From the outside the sheer scale of these buildings, with their soaring towers and spires, presents us with a feat of architecture and human engineering that rarely fails to impress. The real purpose of the building remains a mystery until we venture inside.

Although the entrance to many Gothic cathedrals and churches may be indicated by an impressive doorway surrounded with richly sculpted decoration, the door through which we enter is often quite small. Once across the threshold, if the original stained glass is still intact, we will probably be struck simultaneously by the dimness of the interior and by the brilliant colours of the glass. As our eyes rapidly become accustomed to the change in the quality of light – from the clear light of the world outside to the more mystical light inside – the inner space with its soaring vault becomes more visible, as do other, less immediately obvious details of the interior. Yet when seen from the exterior this same glass that provides the mystical light and intense colours appears to be opaque. Only when seen from the inside does it reveal itself to be what it is – light and colour. It is the same with the mystery of our own inner life – once we are able to see through the apparent opaqueness of our physical body as well as what we refer to, glibly, as the 'real world': a world in which we seldom delve deeply enough under the surface to encounter the mystery of the Life beneath it.

The Gothic Age passed into history, and the generations that followed set their eyes on other things. As a consequence much of the stained glass of the medieval churches and cathedrals was removed to lighten the interior. The style of architecture changed, too, with a return to the classical forms of Rome and Greece, as the human mind turned to reason and order for its inspiration. It was about this time that Western civilization lost touch with its mythical heritage as the world of medieval thought, which had been inspired by the spiritual perception of a divinely ordered cosmos, gave way to the more humanistic philosophies and politics of the Renaissance. Since then the view of the Creation as the continual outpouring of the Spirit or as the eternally recurring *descent* of God into the material universe has gradually been replaced by the notion of a progressive historical and evolutionary *ascent* of man – an ascent that is felt to be the product of human rather than universal or divine intelligence.

This fundamental change in perception has resulted in a prolonged and divisive dispute that has set religion at odds with the world of science as to which of the two – religion or science – exercises ultimate authority over matters relating to the nature of the universe, as well as over the minds and souls of the beings who inhabit it. The Renaissance Church's initial response to what it saw as a threat to its divinely-ordained authority was unequivocal. Those who pronounced ideas that did not accord with its doctrine and teachings were threatened with excommunication or condemned for heresy. Amongst the most immediate results of this zealous defence were the Church's opposition to Copernicus' sun-centred cosmology, the burning at the stake of Giordano Bruno, and the trial of Galileo by the Inquisition. More recent centuries have seen the acrimonious debates of Creationists and Evolutionists at each others' throats.

Meanwhile, and perhaps as a consequence of its mutually-agreed divorce from religion, Western science evolved a perception of the universe that became increasingly opposed to the notion of a creative life-force, the Spirit. Instead it explained the universe in terms of a vast machine in which the component parts functioned according to a series of complex but logical mechanistic laws. These despiritualized laws, which were also applied to human beings, provided a concept of the universe that lacked the sense of mystery that had been a hallmark of the mythical tradition.

3

THE JOURNEY OF A LIFETIME

There has recently been a vogue for colourful 3D posters and books. Maybe you know the ones I mean. From a distance they look as though they are little more than a printed pattern of small, brightly-coloured shapes. But if you hold the pattern up to your nose and then slowly move it away from you, there comes a point at which a coherent three-dimensional image emerges. Some people are able to see the image within seconds. For others it takes a bit longer. Yet others have a problem to see the image-within-the-image at all. The knack lies in looking *beyond* the pattern printed on the surface of the paper, and then, quite suddenly, there emerges, say, a rose, a plane, or an animal. The difficulty lies in focusing the eyes beyond the pattern in the first place.

Like those 3D images, our own life presents us simultaneously with more than one potential image of reality. The difficulty lies in focusing our attention beyond the rich pattern of life's surface. And yet, when we are able to do so, a different reality emerges, although what that reality is remains a mystery until the moment we actually see it. No one else can tell us what it will be like, for life is a process of self-realization, of self-discovery. If we knew what we would find in advance of the realization, the element of *self-* would be removed from the discovery, and along with that the all-important moment of true self-recognition that marks a turning point in our lives.

The mythical journey

The lives of many mythical heroes are often narrated in the form of a journey, itself a metaphor for life. Whilst the form a particular hero's journey may take will vary in its details from one myth to another, broadly speaking there is an underlying pattern common to most heroic myths. The hero is often of humble origins or, unbeknown to himself, of noble birth, having been whisked magically away from his parents or sent away for his own protection to be raised by a humble family. The hero's childhood is often spent learning the skills that will serve him well later in life, or which may at some stage be the cause of his undoing. When he finally sets off into the world he either goes at the request of a ruler, to complete a particular task that has thwarted many before him, or leaves of his own accord in search of a prize, to right a wrong, or to rescue someone from an unpleasant predicament – the proverbial 'damsel in distress'. The quest often ends with him returning home to be reunited with his family, or, as a result of the successful completion of his mission, to win the hand in marriage of a beautiful princess.

In the course of his journey the hero is faced with a number of tests, or rites of passage, each of which has to be accomplished successfully in order for him to proceed to the next stage on the journey towards his goal. The nature and number of the tests again varies from myth to myth. Broadly speaking, they fall into one of three categories. The first entails the overpowering of a 'guardian' – a determined opponent, such as a giant, a demon, a dragon or other fabulous monster – in order for the hero to attain his goal. The second kind of test seeks to hinder the hero's progress by luring or tricking him away from his path. The third kind frequently involves a trial or initiation by water, necessitating the perilous crossing of a river or sea, or a life-death struggle with deep-sea monsters or other malevolent guardians of the deep.

At times it may seem that the world is working against the hero; but in his greatest moments of need an unexpected helper often appears in the guise of a vision, the voice of a god, a wise old man or woman, or an animal or bird. At other times the hero may be in such despair that he fears he will never complete his journey. And then, just as he is on the point of abandoning his quest, he is given fresh encouragement and strength by a reminder of his distant goal. Once again his destination draws him on, and in the final realization of his objective his destiny is fulfilled.

The testing journey of a mythical hero to fulfil his destiny symbolizes the process by which he emerges from the mythical formlessness of the primordial waters, the Womb of Life. The successful overcoming of the obstructive forces that would seek to constrain or detain him as he journeys towards his goal expresses the process of self-realization – a process by which the unformed potential to be a hero is given form, thus manifesting itself as a reality.

Physiologically, this process is much the same as an acorn realizing its potential to become an oak, or a fertilized egg to become a chicken, a fish, or a human being. However, where human beings are concerned, both as individuals and collectively, an additional, psychospiritual process is involved – *the process by which we may become fully human*. With this last point in mind, we can perhaps see the mythical journey as an analogy for our own struggle to be fully human rather than merely existing in the simplest physical, mental, and emotional terms.

The mythical journey is also an allegory for our own spiritual evolution, our inner journey, in which the various trials and initiations that shape the hero express the profound experience of human life as a process of spiritual expansion and integration; a process of being moulded, formed, externally and internally simultaneously, by the combined energies of our outer circumstances and the life-force or Spirit within us. As our spiritual essence expands outwards from our innermost depths, we may experience a change in our perception of ourselves and the world around us. This is because our personal consciousness itself expands as it becomes integrated with the Source of our being. We may even experience at a conscious level the reality of who and what we are – from the inside out, so to speak – rather than simply seeing the image of ourselves that is reflected back to us by our material situation, our thoughts, and our emotions. The latter is our own 'self-image', and *our self-image is perhaps the greatest obstacle facing our unformed spiritual potential*. It is this same self-image that confronts Narcissus as he gazes adoringly at his own reflection in a pool of water.

The myth of Narcissus

The myth of Narcissus is instantly recognizable as myth, so we have little inclination to try to place it in an historical context by looking for the pool by which Narcissus sat.[1] Like many other myths, it serves as a Myth of Origin by providing a charming folkloric explanation for the origin of the narcissus flower. But the myth is now perhaps most commonly cited as a moral tale to illustrate the perils of personal vanity. It has given us the word 'narcissism' – the act of self-worship, of loving oneself, or of loving the image one has of oneself – which, as the myth itself cautions us, can have disastrous consequences for the narcissist.

At another level the myth of Narcissus is much more than a simple moral tale about superficial human vanity. It expresses the profound dilemma that faces us all, for the image Narcissus sees reflected on the surface of the water represents that part of ourselves that we can most readily perceive – our sense of 'me' which arises from the amalgamated experience of 'my' body, 'my' emotions, and 'my' thoughts. Together these constitute our self-image, our self-centred, or egocentric, sense of self – a self that is the centre of its own little universe.

The water in which Narcissus sees the reflection with which he falls in love is of key importance. The fact that water, like breath, is essential for life has resulted in it becoming a universal symbol for life itself. In the present myth the reflection on its surface connects it with the mirror – a symbol for the human *psyche*, the mind or soul – while the image reflected in the mirror represents the same ambivalent relationship between image and reality that we find in Magritte's painting of an apple. From our point of view, there is no doubt as to whose image is reflected on the surface of the water. From Narcissus' viewpoint, there is no doubt either. The image he sees is no illusion. It is *real*. And the reality he sees is the nymph who lives in the pool. The myth also reveals to us the reason why Narcissus falls in love with his own image, but as he himself is unaware of the machinations of the gods, his blindness – both to his predicament and the circumstances that have brought it about – is complete.

A further dimension is added when we consider that from the earliest times a person's name was equated with his or her personal character or destiny – either the name fitted the *persona* the individual had already taken on, or it provided him or her with one *in potentia* for them to grow into. The same tradition appears in the language of myth. The Greek name *Narkissos* is derived from *narkē*, meaning 'numbness', from which come the English words 'narcosis' and 'narcotic'. The origin of the word 'narcissus' is normally associated with the narcotic properties attributed to the plant of the same name. But in naming the youth in the myth 'Narcissus' perhaps the myth-makers sought to personify a state of mind – analogous to one induced by drugs – in which illusion is mistaken for reality. If Narcissus had risked everything by plunging into the water to grasp the object of his devotion, he would perhaps have shattered his self-image and awoken to the binding power of its spell. He would have found himself *in* the mystery beneath the surface. But instead of finding himself Narcissus remains firmly rooted in his world of illusion. Wasting away, he metamorphoses into the flower whose name he bears.

In the same way that Narcissus has eyes only for the image on the surface of the water, our subjective conscious mind sees only what is visible on the surface of life, unaware of the profound depth of the mystery that lies concealed beneath it. In this sense, our surface-only consciousness – our self-image – creates a barrier that separates our outer world from our inner world, our personality from our essence, and ultimately our soul from the infinite spiritual Ground of our being. But this barrier is simply an illusion. In reality there is no separation between our inner and outer worlds.

The gradual diminution of this illusory barrier is allegorized in the various trials and initiations experienced by the hero in the course of the mythical journey, with the successful completion of each trial representing a lessening of the distance that separates us from the deeper levels of our being. As the barrier is progressively eroded our personality becomes increasingly integrated with its spiritual essence, and our microcosmic 'little me' or 'I am' becomes more and more conscious of the macrocosmic 'universal I' or 'I AM' of the One Reality.

Awakening to Reality

At a literal level words such as 'die' and 'dead' refer to physical death. In the language of myth they become ambivalent, simultaneously having several layers of meaning, of which one or more can be applied at the same time. For instance, the seeming physical death of Narcissus is a metamorphosis – a complete change from one mode of existence to another – rather than the full stop at the end of life we normally associate with physical death. In another sense, Narcissus is already dead as he sits looking at his image in the pool of water, for in his torpid state he has no real life in him. 'Death' and 'dying' are also synonyms for the rebirth, the renewal of life, or the transition from one level of experience and perception to another, which comes with the death of illusion and an awakening to the true nature of the One Reality. In the latter sense, death can further signify the fundamental change of perception, or change of mind, that marks the integration of the conscious mind with the deeper levels of consciousness.

In the original Greek of the gospels this awakening to Reality is expressed by the word *metanoia*, which is usually translated by the words 'repentance' or 'conversion'. Because of the close association of these two words with the word 'sin' we generally understand repentance and conversion as marking a change in our moral behaviour, or a superficial change in our everyday ways. In a religious context we even say that someone has converted to this or that religion. Yet such interpretations overlook the deeper implications of these words. Instead of the narrow, moralistic interpretation we normally allow it, the word 'sin' means 'missing the mark' or 'stumbling' *vis-à-vis* our real purpose in life. Likewise, *metanoia* refers to the inner conversion which is concomitant with the integration of our spiritual essence and our human personality, and the realization of our true nature as spiritual beings.

In the latter context *metanoia* can also be described as a process by which we are transformed, refined, or even perfected, by our spiritual essence. As St Paul encourages us to believe, the profound change of mind/perception that comes with *metanoia* is something to be sought after: 'Do not be conformed to this world but be transformed by the renewal of your mind, that you may prove what is the good and acceptable and perfect will of God.'[2] When *metanoia* takes place we are no longer enslaved by the power of our illusory self-image, nor by the surface glamour of the world outside us. Liberated from the worldly whims and desires of our egocentric 'I', our life takes on a new sense of purpose. We become vehicles for our spiritual essence and are open to experience the profound freedom referred to in some spiritual traditions as *the freedom of no-choice.*

The mystical language of religious and spiritual tradition also expresses the numinous nature of *metanoia* as the death of the ego, as the union of the human with the divine, or as 'a transformation of one's whole being; from human thinking to divine understanding . . . and the birth of a "new man"'.[3] The same theme is reiterated by St Paul when he urges us to 'put off your old nature which belongs to your former manner of life . . . and be renewed in the spirit of your minds, and put on the new nature, created after the likeness of God.'[4] At its most profound, *metanoia* can therefore be equated with the experience of knowing and being known by God, because, with the integration of our inner and outer worlds, we experience at a conscious level our inherent unity with the rest of the Creation and with the Source of Life that gives us *being.*

On the other hand, the conscious or even unconscious denial of this same unity draws a veil between us and our original nature, seemingly separating our personality from our essence, and ourselves from the One Reality. It is this sense of separation that gives rise to division and discord, and to the apparently independent existence of the ego-centred personality we call *free will.* Once established, our egocentric 'I' understandably has no wish to see itself die the numinous 'death' that is the price of spiritual integration, union, or rebirth. Perhaps here we have touched on the nub of the mythical predicament of Narcissus: he epitomizes the individual human personality, which, through a misinterpretation of its own free will, cannot see beyond the beauty of its own unique manifestation.

Dante's four levels of meaning and understanding

A misinterpretation of free will can arise in much the same way as the misinterpretation of physical words – that is to say, by understanding both free will and physical words to be ends in themselves. To do so is to ignore our human capacity for understanding: a capacity that extends from the level of the conscious mind to that of inner understanding and insight. So at this juncture it is worth referring to a traditional scheme of meaning and understanding that was advocated by, among others, Dante and St Bonaventure.

According to Dante's scheme there are four principal senses, or levels of meaning, by which books can be understood: the *literal*, the *allegorical*, the *moral*, and the *anagogical*. The literal sense always comes first, because it contains the rest. Without it, it would be impossible to understand the others – not even the allegorical – because with everything that has an inside and an outside, it is impossible to get at the inside unless we have first got at the outside.[5] However, as Dorothy L Sayers points out in the Introduction to her translation of Dante's *The Divine Comedy*, 'the literal meaning is the least important part of it.' Although what she goes on to say concerns itself primarily with Dante's masterpiece, her comments apply equally to the narratives contained in the Old and New Testaments: 'the story with its images is only there for the sake of the truth which it symbolizes, and the real environment within which all the events take place is the human soul.'[6]

The four levels of meaning can be summarized as follows:

1 *Literal* – this is the shell, the outer level, at which the words are understood at their face value, as a record of simple fact or instruction.
2 *Allegorical* – each element of the text is understood as standing for something else.
3 *Moral* – the text can be understood in a way that is relevant to our own lives.
4 *Anagogical* – this is the kernel, the innermost or spiritual level, where understanding becomes direct perception.

The same criteria Dante proposed for books can equally be applied to any other sphere where symbolism and allegory are used – for example, dreams, art and religion. The *literal* level is relatively straightforward. It is the outer form – the physical words, the dream imagery, the iconography of a painting or sculpture, the sacred books and ritual of religion – that must be understood first. If we are unable to understand the physical words, if the dream imagery is blurred, if the subject of a painting or sculpture is unclear, or if we have not read the sacred books or participated in the ritual of religion, then we cannot really say we have begun to understand any of these things at the literal level.

Where our present examples are concerned, at the *allegorical* level we become aware that literature, dreams, art and religion have *meaning*, that there is more to them than first meets the eye. This awareness may come from an external source, such as another person, a book, or a radio or television programme, or it may be something that we sense for ourselves. We understand that the words in front of us, the painting at which we are looking, the events and people seen in our dreams, or the actions performed in religious ritual, all have an underlying meaning. Whilst appearing outwardly to be one thing, we understand them as meaning something else. We may also become aware that these things can have more than one definable meaning, thus enabling them to be interpreted according to a wide range of differing points of view.

At the *moral* level, we may identify with the characters in the book we are reading because they mirror our own thoughts, emotions, or situation. The symbolic images of our dreams perhaps take on a further dimension of meaning as we learn that they provide us with insights into the deeper recesses of our own consciousness. Alternatively, we may empathize freely with a painting or sculpture, or find that the scriptures and ritual of religion give us an increased understanding of the meaning and purpose of our lives.

Finally we come to the *anagogical* level, which can best be described as the end of meaning, because meaning is no longer consciously looked for. Meaning simply *is* – everywhere, and in everything. Instead of looking for meaning, meaning makes itself known, and meaning and understanding become one in a manner similar to that evoked by the following words of the poet and mystic, William Blake. If we are able to put ourselves in the mind of Blake and contemplate his words from within, we may perhaps pass beyond their literal meaning to the images and feelings they inspire in us, thus sharing something of the poet's direct perception of a universe filled with infinite meaning:

> To see a World in a Grain of Sand,
> And a Heaven in a Wild Flower,
> Hold Infinity in the palm of your hand,
> And Eternity in an hour.[7]

Dante's four levels of meaning and understanding can also be seen from another perspective, as levels of understanding that progressively deepen as our perception of ourselves – and the world in which we live – evolves and expands, until our opinions and beliefs about the meaning of things give way to the true understanding that comes with inner wisdom and insight. In that respect, the four levels are not separate from each other. Nor can any one of them be said to be 'better' than any other, because they are all simultaneously present in such a way that each one gives form or meaning to the others.

We can also apply these four levels to the 'book' of our own life in order to understand what we ourselves are writing. In this context, the deepening levels of understanding are analogous to the stages of our progressive awakening to the reality of the mystery beneath the surface of our everyday lives. A more concrete illustration of this process is provided by one of the best known parables from the gospel narratives.

The parable of the Prodigal Son

The parable of the Prodigal Son[8] has a clarity of narrative that renders it less enigmatic than many other parables, with the theme of the young man's journey out into the world and his eventual return home offering us a biblical parallel for the traditional heroic mythical journey. But the similarities seem to end there. Instead of a noble hero, a Ulysses or a Lancelot, who performs courageous feats in the course of fulfilling his destiny, the parable presents us with a seemingly ignominious antihero whose name we do not even know.

There once was a man who had two sons. One day the younger of the two asked his father to give him what would one day rightfully be his, and so the father duly divided his fortune between the two sons. A few days later, the younger son gathered together all his possessions and travelled to a distant country, where he frittered away his inheritance on loose living.

When the son had finally spent all that he had, the country was hit by a disastrous famine, and so, being in great need, the son sought work among the inhabitants of this far-off land. He was sent out into the fields to feed the pigs, and would gladly have eaten the husks on which they were fed because nobody gave him any food for himself.

Eventually, the son came to his senses, acknowledging to himself that even his father's servants had more than enough to eat, whereas he was starving in this distant country. He decided to return home and tell his father that he had sinned before him and heaven, and that, as he was no longer worthy to be called a son, he should be treated as one of the servants.

Having made his decision, the son set off for home. He was still some way off when his father saw him in the distance, and ran to greet him, embracing him warmly. The son confessed to his father that he had sinned before him and heaven, and was therefore no longer worthy to be called his son. But the father instructed his servants to dress his son in the best robe and to prepare a feast to celebrate his homecoming, telling them that his long-lost son had been found – the son he had thought to be dead was alive.

The apparent simplicity of the parable's storyline and subject matter offers us an opportunity to explore three of the four levels of meaning outlined above. (Because of the experiential nature of direct perception, the fourth or anagogical level cannot be illustrated in the same way.) At the literal level we understand the parable simply as it is, as the story of a young man who leaves home to travel out into the world. Having spent all his money, he falls on hard times and returns home where he is welcomed by his father with open arms. Overjoyed at seeing again the son he had thought was dead, the father fêtes his return with a lavish celebration.

At the allegorical level the parable is traditionally understood as an illustration of the love of God, the heavenly Father – a love that extends even to those who, seduced by this-worldly pleasures, forsake Him for a life of sin. According to this traditional interpretation of the parable, turning away from God leads to a period of suffering that continues until the sinner repents, and returns to God asking humbly to be forgiven. As the repentant sinner draws close to God, he finds God drawing close to him in loving forgiveness.

At the moral level, where the parable is understood within the context of our own lives, a similarly traditional interpretation explains that the prodigal son's journey to a distant land represents the distance we have somehow placed between us and God – either by not believing in Him, or, if we do believe in God, by following our own will or way in life rather than the Will or Way of God. As a consequence we remain 'in a distant country' until such time as we do something to reverse the situation. But the question then arises, who or what do we mean by the word 'God'? Furthermore, how do we 'turn' to Him?

For the majority of Westerners, God has become synonymous with institutionalized religion. As a result, the story of the prodigal son is generally both explained and understood solely within that context, with the return home of the wayward son being seen as a turning to God within the institution of religion, as a conversion to Christianity – or, perhaps more precisely, as becoming an active member of the Christian Church. But, following on from what has been said so far in this book, I suggest that the parable is intended to be understood in a much wider context, as an allegorical model for our own psychospiritual journey through life.

When interpreted in this way the parable provides us with a revealing portrait of ourselves. It not only depicts our original spiritual nature and our frustrated search outside ourselves for that which lies within us. It also portrays the potential integration of the outer and inner worlds through the realization of our inherent union with the Spirit. As such, the various elements of the parable – from the father to the husks fed to the pigs – symbolize different aspects of our own psychospiritual evolution.

The son's departure from home epitomizes the beginning of our own journey out into the world as we travel away from the father who personifies the Source, the Infinite Ground, of our being. The inheritance with which we leave home is this life, and, by setting out into the world, we submit ourselves to the equivalent of the trials and initiations that mark the hero's rites of passage. Distracted by material, this-worldly things, we gradually turn our back on our original nature, on our spiritual essence or 'innermost parts', until we eventually perceive ourselves as being *of* the world, rather than merely being *in* it. Metaphorically speaking, we travel to 'a distant country', where we fritter away our inheritance on 'loose living'.

The ambivalent words 'loose living' are a reminder of the moralistic terminology used in the Bible to refer to our relationship with God. Emphasizing the belief in a permanent bond, or union, between God and man, the Old Testament frequently refers to God as our 'husband'. So the prophets' constant castigation of adulterers and harlots is essentially metaphorical, aimed at those who are unfaithful – ie, those who lack faith. While retaining something of this older tradition the gospel narratives also introduce the idea of the Spirit as the bridegroom, thereby indicating a shift in emphasis to the *potential* nature of our union with God, which is no longer seen as an automatic right but as something for which we need to prepare ourselves. The words 'loose living' are therefore intended to convey our potential for an 'adulterous relationship' with the outer world in contrast to seeking the 'true marriage' with the Source of our being. By the same token, the gospels' many references to sinners and prostitutes, adultery and fornication, as well as phrases such as 'this adulterous generation', 'this sinful generation', and 'the woman taken in adultery', are intended to be understood in a very different context to the moral or sexual one we normally allow them. They refer to those of us who, whether intentionally or not, ignore our true spiritual nature and, so to speak, 'marry the world'.

When life is lived solely in the context of our outer relationship with the world, our being suffers spiritual starvation – a state that we find expressed in the disastrous famine that hits the country when the younger son has frittered away his inheritance. The lack of appropriate spiritual food and the inability of the outer world to satisfy our deep inner yearning is further illustrated by the son contemplating eating the husks on which the pigs are fed, as well as by the fact that he is given no 'food for himself'.

Eventually our own sense of spiritual deprivation may become so intense that, disenchanted and disillusioned by our this-worldly mode of existence, we turn back to the Source of our being. Experiencing the change of mind referred to earlier as *metanoia*, we 'come to our senses' and our life undergoes a profound change of direction. Where we had previously believed that fulfilment was to be found solely in the outer world, we now seek it within. Acknowledging our 'sin' – that we had been 'missing the mark' *vis-à-vis* our true path in life – we make the decision to return home. In other words, we turn to the spiritual Source within us. Our decision brings about a rapid transition from a state of spiritual impoverishment to one in which, spiritually speaking, we 'bear fruit'. But the turning of the human personality inward, towards its spiritual essence, is simply our human perception of what is, in reality, the reverse – a process by which our spiritual essence expands to a point at which it integrates fully with our personality. The two sides of this process are illustrated by the reunion of the son with the father, which signifies the union, or 'marriage', of our outer and inner worlds, of our human personality and spiritual essence.

In its function as a teaching story, the parable illustrates that the goal or purpose of our own journey through life is very much closer to us than we think it is. The celebratory feast given in honour of the younger son, who, having been spiritually dead is now alive, is similarly intended to convey the joy we experience at our own homecoming. The second part of the parable, in which we meet the elder son, offers us further insights into our potential evolutionary journey through life.

> When the elder son, who had been working in the fields, came home, he heard the sound of music and dancing, and asked one of the servants what was happening. On being told that his father had ordered a feast to celebrate the return of his younger brother, he became angry, and refused to go into the house.
>
> The father came out and pleaded with his son to come inside, but in reply the latter complained that he had served his father faithfully for many years, obeying his every command, but had never been given the wherewithal to celebrate with his friends. And yet his brother, who had spent his father's money on loose living, was given a great feast in his honour.
>
> 'My son,' said the father, 'you are always with me, and everything I have is yours. It is fitting for us to make merry and celebrate, for your brother was dead, and now is alive. He who was lost, has been found.'

What is it that angers the elder son so much about his brother's return? The cause would appear to be his jealousy over the feast given in his brother's honour, but I suggest his anger is used as a device to illustrate something else more subtle – spiritual materialism. Materialism of this kind manifests itself outwardly every time we feel superior – spiritually, religiously, morally, or physically – towards our fellow beings. In doing so we deny the fact that, whilst each of us is a unique human being, we are all equal in essence.

At a more subtle level, spiritual materialism is a denial of the essential nonduality of existence. From a spiritual perspective, there is no 'higher' or 'lower'. In wishing to place ourselves 'higher' where neither 'high' nor 'low' exists, all we do is reveal our spiritual immaturity and lack of wisdom. We find this particular theme illustrated elsewhere in the gospels when the disciples James and John, the sons of Zebedee, ask to sit next to Jesus in the kingdom of heaven, one at his right hand, the other at his left – a request that is greeted with the response, 'You do not know what you are asking.'[9]

Yet ask we must. As the elder son demonstrates, unless we ask we cannot receive. He felt that he had been a faithful son in staying at home and obeying his father's every command, and yet he had been given nothing – even though, according to the parable, he was offered everything. The paradox is that if we are unable to receive, we cannot be given.

A comparison between the two sons has something else to teach us about ourselves: our journey out into the world is an essential part of our spiritual evolution. It is a journey of profound self-discovery which provides us with the challenges and opportunities, the trials and initiations, that may eventually bring us face to face with who we really are.

How we approach our journey through life and what we learn from it is, however, entirely up to us. Like the 3D images described at the beginning of this chapter, it is up to us to try to see beyond life's rich pattern in order to discover for ourselves the mystery beneath the surface. As we are told in the gospels: 'Ask, and it will be given you; seek, and you will find; knock, and it will be opened to you. For every one who asks receives, and he who seeks finds, and to him who knocks it will be opened.'[10]

4

SEPARATION, REJECTION AND SUFFERING

Like other sayings attributed to Jesus by the gospel writers, the words from the Sermon on the Mount that brought the previous chapter to a close had their origins in the oral tradition. Even though these sayings have now been translated into languages more modern than their original Hebrew or Aramaic, or the common Greek *koine* with which they were first written down, they still retain something of their initial power. That is because the collective wisdom to which they give voice goes straight down into our innermost parts – to our heart, or soul – from where, through 'hearing' the words with our inner ears, we may receive valuable insights into the nature of human *being*.

Our experience of life in the 'real world', however, is very different from the view of life expressed in the myths and teaching stories of the oral tradition. So much so that, unless we can bridge the apparent gulf between the two by hearing what is behind the physical words, the collective wisdom and insights they have to offer us will continue to go unheeded. So, too, will our own inner wisdom and its potential to guide us along our true path through life. In forging a link between these seemingly disparate lives – the outer and the inner – further exploration of the parable of the Prodigal Son provides us with a glimpse of the symbiotic relationship between the two.

The preceding chapter proposed that the parable presents the prodigal son as an antihero, a figure who lacks the noble qualities and virtues associated with the traditional hero. Instead of facing stalwart opponents in life-or-death struggles, or completing various initiatory rites of passage in order to fulfil a pre-ordained quest, the prodigal son appears simply to take his inheritance and travel aimlessly out into the world.

We share something of the prodigal son's anti-heroism in that our own journey through life begins in a similar way. Once we have made our initial entry into the world, we *appear* to have no obvious aim or purpose to our lives. It is as though these things are left for us to provide for ourselves, discovering what they are bit by bit, through a process of trial and error. Once this journey of a lifetime has begun, where it takes us to is determined by the decisions and choices we make *en route*. Although outside circumstances may sometimes seem to dictate the path we follow, it is ultimately we who set our own direction and goals in life. Understandably, we tend to begin in what appears to be the most immediate and obvious place – the physical or material world. As long as we stay happy with what we find there, and with what we are able to achieve – however great or small – our journey remains relatively easy. For we have a simple and unquestioning faith in ourselves and the world in which we live.

The Edenic state of innocence just described provides us with an alternative understanding of the inheritance with which we come into the world – namely, it is in our original nature to be content with who we are and what we have. But once our developing ego begins to feel that this particular inheritance is inadequate for its needs we start to have doubts. We begin to question, to compare who we are and what we have with others, and to want *more*. To want more is to wish for things to be other than they are, thereby creating a situation in which we no longer feel that we are enough in ourselves. It could be said that we have frittered away the inherent happiness and harmony that stem from simply having faith in ourselves and the world in which we live. When this initial inheritance is all spent we tend to look outside ourselves for what we once found inside. In doing so, we begin to experience the different stages of psychospiritual famine illustrated in the parable of the Prodigal Son. In our case we experience these stages as various states of separation, rejection, and suffering.

Separation parallels our apparent separation from the Source of our being. It is allegorized both in the son's setting out into the world and in his finding himself in a distant country, far from home without any means of support. Although this state gives rise to the other two, generally speaking it is the last to be recognized.

Rejection describes what we experience when our material, mental, emotional, or spiritual needs remain unfulfilled, or when we feel a sense of inadequacy because neither we, nor our efforts, receive sufficient recognition. This state is embodied in the son's being sent out into the fields to feed the pigs while nobody gives him any food for himself.

Suffering can be described as the combined effect of the two others. *Suffering arises from the profound deprivation that occurs when we lose touch with our inner resources at the same time as feeling rejected by, or in conflict with, the outer world.* The precise way in which we experience this suffering will differ from one person to the next, affecting one or more of the mental, emotional, or spiritual dimensions of our being. We may even feel its effects physically, because the interdependence of the different dimensions, or levels, of our being means that a dysfunction at one level has the potential to affect others. This state of spiritual famine is represented by the prodigal son's deprivation, far from home with no money and no food for himself. The extreme nature of his deprivation would have been obvious to the parable's original Jewish audience. Not only were pigs regarded as unclean animals, they were also a forbidden food, and yet the son came to a point where he was prepared even to eat the husks they were given to eat. Like the prodigal son, however, the suffering caused by the situation in which we find ourselves may precipitate our seeking to regain the harmonious state of being, the wholeness, which is rightly ours. It is these different aspects of our journey through life in the 'real world' that we shall go on to explore in this present chapter.

Separation

The term *separation* describes that state of being in which our perception of life is dominated by the same dualistic mode of thinking that has led us to divide the One Reality into ever smaller, ever more precisely-defined parts, rather than by that aspect of our mind which sees things in terms of 'wholes'. In a dualistic state our conscious mind focuses its attention on the unrelated nature of things, on the separateness of both objects and events, thus setting itself at odds with our innate sense of their interconnectedness and wholeness. Our dualism also leads us to perceive life as a fundamental *conflict of opposites* – of God/Devil, good/evil, love/hate, friend/foe, positive/negative, male/female. We extend this conflict to all spheres of our existence, peppering our everyday language with the vocabulary of conflict by using words such as 'fight', 'battle', 'struggle', 'overcome', to describe anything from the most mundane activity to personal relationships, the spheres of politics, science, and religion, and even to the world of abstract ideas.

A further effect of our dualistic mode of thinking is the development of our sense of a separate self – our egocentric 'I'. This not only leads us to experience life in terms of 'me' and 'the-world-outside-me', it can also result in an acute sense of isolation, in spite of being surrounded by family and friends, or in the feeling that the circumstances of life are somehow conspiring against us. No longer feeling harmoniously at one with the flow of Life *as it is*, we become like strangers in a strange land. Metaphorically speaking, we have driven ourselves into exile, and the only way to return home is to retrace our footsteps to the Source from whence we came in order to learn who we are and where we have come from. But where or what is 'home'?

Home is the One Reality, the Ultimate Mystery, God, the One, the All, the Absolute – or whatever else we like to call it – which can perhaps be described as a *nondualistic, Self-revealing, Self-knowing state of being.* There is nothing outside itself to see it or know it; not even ourselves, because it is within it that 'we live and move and have our being'.[1] But whilst we may be unable to distance ourselves physically or spiritually from the One Reality, we have done so mentally through our attempts to describe our numinous relationship with it in the only way we know how – that is, from an all-too-human point of view. We have personified the One Reality as a living being – the Supreme Being, in whose image we are made – thus enabling us to experience our bond with the macrocosmic I AM in terms of a profoundly human and personal relationship.

The process of personification has also left us with a profound dilemma. By reducing what is ultimately beyond the comprehension of human reason to the level of a seemingly finite entity, we have placed it within the realm of logical, analytical thought. From there it can readily be posited whether such a Supreme Being – which we in the Christianized West have named 'God' – actually exists or not. However, such argument, which generally seems to hinge around whether or not we believe in the existence of God, would appear to be specious in the extreme, for it is tantamount to arguing about the *fact* of our own existence. By reducing the One Reality to the petty dimensions of a concept that can either be accepted or denied we have also further reinforced our sense of psychospiritual separation and exile. In the process we have placed ourselves in the position of commentators on, rather than active participants in, the numinous experience that marks our true homecoming.

Ultimately, the only way to heal our sense of separation is to change our predominantly dualistic mind-set, for the wedge that separates our humanity from our spirituality, and ourselves from the One Reality, only exists in our mind. Until such time as we do undergo a profound change of mind and awaken to the reality of our true spiritual nature, we remain in a state of separation, which although self-generated is experienced as a sense of rejection.

Rejection

If we momentarily consider the birth of a child as being a rejection or expulsion from the womb and a separation from its mother, then we have a very useful analogy for our own psychospiritual experience of coming into the world. With the latter, it is our *apparent* separation from the Womb of Life that leaves us with a deep-seated sense of rejection, which is further reinforced by our outward inability to bond with the spiritual Source of our being in the way that a newly born child bonds with its physical mother.

The antidote for separation and rejection is love. Parental love thus forms an integral part of a child's nurturing, for it carries with it the qualities of acceptance and approval that provide the infant-child with a sense of security, a sense of *belonging*, in an otherwise new and unfamiliar environment. Yet the need to be loved does not end when we leave our childhood behind us. It remains with us as we progress from infancy through adolescence to young adulthood and on into maturity and the later years of our lives.

As most of us will have learnt through the trial and error of our own experience, human love tends to have conditions attached to it. Both the quantity and quality in which it is given are often used as an instrument of control, either as part of a system of reward and punishment, or as a means of manipulating others in order to get what we want out of a particular situation. Alternatively, when love is not forthcoming or goes unreciprocated, the resultant feeling of rejection can lead us to believe that we are in some way unworthy of love and approval, which in turn may precipitate a feeling of inadequacy, a feeling that we are not enough in ourselves. Paradoxically, our impression of outward rejection is often an echo of our inability to bond with the spiritual Source of our being, as well as of the psychospiritual sense of rejection that stems from an apparent breakdown in our relationship with the One Reality.

The moment when our inherent sense of oneness with the One Reality breaks down is captured evocatively in the myth of the Fall. The mythical eating of the fruit of the 'tree of the knowledge of good and evil' that causes the expulsion of Adam and Eve from the Garden of Eden can be understood as an allegory for the onset of our dualistic mode of thinking, as well as the sense of separateness and opposition brought about by this particular mode of thought. In a similarly allegorical vein, the warning given to Adam that 'in the day that you eat of it you shall die'[2] refers to a spiritual rather than physical death, for in spiritual terminology we 'die' when we either forget, or fail to acknowledge, the essential nonduality of our relationship with the spiritual Source of our being.

As spiritual beings we are *never* separated from, nor are we rejected by, the Source of our being. Both infinite and eternal, the Source does not move. It is we, or rather our minds, that move *within* it, and our feelings of separation or rejection from the One Reality arise in part from a fervent belief in our personal impermanence and mortality. In other words, our belief in the finality of physical death amounts to a rejection of our true nature as spiritual beings.

The gospel writers sought to rectify the belief that death is final by combining the life and teachings of Jesus with a personification that embodies both the spiritual dimension of our being and the Spirit itself. They illustrate the mystery of the latter's eternal nature through the cycle of events we know as the Incarnation, Death, Resurrection, Ascension, and Second Coming. At the same time, through the persecution and rejection of Jesus, the gospel writers offer us a powerful allegory for our own rejection of both our original spiritual nature and our inherent oneness with the Spirit.

The gospel narratives reveal that this rejection ranges from a simple lack of awareness to conscious denial. Popular understanding has tended to interpret these allegories either at a literal or historical level, or in such a way that they relate exclusively to the Jesus of Church doctrine, rather than to the more universal context for which they were originally intended. Recalling the eulogies to Wisdom in Proverbs[3], the Gospel of John opens with a hymn to the Word – (Greek: *logos*) the organizing principle of the universe, the Mind or Thought of God – which refers to our lack of awareness of the true Source of our being:

> The true light that enlightens every man was coming into the world. He was in the world, and the world was made through him, *yet the world knew him not.* He came to his own home, and *his own people received him not.*[4]

A similar lack of receptivity to the eternal presence of the Word/Spirit in the physical world, as well as our inability to hear the 'good news' telling us of it, is conveyed in the following words of Jesus from the Gospel of Mark:

> 'A prophet is not without honour, except in his own country, and among his own kin, and in his own house.' And he could do no mighty work there, except that he laid his hands upon a few sick people and healed them. And he marvelled because of their unbelief.[5]

At a literal level we may take these words to signify the lack of recognition given to the historical Jesus by the people of Nazareth. But at another level these same words apply to ourselves, to our own lack of recognition of the spiritual dimension of our being, and to our inability to hear our own 'prophet' – our inner voice – seeking to make itself and the spiritual core of our being known to us at the level of the conscious mind. When we do become aware of the fuller implications of our spiritual nature, we can perhaps begin to work consciously towards the eventual integration of our human personality and spiritual essence. As our exploration of the myth of Narcissus showed, the process of integration is not always easy, for it is also a process of self-discovery which necessitates the abandonment of our illusory self-image so that the reality it obscures may be revealed.

Suffering

Discarding the illusion of who we think we are in order to be who we really are is a potentially painful process. The physical reality of our mental, emotional, or psychospiritual suffering can be so intense that at times it may feel as though our very being is disintegrating. Yet in one sense the reverse is happening. Instead of *dis*-integrating we are being healed, made into *whole* beings. Our suffering is actually the *re*-integration of our personality and our essence. It is the marriage of the two halves of our split mind, the *re*-union of our divided self, the bonding together of our outer and inner worlds. As such, our suffering is the equivalent of the mythical hero's initiatory rites of passage. It is the process by which we are moulded by our spiritual essence in the same way that the clay is shaped by the potter. In a very real sense, if we knew *why* we suffered, we would not suffer, for the real cause of our suffering is the resistance we offer, at one level or another of our being, to this process of transformation. At the collective level we appear to have lost touch with our original spiritual nature to such an extent that we tend to attribute our emotional and mental stresses, our addictions, dysfunctions, and illnesses to the pressure of living in our modern world rather than to any deeper psychospiritual condition.

By way of contrast, the Hebrew prophets attributed the suffering and misfortunes of the Israelites to the 'wrath of God' punishing them for their sinful ways. But then such threats of divine retribution were perhaps deemed appropriate over two thousand years ago, at a time when the author of Proverbs could assert that the fear of God was considered to be the beginning of knowledge and wisdom.[6] According to the same source, the 'love of God' was also considered to be a cause of suffering, for the seeker of wisdom was encouraged not to despise 'the Lord's discipline or be weary of his reproof, for the Lord reproves him whom he loves, as a father the son in whom he delights'.[7]

In spite of these and many other biblical assertions to the contrary, the ancient notion that suffering is somehow inextricably linked to sin and punishment still predominates in Western religion and in the Western mind. For instance, the myth of the Fall has become the cornerstone of the Church's doctrine of Original Sin, according to which *all* human beings are born alienated from God as a result of what is held to be Adam's rebellion against Him. Reinforced by the teaching that we are permanently subject to some kind of external divine judgement, as well as by the Church's zealous wielding of threats of divine retribution and eternal damnation, one of the long-term effects of the religious emphasis on the inherently sinful nature of human-kind has been the alienation of a large proportion of the population from religion and, consequently, from the collective wisdom at the heart of the gospels.

Whatever the initial theological reasoning behind the doctrine of Original Sin may have been, the deep-seated feelings of guilt and fear it has instilled in the minds of many have strengthened rather than diminished the barrier that separates us from the knowledge – *the good news* – that in essence we are all spiritual beings. The same barrier has been further strengthened by the tendency for religious speakers to present their congregations with a literal, moralistic and fatalistic interpretation of the Fall. Such interpretations draw support from biblical quotations similar to those from the writings of St Paul, which assert 'the wages of sin is death'[8] or 'sin came into the world through one man and death through sin, and so death spread to all men because all men sinned'.[9] When presented in this way, sin is understood solely within a moral context, rather than in the spiritual context of missing the mark *vis-à-vis* our true nature and purpose. As a result, the gospels' references to the word 'death' are assumed to mean physical death, not the metaphorical death that denotes a lack of awareness of the spiritual dimension of our being.

Here we encounter a further contributory cause of our suffering, for a literal interpretation of biblical references to death has reinforced our natural human fear of dying. Yet in the same passages from which come the above quotations Paul also draws our attention to the underlying concern of the gospel message, which is that we all have the potential to live the 'new life of the Spirit',[10] an 'eternal life' which is 'the free gift of God'.[11]

For a different, perhaps more explicit, view of these same themes we can turn to the Far East and Taoist thought:

> The idea of everlasting life has nothing to do with hankering after life. The truth is that actually there is no death. How can there be no death? Because actually there is only one single energy, one all-encompassing motivating force which lies at the root of our life's activity . . .[12]

The Taoist author's reference to 'one single energy, one all-encompassing motivating force' provides us with a description of the Spirit that corresponds closely to the understanding of an increasing number of Westerners, in particular those who have had experience of one or more of the many healing professions whose methods of treatment seek to harmonize the flow of the body's natural energy, or life-force. From the psychospiritual point of view too, when we are no longer in harmony with the stream of life-force or Spirit flowing through us, we suffer. In the allegorical language of the gospel narratives, we become lame, blind, deaf, asleep or even dead, and in order to be healed, to be made whole again, we need to turn to the life-force or Spirit within us.

When I suggested earlier that the gospel writers combined the life of Jesus with a personification of the Spirit, this 'one single energy, one all-encompassing motivating force' which is the Source of our being was what I had in mind. In the present context I would further suggest that the gospel accounts of miraculous healings performed by Jesus were intended to provide us with a timeless allegory illustrating the healing power of the Spirit at work at an inner psychospiritual level. In effect, the turning to Jesus for healing by those who are lame, blind, deaf, dumb or dying, is essentially an allegorical device. In reality they illustrate the process of turning to the Spirit within ourselves in order to be made whole, or given new life, by becoming reunited with the Source of our being.

So far we have encountered two possible ways in which we can respond to our dilemma of living in a world where separation, rejection and suffering, appear to be unavoidable aspects of the human condition. In the case of the prodigal son, his suffering becomes so intense that he reaches a point where he responds to his plight by turning inwards, toward the spiritual Source of his being for healing. In the case of Narcissus, his own blindness to the real cause of his pool-side dilemma is such that he does not respond at all.

Of the two, we tend to choose the response of Narcissus – although it has to be added that this choice is normally not one that we make at a conscious level. Like Narcissus, we unconsciously turn a blind eye to our dilemma, thereby remaining in a state of blissful ignorance that immures us from both our suffering and its cause. At least, we *appear* to turn a blind eye to our predicament. In reality we are in a situation very similar to that presented by the 3D images described earlier. Unable to see beyond the complex pattern of our superficial self-image, we are unaware of the profound mystery lying beneath the surface, waiting to reveal itself. Instead, *our deep-seated sense of separation has led us to create our own version of reality, based upon the wants and desires as well as the opinions and prejudices of our egocentric 'I'.* The alternative response – embodied in the prodigal son – is for us to drop our self-image and with an open mind endeavour to see reality quite simply, *as it is.*

Like so many other things in life, however, the dropping of our egocentric 'I' or self-image appears easier said than done. Our belief that it requires some kind of super-human leap of faith into the void may leave us with a very real sense of fear. And yet there is actually nothing to fear. As Dhiravamsa says: 'If you are free from the "I", what is there to suffer? Who can suffer? Suffering will be unable to arise and at the same time there is nobody to suffer.'[13]

Healing

The allegorical nature of the suffering portrayed in the gospels is perhaps easier to comprehend if we examine one of the accounts of Jesus' healings in detail. The miraculous healing of the Gerasene demoniac,[14] also known as the miracle of the Gadarene Swine, appears in the three synoptic gospels,[15] following immediately on from the miraculous Calming of the Sea. As with many other events related in more than one gospel, the different narratives vary considerably in their detail. (How or why the differences between the gospel narratives came about is open to debate, as are the precise dating and authorship of the gospels themselves.) As a timeless teaching story the healing of the Gerasene Demoniac concerns itself with the intense suffering we can sometimes experience as human beings, and the fact that our suffering can be healed.

The following version of the story has been adapted from the accounts given in Mark and Luke.

After Jesus had calmed the storm, the boat carrying him and the disciples came to the other side of the Sea of Galilee, to the land of the Gadarenes. As soon as he [Jesus] had landed, a naked man possessed by demons came out of the cemetery, where he lived among the tombs. The man had been chained up many times, but he had wrenched his chains apart, and it was no longer possible to restrain him. Night and day he roamed among the tombs or on the mountainside, crying out and gashing himself with stones.

Having seen Jesus in the distance the man ran to him and prostrated himself at his feet. Crying out in a loud voice, he asked Jesus what he wanted of him, pleading with him not to be tormented, for Jesus had ordered the spirit to leave him. When Jesus asked the man his name, he replied, 'My name is Legion,' for he was possessed by many demons. And the demons begged Jesus not to send them into the Abyss.* As there was a large herd of pigs feeding on the nearby mountainside, the demons asked Jesus to let them take possession of the pigs. He gave them leave to do so, and the demons came out of the man and entered the pigs, and the whole herd – which was about two thousand strong – rushed down the steep slope and into the sea, where they drowned.

When the herdsmen saw what had happened, they ran off and told their story throughout the neighbouring towns and country, and a great crowd of people came to see what had happened for themselves. They found the man clothed and in his right mind, sitting at the feet of Jesus. Those who had witnessed what had taken place told them how the man possessed by demons had been healed. Greatly disturbed by what they heard, the crowd of local Gadarene people asked Jesus to leave them, and so he returned to his boat and prepared to leave. The man who had been healed begged to be allowed to go with Jesus, but Jesus sent him on his way, telling him to go home and tell everyone what God had done for him.

Before going on to explore any underlying significance this incident may have, we need first to examine the symbolic imagery of the narrative, which, in the opening paragraph, conveys the extent of the demoniac's suffering. On the one hand the narrative presents us with a distinctly dark side: the darkness of night; the cemetery and tombs, with their direct association with death; the demons, which conjure up the mental picture of a tormented soul; the man bound by chains, and the stones with which he gashes himself. On the other are a number of symbols associated with enlightenment or spiritual freedom: the light of day; the open mountainside, which here suggests a higher plane of existence, for the mountain is a traditional symbol for the meeting-point of the

---

* *Abyss*, the bottomless pit, synonymous with Hell.

human and spiritual worlds; the man, naked and unbound, who has the ability to roam freely, as he wills.

Taken together these strongly contrasting elements can be understood as an allegory for the man's inner turmoil, which results from his being pulled in opposing directions by his inner and outer worlds. The extent of his torment is further illustrated by the legion of demons possessing him. But this portrayal of one man's torment, of one man's state of simultaneous psychophysical and psychospiritual distress, also offers us an image of our own individual and collective suffering as we struggle to become fully human.

To understand the story in this way we need to listen to it with our inner as well as our physical ears. With our physical ears we hear the narrative at a literal level, as an incident that happened almost two thousand years ago, somewhere on the shores of the Sea of Galilee. With our inner ears we may hear it in a very different way, for we potentially recognize the story and each of its elements as pertaining directly to ourselves.

The emergence of the naked man from the cemetery when he catches a distant glimpse of the figure of Jesus – which coincides with Jesus telling 'the spirit' to leave the man – represents our own emergence from the realm of the spiritually dead in response to a prompting of the Spirit within us. The man's prostration at the feet of Jesus signifies a further stage of our response – a profound inner turning towards the spiritual Source of our being in order to be healed, to be made whole, and become *fully* human. But new wine needs new bottles. The 'new life of the Spirit' cannot begin until we have finished with the old life and been freed from the many demons that possess us, and which – like the stones with which the man gashes himself – cause us harm.

Although the precise nature of these demons will vary for each of us, they symbolize whatever it is that obstructs our process of spiritual evolution – arrogance, fear, guilt, greed, resentment, anger, a sense of worthlessness or of inadequacy. Metaphorically speaking, the demons are also the false gods to which we consciously or unconsciously dedicate our lives – power, money, material possessions, our opinions and belief systems, our self-image, etc. The demons can also be equated with the chains that bound the man, for our attachment to our own demons or false gods becomes binding, thus inhibiting our spiritual freedom. It is not until the demons come out of the man and take possession of the herd of pigs, causing their destruction, that we witness the full extent of the man's torment. Similarly, it is only when we have been freed from our own metaphorical demons and false gods that we are able to appreciate for ourselves the hold they once had over us and the degree of suffering they have probably caused us.

After the miracle, the herdsmen rush off to spread the good news of what they have seen, and a large crowd of people gathers to see for themselves what had happened. On reaching the scene, they see the man who had previously run amok sitting quietly and eye-witnesses tell them how he had been healed. But, having both seen and heard, why is the crowd disturbed? And why do they ask Jesus to go away? Here, as elsewhere in the gospel narratives, 'the crowd' embodies our this-worldly reaction to the Spirit, which is one of rejection, or dismissal. This can also be our own potential response when we too are 'called' by the Spirit within us. Like the prophet, the Spirit is not welcome in its own country (the world), among its own people (the collective human race), or in its own house (the individual human being), for once we acknowledge its presence and hear its word, we have no choice but to respond – and responding involves the disturbing process of dying to who we think we are.

As for the man who was healed, why was his request to go with Jesus turned down? Was it really so that he would go home and tell everyone what God had done for him? Translating that in a way that might apply to ourselves, we could say that once we have been healed we have already returned home, for the man's encounter with Jesus/the Spirit represents our transformation, enlightenment, or spiritual rebirth, and the completion of a particular stage of our journey through life. Reunited with the Source of our being, we no longer need to follow the Spirit outwardly because it is alive within us. Open to its guidance, we are following it anyway. In the same way that *hearing* is used as a metaphor for spiritual understanding or insight, perhaps the instruction to the man to go and 'tell everyone what God had done for him' is also intended to be understood metaphorically: as an instruction to lead an outer life that is governed by inner wisdom, and to act with spiritual understanding and insight in our dealings with both the world and our fellow beings.

A final point to mention here is that the transformative process known as enlightenment or spiritual rebirth does not make us any more special than our fellow beings, for our life and our work remain in this world. As the Zen saying goes: 'Before enlight-enment I chopped wood and carried water. After enlightenment I chopped wood and carried water.' In that particular sense, nothing changes at all. In another sense everything is changed. For a crucial part of our process of transformation is the falling away of our separate, egocentric 'I'. The consequent knowledge of who we are and where we come from brings an end to our experience of life as a process of separation, rejection, and suffering.

5

ENLIGHTENMENT AND SPIRITUAL REBIRTH

The paradoxical statement that enlightenment or spiritual rebirth changes nothing and yet changes everything can perhaps be clarified by explaining that the world in which we live does not change. It is we, or rather our perception, that changes, and with that everything alters – even the way in which we experience the world in which we live. For we no longer perceive things in the way we used to. A traditional Zen saying expresses the change of perception thus: 'Before a person studies Zen, mountains are mountains and waters are waters; after a first taste of Zen, mountains are no longer mountains and waters are not waters; after enlightenment, mountains are once again mountains and waters are once again waters.'

A change of perception of the kind we are talking about here comes about through a process of *un*-learning rather than one of learning. Even though learning about enlightenment or spiritual rebirth may be what has initially inspired us to seek the transformational change they represent, there comes a point in our spiritual evolution when we need to acknowledge that merely learning *about* them does not of itself constitute change. Although the potential for profound change is an ever-present reality in our lives, it is often not until our personal circumstances place us in a situation similar to the metaphorical situations of the prodigal son or Gerasene demoniac – a situation in which we seemingly have no choice but to change – that we realize that the opportunity for change is even there. We may even realize that up to that moment we have, so to speak, been living upside-down while all along we were convinced we were the right way up. With this realization a profound yearning for change may be awakened within us.

Marsilio Ficino, the fifteenth-century Italian philosopher and neo-Platonist, expresses the yearning to unlearn and be turned right-side up thus:

> Our life must be converted into its contrary. We must unlearn those things which we have learned; by learning them we have hitherto not known ourselves. We must learn those things we have neglected; without knowing them we cannot know ourselves. We must like what we neglect, neglect what we like, tolerate what we flee, flee what we follow. We must cry about the jest of fortune; jest about its tears.[1]

The profound, revelatory nature of this transformative process is emphasized by the eighteenth-century French Jesuit priest, Jean-Pierre de Caussade. In his treatise, *L'Abandon à la Providence Divine*, he tells us that, if we follow our yearning to its furthest limits, abandoning ourselves wholeheartedly to whatever the present moment brings, 'there is not a single moment when you will not be shown everything you can possibly wish for'.[2]

Spiritual rebirth as revelation

Taking up the same theme, St Paul describes succinctly the before and after of our potential change of perception: 'For now we see through a glass, darkly; but then face to face.'[3]

Like Paul, William Blake connects the change of perception, or *metanoia*, that comes with enlightenment or spiritual rebirth to a moment of profound revelation.

> If the doors of perception were cleansed every thing would appear to man as it is, infinite.
> For man has closed himself up, till he sees all things through narrow chinks of his cavern.[4]

Blake's description of enlightenment as the capacity to see every thing revealed, *as it is*, carries with it the implication that that capacity lies dormant within us, thereby giving us the inherent potential not only to see ourselves as we really are, but also to *be* as we really are – enlightened and all-seeing. Instead, blissfully unaware of our original nature, we live out our lives like Narcissus, held in thrall by an illusion of our own making.

We find our potential for these two modes of existence – one enlightened, the other unenlightened – expressed in numerous ways in the gospel narratives. In Matthew we find the analogy of the lamp hidden under a bushel: 'Nor do men light a lamp and put it under a bushel, but on a stand, and it gives light to all in the house. Let your light so shine . . .'[5] In Mark the analogy is followed with words that echo those of William Blake: 'For there is nothing hid, except to be made manifest; nor is anything secret, except to come to light.'[6] The same idea is also expressed slightly differently, in both Matthew and Luke, in a way that links our enlightened and unenlightened modes of perception with two themes that are frequently represented in the gospels: concealment and revelation. 'For nothing is covered that will not be revealed, or hidden that will not be known.'[7]

The theme of *concealment* relates both to the separation of our inner and outer worlds and the cause of this separation. It implies a lack of spiritual awareness, 'missing the mark', 'blindness', or 'unenlightenment'. It can also be linked to the veil of the mind, or rather the veil that our self-image, opinions, or prejudices, place between ourselves and our original enlightened nature, thus concealing the latter from view. Conversely, *revelation* corresponds to the moment when the veil of the mind is drawn aside, and our blindness gives way to the insight, understanding and wisdom, that come with enlightenment, or spiritual rebirth.

In keeping with mythical tradition we also find the themes of concealment, revelation and enlightenment expressed allegorically in a number of different ways in both the Old and New Testaments – for example, through references to clothing, garments, raiment, robes. Although such references are ambivalent, and their precise meaning may vary from one context to another, in general they provide us with a tangible metaphor for an inner event. For instance, Zechariah relates Joshua's moment of transformation, using 'garments' to represent his states of being before and after the event:

> Now Joshua was standing before the angel, clothed with filthy garments. And the angel said to those who were standing before him, 'Remove the filthy garments from him.' And to him he said, 'Behold, I have taken your iniquity away from you, and I will clothe you with rich apparel.' And I said, 'Let them put a clean turban on

his head.' So they put a clean turban on his head and clothed him with garments . . .[8]

Following the same tradition, the authors of the gospels similarly use garments to allegorize a transformed state of being, as exemplified in the Transfiguration of Jesus, where we are told that 'his face shone like the sun, and his garments became white as light,'[9] as well as in the white robes worn by the righteous in the Revelation to John.[10] A further reference to robes in Revelation involves their 'washing' – 'Blessed are those who wash their robes, that they may have the right to the tree of life'[11] – and from its alternative rendering – 'Blessed are those who do his command-ments' – it becomes evident that the process of revelation, renewal, transformation, here expressed allegorically through garments and robes, corresponds to a state of being in which, having emerged from the restrictive confines of our egocentric 'I am', we become one with the 'I AM' of the One Reality: the Spirit or Divine Will.

This new, transformed state of being differs from our former state to such an extent that it remains incomprehensible to a mind that is still centred in the ego. Indeed, the gospels portray these two states of being as incompatible with each other. That is to say, either we are enlightened, or we are not. We cannot serve both Mammon *and* God, the will of our ego *and* the Divine Will, at the same time. As the parable of the Old and New Garments informs us, the two states simply do not blend together: 'No one tears a piece from a new garment and puts it upon an old garment; if he does, he will tear the new, and the piece from the new will not match the old.'[12]

This process of total renewal associated with transformation also appears in the 'best robe' in which the prodigal son was dressed upon his return home, as well as in the description of the once-naked Gerasene demoniac being 'clothed and in his right mind'. But, as is the case with the Gerasene demoniac, gospel references to 'nakedness' are as ambivalent as those to garments. Perhaps even more so, since a literal interpretation of the Fall has led many to believe that both nakedness and nudity are intrin-sically evil. As a result, when nakedness is combined with the theme of concealment it is often interpreted from the narrowest of moral standpoints. The physical covering up of the naked human body is equated with the covering up of one's shame, one's guilt, or one's sin. However, nakedness also represents a state of primal

innocence – as with Adam and Eve in the Garden of Eden, before
the Fall – in which case it signifies the opposite of shame, for
shame only comes with guilt and the loss of innocence. More
importantly, Adam and Eve's original nakedness provides us with
an allegory for our own original nature. Conversely, their sewing
together of fig leaves to make aprons with which to cover
themselves allegorizes the process by which the development of
our subjective consciousness – our egocentric 'I' – has concealed
that same original nature from us.[13]

The ambivalent nature of mythical language means that in our
attempts to understand the message at the heart of the gospel
narratives we can easily be drawn into merely substituting one
literal meaning for another, rather than delving beneath the surface
of the physical words to discover their potential allegorical, moral
or anagogical meaning. As an example of this kind of parallel
literal interpretation we can turn to the following passage from the
Gospel of Thomas,[14] from which the historian Ian Wilson
concludes that 'Jesus had a striking modern attitude to nudity'.

> His disciples said, 'When will you be revealed to us and when shall
> we see you?' Jesus said, 'When you disrobe without being ashamed
> and take up your garments and place them under your feet like little
> children, and tread on them . . .'[15]

An alternative interpretation of Thomas' reference to disrobing is
given by Anne Bancroft in her book *The Spiritual Journey*, where
she suggests that the passage is one of several pointers to Jesus'
'belief in nakedness as part of what was perhaps an initiation
ceremony' to a mystery cult.[16]

Whatever the historical accuracy of these two interpretations,
they do not take us beyond the literal meaning of the physical
words. They step sideways, so to speak, offering a literal alternative.
By focusing on the messenger rather than the message the latter
becomes further obscured. As a teaching story, each of the elements
in the disrobing incident concerns us directly, even the opening
reference to the 'disciples' of Jesus.

If we approach the figure of Jesus in a mythical sense, as being
both the personification of the spiritual dimension of our being
and the embodiment of the Spirit, we can perhaps understand the
word 'disciples' – followers – as a reference to those who either
endeavour to follow a simple spiritual path in life, or consciously
seek to be guided by the Spirit. In a more general sense it could

even be said that we are all 'followers' of the Spirit, whether we are conscious of it or not. Within that context the disciples' question – when will the Spirit reveal itself to us, so that we can 'see' it? – is very much our own. It gives voice to our profound inner yearning for spiritual revelation and enlightenment. But, as the Spirit that permeates both our inner and outer worlds is invisible, how are we able to 'see' it?

The answer presents us with something of a riddle. For it infers that it is not until we have totally divested ourselves of our 'garments' – everything that either conceals or separates the Spirit from us – that the Spirit will be revealed, filling us with its presence. From this viewpoint the answer can understood as an expression of the process of spiritual evolution and rebirth. It also conveys the reciprocal nature of this process, for the more we divest ourselves of that which veils the Spirit from us, the more it will reveal itself to us.

Thomas' reference to children is equally ambivalent. Similar references in the gospel narratives have inspired many images, some extremely sentimental, of a seated Jesus surrounded by small children. But in the following passage (also from the Gospel of Thomas) it becomes clear that 'being children' describes a defining stage in our spiritual evolution. Having divested ourselves of our 'garments', we are spiritually reborn. We are nurtured (suckled) by the Spirit. Metaphorically speaking, we 'enter the kingdom of heaven'.

> Jesus saw children who were being suckled.
> He said to his disciples:
> These children who are being suckled are like
> those who enter the Kingdom.
> They said to him:
> Shall we then, being children,
> enter the Kingdom?
> Jesus said to them:
> When you make the two One,
> and you make the inner the outer,
> and the outer the inner,
> and the above the below,
> so that you will make the male and the female
> into a single One . . . then shall you enter the Kingdom.[17]

The passage also makes it clear that spiritual rebirth marks the end of our dualistic mode of thinking. Where we formerly perceived things in terms of conflict and opposition, we are now able to experience for ourselves the interconnectedness that permeates all things visible and invisible, and by which the Many *are* the One. Yet the precise nature of enlightenment, spiritual rebirth, or 'entering the kingdom of heaven', is such that it remains a mystery for us until we experience it directly, for ourselves, as *a state of being*.

Spiritual rebirth as self-knowledge

The last point is illustrated in a further passage from the Gospel of Thomas. Its opening warning about the very real danger of being led astray bears a striking resemblance to the passage from Deuteronomy, quoted earlier (*see* pages 26–7). If we understand the kingdom of heaven as being a tangible reality to be sought somewhere 'out there', then our understanding is wide of the mark. Spiritual rebirth is an awakening *from within* to the profound self-knowledge that we are spiritual beings – children, or 'sons' and 'daughters', of the Spirit, the 'Living Father'.

> Jesus said:
>
> If those who guide your Being say to you:
> 'Behold the Kingdom is in the heaven,'
> then the birds of the sky will precede you;
> if they say to you: 'It is in the sea',
> then the fish will precede you.
> But the Kingdom is in your centre
> and is about you.
> When you Know your Selves
> then you will be Known,
> and you will be aware that you are
> the sons of the Living Father.[18]

The last lines express the idea that self-knowledge is more than simply 'knowing ourselves' and being aware that we are spiritual beings. Self-knowledge is concomitant with our *being known*. But what does it mean for us 'to be known'? What is it that 'knows' us?

Earlier I described the perfect nonduality and wholeness of the One Reality as a *Self-revealing, Self-knowing state of being*. If we are able to accept that we 'live, and move, and have our being' within the One Reality, we can perhaps begin to understand that what we know of ourselves and the universe in which we live is an integral part of the One's own Self-revealing, Self-knowing state.

Following on from this I suggest that, in its most profound sense, self-knowledge is the unfolding process by which the One, the Spirit or 'Living Father', knows itself *through* us – through our eyes, and ears, and minds, through our entire being – in such a way that we no longer experience any dualistic separation between subject (the knower) and object (the known), or between knowing and being known.

A similarly nondualistic understanding of self-knowledge is expressed in the following words of St Paul, where it is linked with the idea of a synchronous transition from childhood to maturity, from that which is partial and imperfect to that which has been perfected and made whole.

> For we know in part . . . But when that which is perfect is come, that which is in part shall be done away. When I was a child, I spake as a child, I understood as a child, I thought as a child: but when I became a man, I put away childish things. For now we see through a glass, darkly; but then face to face: now I know in part; but then shall I know even as I also am known.[19]

Paul's words have the quality of a parable about them, for the evolution from child to adult can be understood as referring to either our physical or our spiritual development. From the experience of our own personal physical and psychological evolution, we are able to understand the element of mystery involved – the vagueness of seeing 'through a glass, darkly' – because the unfolding nature of life itself is such that it only gradually reveals its secrets to us as we progress from childhood to adulthood.

As children we have the extraordinary capacity to be filled with a wondrous sense of curiosity by the world around us. We *yearn* to know and understand everything. But then, or so it seems, there comes a point in life when the sense of wonder begins to fade and we no longer want to know with the same intensity. Conditioned by the accumulated experiences of our past, we no longer experience everything as if for the first time. Instead of overflowing with questions our minds become filled with answers, opinions and prejudices. These not only dull our perception of the world around us; they also obscure from our view the light of the Spirit within us. Our physical and mental maturity may convince us that we are fully grown. But in a spiritual sense we are, like Nicodemus, still in the womb.

Spiritual rebirth as a natural process

Nicodemus' visit to Jesus is recorded uniquely in John, where the night-time setting suggests that, spiritually speaking, Nicodemus is 'in the dark'. His lack of spiritual understanding soon becomes apparent from his questions. Nevertheless, he is drawn towards the Spirit (Jesus) in his search for enlightenment and understanding.

> Nicodemus, a Pharisee and member of the Sanhedrin, came to visit Jesus by night, saying to him, 'Rabbi, we know you are a teacher come from God, for no one can do the things you do unless God is with him.' And Jesus said to him, 'I am telling you the Truth when I say to you that unless one is born anew [from above], one cannot know the kingdom of God.'
>
> 'How can a man be born when he is already old? Surely he cannot enter his mother's womb a second time and be born?' Jesus replied, 'I am telling you the Truth when I say to you that unless one is born of water and the Spirit, one cannot enter the kingdom of God. That which is born physically is physical, and that which is born of the Spirit is spiritual. Do not be surprised when I tell you that you must be born anew [from above]. The wind blows where it wills. You hear the sound of it, but you do not know where it comes from or where it is going. So it is with everyone who is born of the Spirit.'
>
> 'How can this be?' asked Nicodemus. Jesus replied, 'You are a teacher in Israel, and you do not understand this? I am telling you the Truth when I say to you that we speak of what we know, and bear witness to what we have seen; but you do not accept our testimony. If I tell you of worldly things, and you do not believe, how can you believe if I tell you heavenly things? And no one has ascended into heaven, but he who descended from heaven, the Son of man who is in heaven.'[20]

The conversation between Jesus and Nicodemus about spiritual rebirth presents us with an allegorical dialogue between the two halves of our divided self – our personality and our essence. The author of John thus highlights the gulf that distinguishes human from spiritual understanding. Not only is this gulf conveyed through the references to worldly and heavenly things, water and the Spirit, and physical and spiritual birth. It is also embodied in the figures of Nicodemus and Jesus. On the one hand we have Nicodemus, 'a teacher in Israel', whose questions parallel our own 'groping in the dark' as we attempt to understand spiritual things in dualistic, this-worldly terms. On the other we have the figure of Jesus, 'a teacher come from God', whose words are both 'spirit and life'.[21]

As with many other ancient languages, the original Greek word for 'wind', *pneuma*, also means 'breath' and 'spirit', or 'life-force'. (We encountered it earlier in the breath of life breathed into Adam in order for him to become a living being.) Together these multiple meanings serve to underline that spiritual rebirth is a natural process. It takes place according to the 'will' of the Spirit rather than any effort of human will. But the question Nicodemus asks in response to Jesus' explanation reflects our inability to grasp the ways of the Spirit with our logical, analytical mind. Such knowledge can be said to come only from the Spirit itself.

Our Westernized mind is such that we *need* to have rational explanations for things. Unless we do, nothing makes sense. Our attempts to define more clearly the simplest of universal and spiritual truths have, however, simply served to embellish them with complex verbal constructs. In the process our dominant dualistic mode of thinking has progressively distanced heaven from the everyday reality of earth until it has now been elevated to a point where it is beyond the reach of most of us. Like the mythical Tower of Babel, our lofty towers of words have ended in confusion and dissension rather than entry to the kingdom of heaven.

In contrast, it was possibly at the simple level of everyday activity that the life-giving rise and fall of our own in-breath and out-breath first inspired our ancestors to equate the Spirit with the primordial Breath of Life – the life-giving 'Breath of God', the continuous movement by which the One manifests as the Many while never ceasing to be the One. In the Judaeo-Christian myth a similar movement is frequently expressed as one of 'ascent' and 'descent', in which our ascent towards heaven is rendered possible by a corresponding descent from heaven towards us. The movement is epitomized in Jacob's vision of a ladder set up on earth, with its top reaching up to heaven, and angels ascending and descending on it.[22] We also encounter it in the closing lines of the conversation between Jesus and Nicodemus. Here the idea that spiritual rebirth is a natural process, initiated 'from above', is expressed as an ascent *into* heaven and a descent *from* heaven by that which is *in* heaven – namely, the Son of man. But who, or what, is the 'Son of man'?

The Jewish scholar and historian of Christian origins, Hugh Schonfield, points out that the term 'Son of Man' was in use before the time of Jesus as another name for the Messiah. According to Schonfield, Jesus' own usage of the title echoes the language of the *Similitudes of Enoch*, in which Enoch recounts his heavenly visions of the apocalyptic Last Times. In the *Similitudes* the Son of Man '. . . is named and hidden from the beginning in the secret thoughts of God, finally to be revealed in the Last Times as the ideal Man who will justify God's creation of the world.'[23] Schonfield goes on to tell us that at the end of the *Similitudes* Enoch is told that in his vision of the Son of Man he has seen 'an image of his own righteous self'. He concludes by saying that the Son of Man/Messiah would embody the 'perfect righteousness which God from the beginning designed for humanity'.[24]

The complex terminology of the doctrine surrounding the Son of Man is in stark contrast to the simplicity of the sayings of Jesus recorded in the Gospel of Thomas. For this reason the messianic ideal it presents us with can easily appeal to the head more readily than the heart. What really concerns us here, however, is the implication that the Son of Man is the personification of our original spiritual nature. As such the Son of Man/Messiah refers to that mysterious, perfected state of being that exists *in essence* in all of us, waiting to make itself known – i.e. waiting to be 'born' – at a more tangible level of reality. When our personality does become one with our essence, it transforms us, 'lifting us up' naturally to another level of being. In other words, when that state of 'perfect righteousness which God from the beginning designed for human-ity' manifests itself within us we experience for ourselves the coming of the Son of Man, the Messiah/Christ. Spiritually reborn, we enter the kingdom of heaven.

The looking-glass mind

In his account of the night-time conversation between Jesus and Nicodemus about spiritual rebirth the author of John not only encapsulates the very essence of the gospel message; in the figure of Nicodemus he presents us with an illuminating personification of our own search for spiritual fulfilment. Like Nicodemus, we tend to look for what we are looking for in our mind. Yet looking in our mind is rather like looking in a mirror. All we see is ourselves – our own thoughts – looking back at us. However, if we wish to pass through the seemingly opaque images reflected back to us by our mind, we can perhaps learn something from Alice, the young heroine of Lewis Carroll's children's classic, *Through the Looking-Glass*. As she stands in front of the fire, holding her kitten and looking into the mirror, she says:

> 'Oh, Kitty! how nice it would be if we could only get through into Looking-Glass House! I'm sure it's got, oh! such beautiful things in it! Let's pretend there's a way of getting through into it, somehow, Kitty. Let's pretend the glass has got all soft like gauze, so that we can get through. Why, it's turning into a sort of mist now, I declare! It'll be easy enough to get through –' She was up on the chimney-piece while she said this, though she hardly knew how she had got there. And certainly the glass *was* beginning to melt away, just like a bright silvery mist.
> In another moment Alice was through the glass . . .[25]

Since Lewis Carroll first sent Alice and her kitten through the looking-glass over a hundred years ago, myriad children and adults have followed them through it in their imagination to meet the Red King and Queen, Tweedledum and Tweedledee, the Walrus and the Carpenter, Humpty Dumpty and the countless other characters who live on the other side of the glass. As with Carroll's earlier book, *Alice's Adventures in Wonderland*, which begins with Alice falling down a rabbit hole, the passage through the looking-glass is a simple device to transport us into the world of the imagination – a world which, for Alice at least, becomes as real as the world this side of the glass. At the end of the story, however, when Alice awakens to find it was all a dream, she asks who it was that had dreamed it all. Was it her, for it was she who had dreamed about the Red King? Or was it the Red King, because she had been a part of his dream, too?

Whoever's dream world it is that we really enter as we go through the looking-glass – Alice's, the Red King's, Lewis Carroll's or our own – the story illustrates the human mind's ability to pass from waking reality to dream, from the 'real world' to the world of our imagination, and back again. Now, whether these different realities exist simultaneously, side-by-side like so many parallel universes, or whether they are merely different aspects of a single reality, is also a thing of the mind.

Normally the only things we see reflected in our looking-glass mind – our thoughts and the information gleaned from the input of our physical senses – derive from our subjective conscious mind. Occasionally we can use our mind to reflect an image that we ourselves call up from our personal unconscious – for example, the pleasant memory of some past experience. On other occasions, without us appearing to exercise any conscious recall, we may find the image of a long-forgotten, possibly repressed, experience suddenly emerging from the depths of our personal unconscious to impose itself upon the surface of our conscious mind. But these layers of personal consciousness are merely one side of our looking-glass mind. If, like Alice, we can pass through the looking-glass, we will encounter further layers of consciousness. Universal in nature, these extend beyond the layer of the collective unconscious into the universal sea of consciousness that we variously call Wisdom, the Divine Intelligence, the Universal Mind, or the Mind of God.

The analogy of an iceberg will perhaps help to clarify this last point. Normally all we see of an iceberg is the tip; the rest of it is out of sight beneath the surface of the ocean. Similarly, all we normally experience of consciousness, of the Universal Mind, is merely the tip – the subjective conscious mind – which, because it can see no further than itself, believes itself to be the whole iceberg. A return to our original spiritual nature involves the gradual demise of the self-centred bias of the conscious mind, and a turning upside-down, or inside-out, of our perception whereby the conscious mind becomes fully re-integrated with the universal consciousness that is the Source of our being. In this transformed state of mind the tip (the conscious mind) no longer perceives itself to be the whole iceberg. It realizes that it is merely the most prominent manifestation of an infinite sea of consciousness that permeates all things, from the minutest particles of matter to the vast, seemingly empty spaces of the universe.

That same sea of consciousness resonates within us, drawing us to herself like some primordial call of the ocean. As the following words of St Augustine would seem to suggest, she is the source of the true *sophia perennis*, which, in making itself known to us through the collective unconscious, reminds us of who we are and where we come from: 'Wherever you turn, by certain traces which wisdom has impressed on her works, she speaks to you, and recalls you within, gliding back into interior things by the very forms of exterior things.'[26]

If St Augustine's words express what lies on the far side of our looking-glass mind, the view from this side was evoked in the words Abbot Suger inscribed on the gilded west doors of the twelfth-century abbey of St Denis, near Paris: 'The dull mind rises to truth through that which is material and, in seeing this light, is resurrected from its former submersion.'[27] The physical world portrayed in the gospel narratives is likewise imbued with a light of truth that has the capacity to take us beyond the limited horizons of our conscious mind.

The looking-glass mind and the iceberg and its tip provide us with helpful analogies to illustrate our potential for two fundamentally different modes of consciousness. And because consciousness is inextricably bound up with the way in which we experience things, we also have the potential to experience two modes of *being*. With the one we are governed by the desires and opinions, the thoughts, concerns and fears, of our ego-centred subjective consciousness, our finite 'I', our 'I am'. With the other we are a means of expression for the eternal and infinite I AM, the Spirit: the dynamic flow of energy, the 'all-encompassing motivating force' that *is* the One Reality. We shall go on to explore these two modes of consciousness/being and, more specifically, the transition from the first mode to the second, in Part Two within the context of the Judaeo-Christian myth and the gospel narratives.

PART TWO

Through Meaning to Being

To be what we are and to become what we are capable of becoming,
is the only end of life.

Robert Louis Stevenson

6

THE JUDAEO-CHRISTIAN MYTH

There can be little doubt that the mythical core common to both Judaism and Christianity – which expresses itself through the themes of the Old and New Testaments, in particular the Pentateuch[1] and the gospel narratives – has had a formative influence on our collective psyche and on the evolution of Western thought. In turn the dualism of Western thought has influenced our understanding of the Judaeo-Christian myth. It has also influenced the evolution of Western religion, leading to the predominantly exclusive, proprietorial attitude adopted by the Christian Church towards both the all-pervading Spirit and the One God.

On the one hand, at its extreme this proprietorial attitude has led the change of mind or conversion of *metanoia* to be interpreted narrowly as a conversion to the Christian religion, the Bible to be proclaimed as the only legitimate 'word of God', and the Church to adjudge itself as having sole authority in matters spiritual. On the other, the exclusive attitude of the Church has led countless numbers of people who believe that religion and spirituality are one and the same thing to turn away from religion – especially in its institutionalized form – and in so doing unwittingly turn their back on their spirituality, the spiritual dimension of their being.

But religion and spirituality are *not* the same thing. As many centuries of religious wars the world over have shown, religion has the potential to set individual against individual and nation against nation; whereas spirituality is something that we have in common. It is the one thing that unequivocally unites us all. It is that which motivates the love and compassion we manifest towards our fellow beings, especially when they are in pain or distress. To turn our back, even unwittingly, on our spirituality is to deny the reality of who we really are.

Our spirituality – the spiritual dimension of our being – yearns to express itself. This is why we have within each of us an innate need for spiritual evolution and fulfilment. If that need remains either ignored or unfulfilled, it has the potential to set us at odds with ourselves in what can best be described as an inner tug-of-war: our spiritual essence endeavours to guide us along our true path in life while our ego doggedly takes us off in another. But there is nothing new about that particular predicament. It is the fundamental dilemma that has faced us ever since we developed our subjective personal consciousness, our sense of 'I am', several thousand years ago. A peculiarly human dilemma, its essential dichotomy was expressed in no uncertain terms some two thousand years ago in the Gospel of Thomas: 'Jesus said, "If you bring forth what is within you, what you bring forth will save you. If you do not bring forth what is within you, what you do not bring forth will destroy you".'[2]

The message contained in those words applies to us all, both as individuals and collectively, and it perhaps opens the way to understanding why it is that the modern Westernized world appears to be in a permanent state of quasi-crisis. We have reached a stage in our evolution where – motivated collectively and individually by materialistic rather than spiritual values, by self-interest rather than philanthropy – we are at odds with the very core of our being. In effect, what we generally perceive to be the negative but more or less acceptable side-effects of our modern way of life – stress, violence, discord and dysfunction, the increasing polarization of society, the exploitation of natural resources to the point of exhaustion and of our fellow creatures to the point of near-extinction – are nothing other than a mirror of our impoverished psychospiritual condition. The chaos we see around us is merely the reflection of a confusion within. By the same token, both the underlying dissatisfaction with the society we have created and the widely articulated desire to 'change the world' are the natural, external expression of an unconscious yearning for spiritual evolution and inner change.

Like the younger son in the parable of the Prodigal Son, many people have responded to finding themselves caught in the spiritual famine of the 'distant country' our society has become by consciously setting out in search of spiritual food. Others have perhaps embarked on the same quest more intuitively, in answer to a prompting from within themselves. Some from both groups have successfully found the spiritual fulfilment they are looking for within one or other of the mainstream Christian churches or spiritual traditions. Others have turned their search for spiritual fulfilment to other religions or spiritual movements. Yet others, perhaps in the belief that religion itself is largely responsible for the current state of Western society, have acquired a distrust of religious and spiritual traditions in general. Instead they have turned their search for spiritual expression to the ubiquitous New Age movement. Or else they have abandoned the search altogether.

The point I wish to make here is that the Judaeo-Christian myth is embedded in our collective and individual psyche so deeply that it has become an integral part of our Western psychospiritual roots. For those of us who have been brought up with its symbolic language and imagery, it continues to affect our understanding of the spiritual dimension of our existence in many different ways, both positively and negatively, *whether we actually subscribe to the myth or not.*

The essential point is that we do not necessarily have to believe in the literal truth of the myth in order to subscribe to it at an unconscious level. It is part of our collective unconscious. It could even be said that it was our collective unconscious that gave birth to the myth in the first place, in order to define for us our place within the overall scheme of things.

But we tend to forget that the Judaeo-Christian myth is not entirely our own. We have adopted at least part of it. The Judaeo-part has its origins in the distant past of the Middle East and was defined by the evolving needs and experience of a specific social grouping that at first comprised the tribes of Israel, then the kingdoms of Israel and Judah, and later the Jewish people. Yet beneath its powerful evocation of a particular people's evolving understanding of their relationship with themselves and their God, the Jewish myth offers us profound insights into our own human psyche as it struggles to resolve the apparent dualism of its physical and spiritual natures.

It was out of this same cultural and mythical background that the particular literary form we know as the gospels emerged some two thousand years ago. It offered a renewed definition of our human place within the overall order of things, influenced by the more cosmopolitan nature of eastern Mediterranean civilization as well as the religious and philosophical thinking of the time. Although they had their roots in Jewish mythical and religious tradition, the gospels appeared to be more universal in both their message and appeal; they were seen to be addressed to Gentile as well as Jew. Furthermore, the time-scale of their setting had an unprecedented immediacy about it, which gave the impression they were more or less contemporary with the events they described. Possibly because of their proximity to current history, it was not long before the focus of attention had shifted from the spiritual nature of the message to the historical existence of the messenger. With the further passage of time the gospels' original message that we are spiritual beings has come to be presented in such a way that it has increasingly convinced us we are not.

How that shift in emphasis came about is not really at issue here. It has happened. What is important is that it reveals our seeming lack of any real sense of identity, of who we are, where we come from, and what our purpose is in being here; in other words, a fundamental lack of any real self-knowledge. For that reason this second part of the book explores the gospel narratives as I feel they were originally intended to be understood – as a manual of self-knowledge, a myth of Being, that has the potential to transform our lives by giving us a renewed sense of meaning and purpose. First, however, we shall examine the two themes from the Judaeo-Christian myth that have perhaps had the most negative influence on both our individual and collective psyches – the Fall and the Last Judgement – in order to understand them for what they really are.

A fall from grace?

In its account of both the origins of the universe and the origin of human life, the Judaeo-Christian myth offers us a point on which to focus in our own collective and individual quest for self-knowledge, in our search to both know and *be* who we really are. As with the myth of the Heroic Journey, there is a starting-point to which we eventually return. In naming that starting-point as the mysterious life-force or Spirit of God that permeates all things, giving them both form and life, the Judaeo-Christian myth sets out to explain the mystery of our existence from a nondualistic, *spiritual* point of view. In doing so it also expresses the idea that our origins stretch back to the Creation of the Universe, when on the sixth day 'God formed man of dust from the ground [matter], and breathed into his nostrils the breath of life [spirit]; and man became a living being'.[3]

In reminding us of our original spiritual nature, the author of Genesis also draws attention to the primary source of our human dilemma: our dualistic mode of thinking, which tends to divide us from the One Reality 'within which we live and move and have our being'. That dilemma is expressed in what has become known as the Fall: Adam and Eve's expulsion from Paradise. The mythical account of the Fall is well enough known for it not to need retelling here. But one detail is relevant in the present context: 'the tree of the knowledge of good and evil', whose fruit brought about the Fall.[4] The tree echoes the dualism that is an essential part of the Genesis creation myth, in that there is light and darkness, a Heaven and an Earth, a God and Man, man and woman, and then good and evil.

Prior to the Fall the knowledge of good and evil had apparently been the prerogative of God, for when the serpent enticed Eve into eating the fruit of the tree, he said to her: 'You will be like God, knowing good and evil.'[5] The implication here is that before we ate the fruit we had neither known, nor had the need to know, the difference between the two. We had simply and dutifully followed God's commands. From here it is but a small step to come to the same conclusion as that proposed by Julian Jaynes (whose theory on the origins of consciousness was referred to in Chapter 1). The myth of the Fall was 'a narratization of the break-down of the bicameral mind and the coming of consciousness'.[6] It was 'the groping of newly conscious men to narratize what has happened to them.'[7]

In other words, Adam and Eve's apparent loss of innocence and their expulsion from Paradise were the myth-makers' way of accounting for a naturally occurring stage in our evolutionary process. The Fall was simply fulfilling its primary function as myth by providing the emerging new consciousness with a sense of place and purpose within the overall scheme of things. From an evolutionary point of view it could even be said that we didn't *fall*;

we were *pushed* into 'eating the fruit'. But as it was unthinkable that their God could do any wrong, our ancestors appear to have blamed themselves for the consequences of an evolutionary change in consciousness – which is a bit like blaming ourselves for standing upright simply because we evolved from being a four-legged animal to one with two.

The change of consciousness also brought with it the need for reassurance – a need to know that we had not been totally abandoned by the God who once whispered words of wisdom to us as he guided us along our path through life. In articulating the idea of God's promise of *a binding covenant between Man and God*, the myth-makers gave voice to the hope of our post-bicameral ancestors that the gods would return, and that whatever they might have done to make the gods forsake them would be forgiven. The covenant also implied that there were those who knew God intimately, and it was to them that God revealed the nature of the relationship that bound his people to him. His intimates then passed on the knowledge they had been given to their fellow human beings. As the myth itself unfolds the covenant is frequently renewed, or restated, to reflect our changing under-standing of our relationship with God and the world in which we live. Its outer form also alters in keeping with the changes brought about by social and cultural evolution.

The first such covenant was revealed to Noah after the waters of the Flood had subsided. It set the pattern for later covenants in that it included a small number of observances for us to keep as our part of the bargain. In contrast to the exclusivity of later covenants, the promise to Noah was both universal, extending to 'every living creature', and everlasting, 'for all future generations'. Possibly due to the fact that we were then closer to the natural world, God's sign of the covenant was the rainbow.[8] Unlike the covenant with Noah, which was made without ceremony, the first of the two covenants made between God and Abraham was preceded with a ritual sacrifice, while the second required a clear sign of acceptance: Abraham, and his descendants after him 'throughout their generations', were to be circumcised.[9]

The covenant revealed to Moses on Mount Sinai was far more extensive than earlier covenants. It not only saw the setting up of a code of religious law, with ritual observances and a priesthood. It also contained a comprehensive list of social and moral rules which together were destined to become the mainstay of the Torah or Mosaic Law. The Sinai covenant appears to mark a change in the perception of our relationship with God: it was now *conditional* upon the Israelites faithfully following God's commandments. The latter were backed up by a sequence of escalating threats, which carried with them the idea of a potentially angry and jealous God who would sit in judgement on his people and punish them with divine retribution should they transgress his laws.[10]

The sense of guilt and self-blame that had accompanied the Fall found itself reiterated in the Israelites' bewailing the misfortunes that befell them because – as they saw it – they had broken the covenant. By not 'hearkening to the Lord' they had wandered away from his commandments. At some point in time the guilt became interwoven with a growing belief in an angry and jealous God, who constantly cajoled, threatened and even punished his Chosen People in his attempts to get them to follow him. Eventually these various strands culminated in visionary prophecies concerning 'that Day', the Day of Wrath or *Dies irae*, the day on which time and history will come to an end and God will manifest himself in the world and reign over it in person, thus bringing to an end its misery and suffering.

The Last Times

According to the portentous visions of the prophets, 'that Day' will manifest as some kind of apocalypse, or a series of momentous apocalyptic events which will themselves constitute the Last Times. The ominous nature of some of these prophecies are to be found in Ezekiel's references to the day of 'doom',[11] in Daniel's promise of 'a time of trouble, such as never has been',[12] or in Revelation, with the opening of the seals that release the Four Horsemen of the Apocalypse.[13] There were also visionary prophecies of a Final Resurrection as part of the Last or Divine Judgement, which would take place before God seated on his throne,[14] when 'the books would be opened' and 'the dead' would be judged 'by what was written in the books, by what they had done'.[15]

The Resurrection and its accompanying Judgement appealed to the artists of medieval and Renaissance Europe who used them to decorate the doorways of their cathedrals and churches.[16] They also portrayed them in dramatic paintings of *The Last Judgement*, such as those by Hieronymus Bosch in the Akademie der bildenden Künste, Vienna, and Michelangelo in the Sistine Chapel, Rome. The combination of themes provided artists and their patrons with abundant material for their creative imagination, as evidenced in the many vivid images of the archangel Michael holding a pair of scales in which he weighs the souls of the resurrected. Once judgement has been passed, the Damned are subjected to all manner of tortures and obscenities as they enter the gaping jaws of Hell. For the Blessed it is a very different story: they are either welcomed into the bosom of Abraham or ascend towards the company of saints.

The events surrounding the Day of Judgement, as well as the belief that it refers to some future time when the world itself is doomed to end, have left a profound mark on our collective and individual psyches. (How many of us harbour the conscious or unconscious desire to go to Heaven when we die, even if only to avoid the fires of Hell and eternal damnation?) Yet although apocalyptic pronouncements about the Last Times and a Final Judgement initially may have arisen out of the sense of guilt instigated by the apparent departure of the gods, they also carry with them the implication that the Last Times are much closer

Figure 1 The Last Judgement (second half of 13th century), from the central tympanum on the west front of Bourges cathedral

(To the right of the archangel Michael, demonic figures drive the Damned towards a cauldron bubbling over the flames issuing from the jaws of Hell. Demons fan the flames with bellows while toads and snakes on the cauldron's rim prepare to devour their victims. To the left, angels escort the Blessed towards the door of Heaven. St Peter waits at the door to show them in to the bosom of Abraham; above the door angels hold out crowns to place on the heads of the Blessed.)

than their futuristic descriptions might lead us to believe. Behind their ominous portents of doom they seek to express the idea of a new or Final Covenant, an ultimate understanding of our relationship with our Creator.

In order for that new understanding to come into being, the old has to pass away – not just superficially, but fundamentally, through the profound change of mind expressed by the Greek word *metanoia*. As the old is characterized by its dualistic belief (held consciously or unconsciously) that God is purely external and distant, an essential part of establishing the new is to get God down on Earth. And not only moving around on Earth, but moving and living *within* his people.

To avoid possible confusion it needs to be made clear that the old and new covenants I am talking about here are not the same as the Old and New Testaments. The latter denote the bi-partite division of the Christian Bible; the former express our potential to experience our relationship with the One Reality in one of two ways which correspond to two modes of consciousness or *being*. The 'old covenant' denotes a mode of consciousness/being governed by our dualistic sense of 'I' and 'other-than-I'. The 'new covenant' alludes to a mode of consciousness/being in which, no longer dominated by our egocentric 'I', we experience the essential nonduality of the One Reality.

Our potential for this second mode is a recurring theme in the books of the Old Testament. It is hinted at in the passage from Deuteronomy quoted earlier (*see* pages 26–7). There we are told that God's commandment 'is in your mouth and in your heart, so that you can do it'. The new covenant is expressed more fully in Jeremiah, where it is clearly connected to the Last Times, to *those days*. In contrast to the judgemental 'angry and jealous' God of Leviticus,[17] this is a forgiving God, intimate knowledge of whom is not transmitted from one human being to another, but directly, by God himself, to everyone.

> Behold, *the days* are coming, says the Lord, when I will make a new covenant . . . [and] *after those days*, says the Lord: I will put my law within them, and I will write it upon their hearts; and I will be their God, and they shall be my people. And no longer shall each man teach his neighbour and each his brother, saying, 'Know the Lord', for they shall all know me, from the least of them to the greatest, says the Lord; for I will forgive their iniquity, and I will remember their sin no more.[18]

The essential point here is that *those days* coincide with an ultimate knowledge of God, because *after* those days: (1) God will rule directly, from inside people's hearts, not from a throne in heaven; (2) God will be the One Teacher, within us, and therefore (3) the dualism that separates Man from God will come to an end; and finally, (4) with the knowledge of God within us, there will be no more sin – that is, no more erring from the Way of God – and therefore no more judgement. The difference in the *before* and *after* of the Last Times lies in the fundamental change of mind-set referred to above. As an event in time, the Last Times is essentially a psychospiritual not an historical phenomenon.

But what of the Final Resurrection, with its visions of the dead being summoned at the sound of the last trumpet to face the Final Judgement? One thing is certain: the image of the dead rising out of graves or coffins has impressed itself on our collective psyche to such a degree that it literally haunts our unconscious. The unnatural phenomenon of the physically dead coming back to life has become a popular theme of horror stories and films, from where it brings our unconscious fears to the surface, as well as reinforcing our own very real conscious fear of death and what will happen to us afterwards. Perhaps it is a combination of these factors – not knowing what happens to us after we die, and the realness of our own fear of death – that enable the concept of a Final Resurrection to hold us in thrall.

From a literal standpoint, as part of the Last Times, the Final Resurrection means exactly what it says. At some point in the future we shall be raised from the dead and judged according to the deeds we did while we were alive. Once judgement has been passed we will be sent to Heaven, to Hell or to Purgatory. But biblical references to 'the dead' are generally used allegorically, to signify those who, although physically alive, have no spiritual life in them.

A striking example of this particular usage is found in Ezekiel, where in a vision the prophet is shown a valley filled with dried bones. The bones are those of the exiled Israelites, who lament their fate, crying out, 'Our bones are dried up, and our hope is lost'. In the vision the bones come together and are progressively covered in sinew, flesh, and then skin, but there is no breath (spirit) in them until God commands breath to enter them, at which they come alive and stand up. God then tells the prophet to prophesy to the Israelites, saying: 'You shall know that I am the Lord, when I open your graves, and raise you from your graves . . .

And I will put my Spirit within you, and you shall live.'[19] In keeping with the underlying theme of the Last Times, here *resurrection* is equated with knowledge of God, which is also the acknowledgement and/or realization of our original spiritual nature.

Following on from the above, I suggest that to be 'raised from the dead' means to come alive, to be enlightened, or to fulfil our spiritual potential and be transformed into a new state of consciousness/being. In that context the Final Resurrection can also be understood as that moment in time – whenever it may be – when all of humankind becomes enlightened. When seen in that light the Last Times are an event that need no longer fill us with fear; they are something to look positively forward to.

The Last Times in the gospels

When we forget that the vivid language of the Last Times is intended to be understood allegorically, our attention is taken away from the present and directed towards the future. And yet we cannot escape the present moment, for that is the point in time at which we always are. It is the only time there ever is. It is the only time in which we can ever *be*.

The importance of *being in the present moment* is a recurring theme of the gospel narratives, for they are constantly drawing us back into it by either direct reference or allusion. As a consequence, if we approach the narratives as relating a sequence of historical events that happened once upon a time, we miss the eternal timelessness of their message – a message that we can only ever experience by being in the present. Certainly, if we look for the dimension of future time in the events narrated in the gospels, or in the potential events to come, we will find it. But then we will in some way be emulating those characterized in the gospels as looking for signs of the times.

To the Pharisees who ask Jesus when the kingdom of God is coming, he replies that it is not coming with any visible signs.[20] To those who ask him to give a sign from heaven, Jesus responds by saying that we may be able to predict what the weather will be by interpreting the signs in the sky, but we cannot interpret the signs of the times. He adds enigmatically that the only sign there will be is the sign of Jonah.[21] Jesus uses the analogy of the weather forecast on another occasion, ending with the question, 'Why do you not know how to interpret the present time?'[22] Whilst his question carries with it the implication that the times are *now*, the gospels tell us elsewhere that we do not know when the time will be.[23] They also remind us that the coming of the Son of Man is itself a sign of the times.[24] Perhaps the final word on the subject is contained in Matthew: 'Of that day and hour no one knows . . . but the Father only.'[25]

According to Matthew, we are unable to predict when the Last Times will happen. Nevertheless, he sheds some light on their possible timing in a parable that brings together a Final Judgement and entrance to the kingdom of heaven in one event.[26] At the moment of judgement/entry, the King will 'separate the sheep from the goats', placing the sheep to his right hand, the goats to his left. He will then say to those at his right hand:

> 'Come, O blessed of my Father, inherit the kingdom prepared for you from the foundation of the world; for I was hungry and you gave me food, I was thirsty and you gave me drink, I was a stranger and you welcomed me, I was naked and you clothed me, I was sick and you visited me, I was in prison and you came to me.' Then the righteous will answer him, 'Lord, when did we see thee hungry and feed thee, or thirsty and give thee drink? And when did we see thee a stranger and welcome thee, or naked and clothe thee? And when did we see thee sick or in prison and visit thee?' And the King will answer them, 'Truly, I say to you, as you did it to one of the least of these my brethren, you did it to me.'[27]

Conversely, those on the King's left hand have done none of these things. The King tells them that in not doing them 'to one of the least of these, you did it not to me.' As a consequence of their (non-)actions entry to the kingdom is not for them. In making a direct connection between (1) a Final Judgement, (2) entry to the kingdom of heaven, and (3) our present actions, the parable shows these three things to be synchronous. But in order to convey that to our linear mode of thinking, their synchronicity is narratized in the form of a parable. If the parable's message about the underlying unity of existence (including the dimension of time) really goes home, it has the potential to awaken us to the reciprocal consequences of our present actions: what we do or do not do to others is what we do or do not do to ourselves. In the end it is not the King who separates the sheep from the goats. It is their own actions or non-actions.

The idea that ultimately we are on the receiving end of our own actions can be linked to the theme of judgement expressed in a saying from the Sermon on the Mount. The sermon hints at the part we ourselves play in postponing to some future date our own realization that all is One: 'Judge not, that you be not judged. For with the judgement you pronounce you will be judged, and the measure you give will be the measure you get.'[28]

Here we have a key to understanding the Last Judgement, which, as part of the Last Times, is concomitant with ultimate knowledge of God. The ominous air of finality surrounding the Last or Final Judgement has nothing to do with it being an event envisaged as taking place somewhen in the future, somewhere at the end of historical time. Its finality is due to it simply being the *last* judgement – that is, the last time we judge, and are judged (by ourselves) in return. It is a reversal of the Fall, the moment when consciousness emerged. It was then that we ate 'the fruit of the tree of knowledge of good and evil' and began to evolve the judgemental, dualistic mode of thinking that has gradually separated us from ourselves, from our fellow beings, and from the One Reality. That separation is perpetuated each time we (consciously or unconsciously) judge a person right or wrong, or better or worse, in relation to ourselves. The same also applies to things or events. For each time we make a judgement we set ourselves apart from the One Reality of which we are a part. The day we pass judgement for *the last time* marks the transition from the dualistic mind-set of the old covenant to the nondualistic of the new embodied in the Jesus of the gospels, who says, 'I judge no one.'[29] And of the revelatory nature of that day, he says: 'In that day you will know that I am in my Father, and you in me, and I in you.'[30]

By way of concluding this exploration of the Last Times, I suggest that the apocalyptic *end of the world* associated with them provides us with a mirror image of the Creation myth in Genesis, where an evolutionary change of consciousness was narratized as the Fall. In other words, the Last Times marks the end of our perception of life on earth as little more than a time of judgement and suffering. *Dies irae* denotes the mind-bending moment when our current dualistic mode of consciousness is transformed into one that is nondualistic, and our current understanding of ourselves and the world in which we live comes to to an end. Even

'heaven and earth shall pass away'[31] as our 'I am' becomes one
with the I AM, the One that is the 'Alpha and Omega, the
beginning and the end, the first and the last'.[32]

The old and the new

The transformation of consciousness and being associated with
both the Last Times and 'old' and 'new' covenants is embodied in
the statues of two women set amongst the thirteenth-century

*Figure 2a) The Church of the New Covenant (c1230) from the south
portal of Strasbourg Cathedral*

Gothic sculpture that decorates the façades and portals of a number of French cathedrals.[33] Although varying in style from place to place, the statues follow the same broad pattern. The head of one droops downwards, a blindfold bound tightly over her eyes. With one hand she holds on to a broken spear; from the other dangles a stone tablet. The second wears a crown. Her head is held erect and her eyes look boldly in front of her. In one hand she holds a tall cross, in the other a chalice. The body language of the two figures speaks volumes.

Tradition identifies these two statues as a symbolic portrayal of the triumph of the Church over the Synagogue, for in their hands

Figure 2b) The Synagogue or Old Covenant (c1230) from the south portal of Strasbourg Cathedral

they hold the symbols of the old and new laws or covenants: the stone tablet of the Mosaic Law and the chalice of the blood of Christ. Their other attributes – the crown and cross; the blindfold and broken spear – complete the visual analogy. The widespread portrayal of these two figures in either stone or stained glass on the cathedrals and churches in towns across northern Europe, seems to have coincided with the wave of anti-Semitism, which, fired by vicious rumour and accusations of deicide, swept through Euro-pean countries during the Middle Ages. If popular imagination needed proof of the superiority of Christianity over Judaism, or of Christian over Jew, it was there for all to see.

But interpretations of that kind merely serve to reinforce our human tendency to perceive the world, including religion and spirituality, in terms of division, opposition and conflict. For an alternative understanding of what these two figures represent we need to turn to the original source of their inspiration. This is to be found in the gospel narratives and the spirited confrontations between Jesus and the religious leaders of his time – the scribes, Pharisees, Sadducees and priests – whom he frequently chastises for their strict observance of the Mosaic Law. Taking up the same theme in his series of Letters to the various early Christian communities, or 'churches', St Paul announces a new covenant that lies not in the Mosaic Law – the stone tables of testimony delivered to Moses on Mount Sinai – but in the Spirit:

> . . . for the written code [the Law] kills, but the Spirit gives life. Now if the dispensation of death, carved in letters on stone, came with such splendour that the Israelites could not look at Moses' face because of its brightness, fading as this was, will not the dispensation of the Spirit be attended with greater splendour? . . . But their minds were hardened; for to this day, when they read the old covenant, that same veil remains unlifted, because only through Christ is it taken away. Yes, to this day whenever Moses is read a veil lies over their minds; but when a man turns to the Lord the veil is removed. Now the Lord is the Spirit, and where the Spirit of the Lord is, there is freedom. And we all, with unveiled face, beholding [reflecting] the glory of the Lord, are being changed into his likeness from one degree of glory to another; for this comes from the Lord who is the Spirit.[34]

Whilst Paul may at first appear to be outlining the fundamental difference between Judaism and an emergent Christian religion, he is simply restating – as the Hebrew prophets had done before him – our potential for a new relationship (or a new understanding of our present relationship) with what we have come to call 'God'. As before, the essence of the 'new covenant' lies in its open declaration that knowledge, or direct experience, of the One Reality comes through the Spirit within us, not through the ritualistic observance of religious law.

It was this direct experience, this intimate 'knowledge of God' that those who announced the covenants endeavoured to pass on to their fellow beings. But as Paul's references to the 'old covenant' of Moses demonstrate, our understanding of what they are passing on is often wide of the mark. After his meeting with God on Mount Sinai (a mountain is a traditional symbol for the meeting-place of heaven and earth, of gods and mortals) the Israelites had asked Moses to cover his face with a veil. Its dazzling brightness was such that they could not look at him directly. As Paul points out, however, the veil is more one of the mind than a physical reality. It represents the essential difference between two perceptions of our relationship with God. The one contemplates God from a distance, blind to the spiritual presence within ourselves; the other experiences that same spiritual presence directly, having been transformed by it. Without that process of transformation – spiritual rebirth, or the 'coming of the Messiah/Christ' – the veil of the mind remains unlifted.

When seen within the above context the statues of the two women embody two perceptions of our relationship with God that are crucial for our understanding of the myth of Being at the heart of the gospel narratives. They not only present us with a powerful visual analogy for the transition from spiritual darkness and suffering to spiritual enlightenment and freedom. They also give tangible form to two modes of consciousness, to two modes of being. The one dualistic, inwardly mourns its divided self and its separation from the God with whom it yearns to be reunited. The other nondualistic, owes its vitality and outer vibrancy to the Life or Spirit within it, and with which it resonates in unison throughout the entirety of its being.

The first mode of consciousness/being has its origins in the evolutionary change in consciousness that originally gave birth to the myth of the Fall. It yearns to be reunited with the God who once guided it unfalteringly through life, according to the Way of the Lord. Weighed down with guilt, shame and self-recrimination, it prays for its God to return to it and forgive it its sins. That is the point of departure from which the gospel narratives begin.

Taking up the dualistic man-and-God terminology of the old consciousness the gospel authors narratize the emergence of the new. In the everyday language naturally common to both modes, the two are presented side by side so that we are able to appreciate the differences between them. The new nondualistic, spiritual consciousness is embodied in the figure of Jesus; the old dualistic, man-and-God consciousness is characterized by the myriad cast of characters around him. As we read through the gospel narratives we are also able to experience for ourselves the incompatibility between the two modes; not only in the way that the apparent conflict between the two is expressed through the physical words, but also in the way in which we understand what the words themselves are actually trying to tell us. A closer study of the image presented by the two statues will help us understand what this is.

Taken together the two women depict our two worlds: the inner and outer, the spiritual and human. The woman who looks boldly ahead is the embodiment of our inner world. As the personification of our original spiritual nature in all its glorious perfection, she is a tangible expression of who we really are, if we were only able to see it. The other woman represents our outer world. In the blindfold that covers her eyes we have a concrete image of the veil referred to by Paul. This veil, which can be equated with the egocentric 'I' of our subjective conscious mind, conceals from us our spiritual essence and the knowledge of who we really are. Furthermore, by becoming a veil between our humanity and our spirituality, our ego-centred mind has also given birth to both the fiction and the reality of our divided self.

From a nondualistic, spiritual viewpoint there is no such division. Our outer and inner worlds are one. The blindfold is a visual allegory for a state of spiritual blindness, of unenlightened existence, while the state itself is conveyed in the air of despondency the woman exudes through her body language. Conversely, the unveiled eyes of the second woman evoke the insight that comes with enlightenment. Here it is worth comparing the two women with the figures of the Damned and the Blessed from the Last Judgement. For although the artistic styles are very different, the modes of being they represent are strikingly similar. On one hand we have the embodiment of a state of inner torment and despair; on the other a state of bliss.

But hell and heaven are neither 'down below' nor 'up above'. Nor do they lie in the future. They are here, now. In effect, the state of being embodied in the Damned and the blindfold woman represents our human struggle to *become* who we really are. Between them these two figures also offer us an image of the demise and death of the ego that are an essential part of our becoming. In contrast, the blissful state portrayed by the Blessed and the woman with the unveiled eyes shows us how we already *are*, even now, at the level of *being*.[36] Furthermore, these two figures personify what it means to be fully human. For their enlightened state is the fulfilment of the process referred to as transformation, or spiritual expansion and integration.

This process begins when our spiritual essence incarnates, manifesting itself physically as human form, and concludes when it integrates fully with the individual conscious mind. By that stage the ego, our personal sense of 'I am', has diminished to such a degree that with the fusion of the three levels of our being – body, mind and spirit – we become a spontaneous vehicle for the universal I AM of the Spirit. In doing so it could be said that we have fulfilled our purpose, for our spiritual and physical natures

a)   b)

Figure 3a) Two of the Blessed from the central portal on the west front
of Notre Dame, Paris (first half of the 13th century)

Figure 3b) One of the Damned from the central tympanum on the
façade of Autun cathedral, by Giselbertus (before 1145)

become integrated into a harmonious whole: we have become a fully human being.

What that means for us at a personal level can perhaps best be described by saying that with the demise of the ego we experience simultaneously the fullness of both our human individuality and our inherent spiritual interconnectedness with the myriad aspects of the One Reality. There is no longer an ego to say 'we' are. We simply are. That is what is meant by a state of pure *being*.

In brief that is what the gospels are trying to tell us. In doing so they are simply reminding us, from the outside in, of who we are and where we come from. In effect they are a message to ourselves from ourselves, a message to the conscious mind from the universal sea of consciousness in which we have our roots. The purpose of that message is to heal our sense of being a divided self: to heal the divisions that appear to separate our humanity from our spirituality, and our conscious mind from the deeper levels of consciousness. The problem was (and still is) to get the message home; to get it 'into our guts' (our innermost parts) in such a way that it not only awakens us to the divisions that gave birth to the notion of a divided self, but will also heal those divisions in the process. That is why the gospel narratives are *not* intended to be understood at their face value. By seeking out their deeper meaning we may eventually be brought to a new understanding – not just of the gospel message, but also of ourselves.

As a prelude to getting at that deeper meaning we can use a simple diagram to illustrate how our understanding of the gospel story relates to the two 'covenants' or modes of consciousness/being described above. According to the traditional dualistic man-and-God interpretation of the gospel message, the historical Jesus acts as the intermediary between us and God. His sacrificial death on the cross is a once-and-for-all-time redemptive act by which we are saved from the misery of our sinful earthly existence. That God sent his only Son into the world to die for our sins is not only a powerful sign of his active Presence in the world. It is also a living testimony to the all-embracing love he has for his People. Because of this the Crucifixion has understandably become the central point of the gospel story and a point of focus in the life of every Christian.

If we translate this into a symbolic image (*see* figure 4a opposite), the Crucifixion and our redemption through the death of Jesus are marked by the apex of the triangle. It is the high point in our life, so to speak, at which we are 'lifted up' to a new relationship with God. The baseline of the triangle corresponds to the 'this-worldly' physical plane of our existence, which begins with our physical birth and ends in death. Nevertheless, the diagram depicts our human view of what is essentially a spiritual reality. For as Plato said: 'Is not the whole of human life turned upside down: and are we not doing, as would appear, in everything the opposite of what we ought to be doing?'[36] To understand the gospel message from the standpoint of our original spiritual nature, we need to reverse the point of view symbolized by figure 4a, turning it upside-down as in figure 4b.

In the first image the baseline of the triangle represented the tangible, this-worldly reality of our physical existence. In the second it represents the spiritual dimension of that same existence, which begins and ends in the Spirit. The three points of the triangle correspond to the principal events of the gospel story. At one end of the upper line is the Incarnation, at the other the Ascension. As in figure 4a, the apex of the triangle represents the Crucifixion. But the incarnation and ascension described in the gospel narratives are now our own. They denote our emanation from (our physical birth) and our return to (our physical death) the Spirit. The death on the cross is also now our own. It signifies the moment when, as spiritual beings, we become fully human. And the integration of the spiritual and human dimensions of our being bring to an end our apparent duality and its attendant perception of human life as little more than a process of toil and suffering.

If the two triangles are now superimposed as in figure 4c, they

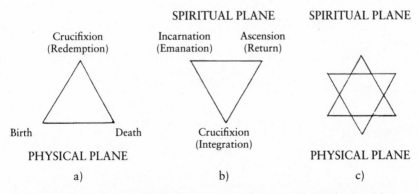

Figure 4 The gospel message from a) human, b) spiritual, and c) non-dualistic standpoints

become the six-pointed star, or Seal of Solomon. This traditional symbol represents in visual form the integration of heaven and earth, the spiritual and material planes. The six points of the star symbolize the inherent perfection of the One Reality, which is similarly expressed in the Six Days of the Creation. But there is also a seventh point, the most important one, which remains unmarked. Corresponding to the Seventh Day of the Creation – the day of rest, or symbolic day of completion – the seventh point is the still point at the centre, around which all else turns. Given voice in the words, 'Be still, and know that I am God',[37] this point of stillness comes into being when the previously separate worlds of 'heaven' and 'earth' – our own inner and outer worlds – are united harmoniously as one. That union, which involves us *dying to what we think we are so as to be born again as we really are* is symbolized from both the human and spiritual standpoints in the death on the cross. But it is far more than a symbolic death. It is simultaneously the fulfilment of our original nature and the profound healing of our divided self.

7

BEHOLD THE SPIRIT!

One of the problems that faced the authors of the gospel narratives was the dimension of time. From the human point of view, time, the fourth dimension, is an essential part of our experience of the One Reality: it simply takes us time to experience things. In the same way that we measure the surfaces of the physical world in inches, feet and miles (or centimetres, metres and kilometres), we also measure the way we experience our lives in days, months and years, or past, present and future. If we go on a journey from A to B, for example, we can measure the distance we are going to travel and from that we are able to work out roughly how long our journey will take.

Things look very different from a spiritual viewpoint because the Spirit is both eternal and infinite. That not only means that it goes on and on through time and space, without ever ending. It also means that it has neither beginning nor end. And because it is One and indivisible the Spirit is both its own cause and effect. That is why, from a spiritual perspective at least, there is only *now*. Whereas a physical journey takes us from A to B in, say, five hours, our spiritual journey begins at A and returns to A without ever leaving it, and the time it takes is also A. Perhaps the nature of the journey becomes a little more clear if we say that it is a journey in *depth*, a journey of self-realization in which a pre-existing potential becomes a reality.

Perhaps it would further help if we drop the word 'journey' and use 'fact' instead. From a spiritual viewpoint, the *fact* is we are spiritual beings. From a human viewpoint, it takes us time to realize the fact. The actual realization may occur all at once, in a flash, or it may take place gradually over a number of years; it may happen when we are three or when we are 93. But our concept of linear time is merely a human construct: a framework we have evolved to help us both understand and live within the eternity of the One Reality, to help us define the smaller, human reality we call 'the real world'. In reality neither time nor timing are that important. It is the realization of the fact that matters; and the only 'time' we can ever realize the fact is *now*.

That was the problem that faced those who composed the gospel narratives: how to portray *in* time that which is eternal? For the more traditional wisdom sayings, stories and parables of the oral tradition there was no such problem. They were not only short enough for time not to matter; those who heard them knew that they were not simple human history. Like traditional creation myths and myths of origin, they expressed the profound and timeless mystery of Life that lies beneath the surface world of everyday human experience. But times had changed. The authors of the gospels were living after recorded history had begun. Our attention was shifting from the mystery beneath the surface to focus increasingly on the waves and ripples of its everyday events. In the process the One Reality was being shrunk to fit into the four-dimensional world of human experience. For those who composed the gospel narratives, that four-dimensional world was obviously the place in which their spiritual story needed to begin. The problem was how, and when?

The canonical Gospels show four different solutions to the problem of how and where to begin. Matthew provides a genealogy from Abraham to Jesus, followed by an angelic annunciation to Joseph in a dream, and a virgin birth; Mark starts later on in time, with John the Baptist and the Baptism of Jesus; Luke begins with angelic annunciations to Zechariah – the elderly father of John the Baptist, whose wife Elizabeth then conceives – and to Mary, the mother of Jesus, followed by the births of first John then Jesus; he also includes a genealogy tracing Jesus' descent back to God. John opens with a prologue describing the incarnation of the Word, or the Light, which is interspersed with verses about John the Baptist who came 'to bear witness to the light'. Where to end presented less of a problem. Although the four gospels differ slightly in their account of events, they all include the discovery of the empty tomb followed by a number of post-resurrection appearances. Both Mark and Luke conclude with the ascension of

Jesus to heaven, an event that is also related at the beginning of the Acts of the Apostles.

The problem of time was not quite the same for those who were later to portray the gospel narratives in visual terms. Until the Renaissance – when art began to do little more than reproduce the visual realism of our four-dimensional world – it was common practice to incorporate the different stages of an event into the same painting or sculpture. In this way the artist could collapse time into one moment in a manner that was far beyond the scope of the linear written form of the gospels.

As an example we can take the panel illustrating *The Annunciation*, by the fifteenth-century Master of the Life of the Virgin, in the Alte Pinakothek in Munich (*see* page 102). The dominant figures of the Virgin Mary and the archangel Gabriel are in the foreground, while floating behind and above them towards the top of the painting is the much smaller figure of God the Father surrounded by angels in a golden heaven. A beam of light descends from God towards Mary. On the beam of light just above Mary's head is a dove, symbol of the Holy Spirit. Higher up on the beam is a tiny figure: the already perfectly formed Christ-child, who, although descending towards the this-worldly space occupied by Mary and Gabriel, has not yet quite left the realm of heaven. Even so, he holds in his hands the Cross on which he is destined to be crucified. The clasp on the archangel's cloak shows the child's ultimate destiny, his heavenly enthronement. In this one scene the artist has managed to portray the spiritual journey (A to A, in A) as a single event. Our end is in our beginning.

As the fully adult Jesus (our mature spiritual nature) of the gospels says: 'I know whence I have come and whither I am going, but you [our immature human nature] do not know whence I come or whither I am going.'[1] If we look closer at the panel, we can see that the painter has collapsed the dimension of time even further, for secreted away in its decorative detail we find Moses, Solomon and the Queen of Sheba, the four evangelists (in symbolic form), as well as the apostles Peter and Paul. Our human concepts of time and space no longer apply in the spiritual dimension of *now*.

Figure 5 The Annunciation, by the Master of the Life of the Virgin,
Cologne School c1460-1490

(Moses, Solomon and the Queen of Sheba are among the saints
embroidered on the archangel's robe; Christ enthroned, surrounded by
the symbols of the four evangelists, is depicted on the clasp below the
archangel's face; Saints Peter and Paul are portrayed in the carved
bench-end on the left.)

The Gospel of John and the Incarnation of the Word

In spite of the obvious difficulties of conveying a sense of the
eternal now in physical words, the writers of the gospel narratives
set out to achieve it as best they could. The style adopted by the
author of John sets his gospel apart from the others, especially in
its opening verses, which take the form of a prologue, a hymn to
the Word, or even an antiphonal chant.[2] Its intertwining themes
offer us a verbal allegory of both an incarnation and a return, in
which the more abstract verses express the progressive descent of
the Word into the world until it takes bodily form, while the verses
about John the Baptist articulate a human view of our ascent
towards the unknowable mystery of God.[3]

Whereas 'the Word' is the standard English translation of the Greek *logos*, its translation into French as '*Le Verbe*' (the Verb) – rather than the more literal '*Le Mot*' (the Word) – holds the key to a slightly different understanding of the Word. In grammar lessons at school I was taught that a verb was a 'doing word'. *Le Verbe* seems to provide a powerful image of an *active* Word, of the Word itself as the creative force that gives things *being*, as when God said: '"Let there *be* light"; and there was light.'[4] The power of the Word as the creative force is expressed perhaps even more clearly in the *Qur'an*, where we are told that God 'need only say "Be", and it is.'[5]

The author of John expresses the creative power of the Word in terms of Life and Light: 'In him [the Word] was life, and the life was the light of men.'[6] In the next stage of his mini-Creation he adds: 'The true light that enlightens every man was coming into the world,'[7] which conveys the idea that we are *in essence* already enlightened. By contrast, those who compiled the synoptic gospels sought to express the same idea of our original enlightened state in more mythical terms, mirroring the original creation of Adam with the creation of a new man, a perfect archetypal Man, both conceived by and one with the Spirit – an idea that is also expressed in John, with the words: 'And the Word became flesh and dwelt among us.'[8]

A similar idea is put into words in the Old Testament theme of the potter and the clay (*see* Chapter 2, page 25). If we turn around our understanding of the process by which the potter forms the lump of inanimate clay into a pot, and say that in order to take on the form intended for it the clay *allows* itself to be shaped by the potter, we begin to have an analogy for both our own physical journey through life as well as the way in which the Spirit/Word works *through* us. The latter is an actively passive process: one of being rather than doing, of grace rather than effort. It is not something our ego can 'will' into happening. On the contrary, it is by dropping our egocentric sense of 'I' and surrendering wholeheartedly to the Source of Life within us that we become one with its creative power: the Spirit/Word. By simply *being*, we become the word 'Be' in action.

To emphasize a point made previously: a fundamental part of our dilemma is that once we have come into the world we tend to lose sight of the spiritual Source of our being. With that we also lose sight of the purpose of our existence. The primary function of the gospel narratives is therefore to remind us of who we are and where we come from. Of the three synoptic gospels Luke is perhaps the most successful at presenting us with the whole story, but the symbolism he uses is complex. If we still had a genuine sense of myth and symbol, we would both hear and understand Luke's symbolism at an unconscious archetypal level. Instead, we have to dig out the meaning from behind the words by using yet more words. That is what we shall be doing in this chapter and the next. For that reason they take a slightly different form to further chapters in this second part of the book. Whereas later chapters concern themselves more with the gospels' characterization of the two modes of consciousness/being described at length in Chapter 6, this one goes on to explore the multiple layers of meaning contained in the opening chapters of Luke.

The Gospel of Luke: From Annunciation to Temptation

The author of Luke begins his gospel with the words: 'Inasmuch as many have undertaken to compile a narrative of the things which have been accomplished among us . . .', and then goes on to dedicate his own version of the gospel to someone he calls 'most excellent Theophilus' with the adjunct 'that you may know the truth concerning the things of which you have been informed'.[9] Popular Christian exegesis holds that Theophilus was an unknown Christian, possibly a Roman, of some social eminence.[10] It is likely that the author had someone else in mind. When the name Theophilus, or *Theo-philus* is translated into English it becomes 'lover of God', and it is probably in this sense that we are intended to understand it. That is to say, the author of Luke dedicates his gospel to *each and every* 'lover of God' – including ourselves – with the expressed intention of disclosing some kind of 'truth' relating to the narratives mentioned in his opening sentence. In spite of its author's declared intent, the parabolic nature of the gospel genre is such that whatever truth is revealed in Luke, it will not be found in a literal interpretation of the physical words.

After the opening dedication the first three chapters of the gospel are carefully orchestrated to provide us with an allegorical account of the progressive Self-revelation of the Spirit. They take us from the angelic annunciations of the births of John the Baptist and Jesus to Jesus' Temptation in the Wilderness. In doing so the sequence of events narrated here parallels the Incarnation of the Word that unfolds in the opening verses of John. The principal difference between the two versions is that Luke uses the traditional symbolic imagery of everyday events, which would perhaps have been more accessible to the minds of ordinary folk than the abstract concept of the *Logos*. Because both the mythical and contemporary historical settings for the gospel are essentially Jewish, as was the background of the audience for whom the gospels were originally intended, we shall frequently need to turn to the verbal imagery of the Old Testament and the Hebrew or Jewish myth to uncover something of the underlying meaning. In the following exploration of Luke's narrative, verses from John's Incarnation of the Word have been inserted where appropriate to illustrate the synchronous nature of the two accounts. At the same time they provide an additional commentary on the events themselves.

Two Annunciations and two Births

Following its opening dedication, the first chapter of Luke takes the form of a prologue to the birth of Jesus. The events that take place between the twin conceptions and births of John the Baptist and Jesus and their appearance on the banks of the Jordan present us with two interwoven strands. Between them they portray the old dualistic man-and-God consciousness and a new mode of consciousness/being vitalized by the Spirit/Word within us. In essence that is the story that unfolds in all the gospel narratives. But the nature of the gospels is such that the whole of the story and each event within it offer us an opportunity to awaken to our own divided self. As we shall see, the awakening to the new mode of consciousness does not necessitate the forceful shattering of the old. The new emerges from within it, naturally. The old is merely a veil, a looking-glass, through which we see but dimly the wholeness that lies beyond.

The author of Luke begins his story with the strand that represents the old consciousness and the appearance of the archangel Gabriel to Zechariah. As an embodiment of our man-and-God dualism, Zechariah is an elderly priest. He and his wife Elizabeth are described as 'childless and advanced in years', an allegorical state that expresses the idea of not hearing the word of God, of being barren and unfruitful like the wilderness. Gabriel informs Zechariah that he and Elizabeth will become the parents of a son, whom they are to name John. '*There was a man sent from God, whose name was John.*'[11]

In Hebrew the name John means 'God is merciful', but Zechariah does not believe the 'good news'. Because of this Gabriel tells him that he will be unable to speak until such time as the prophesied event has taken place. Ironically, the man who neither hears 'the word', nor believes it when he does hear it, is told that he will not utter a word until 'the word' has been fulfilled.

Using a phrase that reminds us of the Last Times, the author tells us that 'after *those days*'[12] Elizabeth conceives. He then introduces us to the second strand – representing the new nondualistic consciousness – when, in the sixth month of Elizabeth's pregnancy, Gabriel goes to Nazareth in Galilee. There he appears to a virgin whose name is Mary and announces that she will 'conceive and bear a son', whom she shall name Jesus. (The reference to Mary being 'a virgin' is connected with the fulfilment of a prophecy from Isaiah, quoted in Matthew: '"Behold, a virgin shall conceive and bear a son, and his name shall be called Emmanuel" (which means, God with us).'[13]) For the fuller implications of Mary's response to Gabriel – 'How shall this be, since I have no husband?'[14] – we need to turn to the Old Testament. There the use of the word 'husband' as a simile for God suggests an alternative meaning for the word 'virgin': as someone who has no knowledge of God. But first we need to look at the word itself.

Much ink has already been expended on the fact that the original Hebrew of Isaiah uses the word *almah*, which appeared in the Septuagint (the oldest Greek translation of the Old Testament) as *parthenos*. As a result *parthenos* was the word used in the common Greek with which the gospels were first written down. Since then commentators have debated the different meanings attributable to the two words: the Hebrew *almah* can be translated as 'young woman', 'maiden', 'girl' or 'virgin', whereas the Greek *parthenos* normally translates only as 'virgin'. The essential difference in meaning, however, is that the former (*almah*) is used socially to describe an unmarried female – that is, a young woman who has 'no husband' – the latter (*parthenos*) is used in a strictly biological sense.

We find a possible source for Luke's own use of the word 'virgin' in Jeremiah. There the prophet announces a 'new covenant' in which the 'virgin Israel' (ie, a husband-less, or God-less Israel) is promised a time of fruitfulness to follow the barren time she has endured through having forsaken her God.[15] As the Hebrew and Aramaic forms of the name Jesus mean 'he will save', or 'saviour',[16] Luke's Jewish-orientated audience would have understood Mary to be the personification of Jeremiah's 'virgin Israel', whose salvation lay within her, in the intimate knowledge of God that was central to the new covenant/consciousness announced by the prophets. Her response to the angel's announcement that she will conceive a son would have been understood as: 'How shall I bear fruit, since I have no knowledge of God?'

Gabriel's reply to Mary/Israel's question describes how the new 'covenant' that will bring about the spiritual regeneration of Israel is to be made: 'The Holy Spirit will come upon you, and the power of the Most High will overshadow you; therefore the child to be born will be called holy, the Son of God.'[17] But the nature of the gospel message is such that the angel's reply can be applied at a more personal level, to our individual spiritual re-birth. And the making of the new covenant/consciousness is exemplified in Mary/Israel's words – 'Behold the handmaid of the Lord; *be* it unto me according to thy word.'[18] – as a process of surrendering to the Spirit of God within us. For both the commandment of God, and his 'word' – the pro-creative word '*be*' – are merely further synonyms for the Spirit/Word of Life within us. As the simple words of the psalmist remind us, the timing of the new covenant/consciousness, of that numinous moment of Self-revelation and Self-knowledge is always *now*: '*Be* still, and know that I am God.'[19]

The two strands of the old and new are now woven together as the author of Luke tells us that 'in *those days*' after the angel's departure Mary goes quickly to visit her kinswoman Elizabeth. When Mary enters the house of her relatives she greets Elizabeth, who is filled with the Holy Spirit while her child leaps in her womb. '*He came for testimony, to bear witness to the light.*'[20]

When the time comes and Elizabeth gives birth, her neighbours and relatives join with her in rejoicing because 'God has shown great mercy to her'. At the ceremonial naming of the child, the relatives wish to name him Zechariah, after his father. But his mother says, 'No; he shall be called John.' (The Hebrew meaning of the name John – 'God is merciful' – provides us with a pun on the earlier rejoicing of the neighbours and relatives.)

After the naming of the child, Zechariah regains his speech, thereby fulfilling the angel's prophecy. But there is another play on words here in this unfolding story of the two 'covenants', for the 'good news' that Zechariah refused to believe was that 'God is merciful' even to those who cannot hear his word, and now 'God's mercy' that came with the naming of the child is extended to the old priest.

The author of Luke marks the conclusion of a particular stage in the progressive Self-revelation of the Spirit with a brief comment or afterword. When taken together the changes of wording in these concluding comments appear in themselves to sum up the process unfolding before us. The first of them comes with the birth of John, concluding the first chapter with the words: *'And the child grew and became strong in spirit, and he was in the wilderness till the day of his manifestation to Israel.'*[21]

We now come to the birth of Jesus. Apart from being set in Bethlehem, David's city, in accordance with Messianic expectation that the Messiah/Christ would be from the house of David, this birth is presented in a way that seems intentionally to parody our own everyday awareness of the spiritual dimension of existence. Compared with the lengthy description of the events surrounding the birth of John, it is an insignificant birth with the child being laid in a manger because there was 'no place . . . in the inn'. There is no star, the astrological portent that brought wise men from the East announcing the birth of the king of the Jews; no jealous Herod who massacres all the boys aged two or under in Bethlehem and the surrounding region; there are not even the rejoicing neighbours and relatives that were present for the birth of John. *'The true light that enlightens every man was coming into the world. He was in the world, and the world was made through him, but the world knew him not. He came to his own home, and his own people received him not.'*[22]

Although the incarnation of the Spirit/Word is ignored by the world, the news is heard by some: the shepherds, who are 'keeping watch over their flock by night'. But the angelic nature of their night-time revelation and 'the glory of the Lord that shone around them' indicate that their knowledge of the event does not come from the world. '*The light shines in the darkness, and the darkness has not overcome it.*'[23]

In Luke's narrative there are as yet no eye-witnesses to the presence of the Spirit in the world. The shepherds have only heard of it from the angels, and their hearing, or understanding, of the good news is followed by what seems to be Luke's concluding statement for this stage in the Spirit's progressive Self-revelation. On this occasion it is uttered by 'a multitude of the heavenly host praising God and saying, "*Glory be to God in the highest, and on earth peace among men with whom he is pleased!*"'[24] Having heard the good news, the shepherds now go to Bethlehem to see for themselves the infant who is the embodiment of the 'good shepherd'. The transformation from 'hearing' to 'seeing' is illustrated in the next episode in Luke's story.

The Presentation in the Temple

Following the shepherds' departure, the author of Luke passes over the circumcision of Jesus in one verse before bringing together the two strands of his narrative in the Presentation in the Temple.[25] According to religious law, if a child was the first-born of its mother it was to be consecrated to God.[26] And so, after the legally required period of purification had been completed, Mary and Joseph take Jesus to the temple in Jerusalem to make their offering and present their first-born child of God. The temple setting and the religious ceremony that takes place there embody the old man-and-God covenant/consciousness while the infant Jesus personifies the new. But the presence of the child in the temple has an additional significance. For the gospel writers the temple is a synonym for the human body.

Luke tells us that Simeon, a devout old man who has previously been told by the Spirit that he would not die until he has seen the Messiah, is inspired by the Spirit to enter the temple. When Mary and Joseph enter the temple with the child Jesus, Simeon takes him in his arms, praises God, and utters the words now sung as part of the *Nunc Dimittis*: 'Lord, now lettest thou thy servant depart in peace, according to thy word; for mine eyes have seen thy salvation which thou hast prepared in the presence of all peoples . . .'

The name Simeon involves a play on words derived from Genesis, where Jacob's second son by Leah is given the name Simeon, 'because the Lord has heard' (Hebrew *shama*).[27] As with his name, the words that Simeon speaks are also of Old Testament origin and echo those spoken by Job. At the end of his time of testing, Job says to God: 'I had heard of thee by the hearing of the ear, but now my eye sees thee.'[28] A further play on words is present in Simeon's 'my eyes have seen *thy salvation*' and the name of the child he sees: Jesus, also meaning 'saviour' or 'salvation'. When these elements are taken into consideration, Simeon's recognition of the Messiah can be seen to offer us an allegory for the transition from spiritual insight (*hearing*) to direct spiritual experience (*seeing*). This transformation from one state of being to another is borne out in Simeon's own reference to his 'peaceful departure' (enlightened bliss) and 'death' (of the ego), foretold by the Spirit as not occurring until he had 'seen the Messiah'. For if we interpret these words according to their spiritual meaning they express the profound process of spiritual awakening and rebirth.

Also present is Anna, a prophetess. She never leaves the temple, spending all her time there fasting and in prayer night and day. Coming up at the very moment of Simeon's revelation, she too recognizes the true nature of the infant, gives thanks to God, and proceeds to proclaim the good news of his presence to all who awaited the salvation of Jerusalem.[29] '*To all who received him, who believed in his name, he gave power to become children of God.*'[30]

By including Anna the author of Luke provides three views of the same event, each of which offers us an insight into our own individual and collective spiritual evolution. First, we have Mary and Joseph who take their child to the temple to dedicate him to the Lord, as a child of God, in strict observance of the Law. Theirs is a formal religious gesture, with a profound underlying meaning of which they are apparently unaware: our *re*-cognition of the Spirit within us. (As we shall see in the next section, they seem to be oblivious to the true nature of their child, even though they may have been 'told by angels'.) Second, we have the spiritual awakening and rebirth of Simeon that comes with his recognition of the Spirit of God incarnate in the world. But as his inspired visit to the temple shows, the Spirit/Word acts independently of both human will and religious law; it reveals itself spontaneously to those who are ready to 'hear' it. Third, there is Anna. In announcing the presence of the Spirit to all who are looking for spiritual fulfilment she places the personal revelation personified by Simeon in a wider context. Spiritual fulfilment is available to everyone who truly seeks it.

In presenting us with this contrast between outer gesture and spiritually inspired response, Luke illustrates the distinction between the two strands that are the underlying core of his story: the dualism of the old man-and-God understanding of our relationship with the One Reality and the nonduality of the new spiritual consciousness. With the one we are governed from the outside by the observance of social and religious laws and from the inside by the will and desires of our ego. With the other we are simply vehicles for the spontaneous self-expression of the Spirit, the Source of our being. The event concludes with the words: *'The child grew and became strong, filled with wisdom; and the favour of God was upon him.'*[31]

It is significant that the infant has not yet spoken for himself.

In my Father's house

We learn little from the gospel narratives about the years between Jesus' infancy and his appearance on the banks of the Jordan, where, according to the gospel story, he is baptized at the age of 30. Except for one incident that takes place when he was 12, recorded exclusively in Luke, where Jesus was and what he did in the intervening years remains a tantalizing mystery that invites conjecture and speculation. But speculation about the mystery of those 'silent years' is looking for the messenger rather than the message. If we examine the mythical elements in Luke's narrative concerning Mary's and Joseph's search for the 12-year-old Jesus, we will find that this event (which follows immediately after the Presentation in the Temple) expresses an intimate spiritual moment:

> Every year Jesus' parents went to Jerusalem for the Passover festival. When he was twelve years old they went up as usual, and after the festival was over they set off on the return journey, but, unbeknown to his parents, the boy Jesus stayed on in Jerusalem. Assuming him to be travelling with the rest of their party, they had completed a day's journey before they looked for him amongst their relatives and

acquaintances. They were unable to find him, and so they returned to Jerusalem to search for him there.

Three days later they found him in the Temple, sitting amongst the teachers, listening to them and asking them questions, and everyone who heard him was amazed, both at his understanding and by his answers. His parents were astonished when they saw him, and his mother said to him, 'Son, why have you treated us like this? Your father and I have been searching anxiously high and low for you.'

'Why did you look for me?' he asked them, 'Did you not know that I must be in my father's house?' But his parents could not understand what he said to them.[32]

According to Hugh Schonfield, the author of Luke drew on various non-biblical sources, including the works of the Jewish historian Josephus. He suggests this episode in the temple may have been inspired by the following passage from Josephus' autobiography: 'While still a mere boy, about fourteen years old, I won universal applause for my love of letters; insomuch that the chief priests and learned men of the city [Jerusalem] used constantly to come to me for precise information on some particular of our ordinances.'[33] If Schonfield's explanation is correct, then in adapting Josephus to suit his own purposes the author of Luke has woven into it several additional elements to give it an entirely different connotation. An erstwhile historical event has become a timeless teaching story.

Of fundamental importance in Luke's unfolding narrative this is the moment when the infant Spirit/Word spontaneously reveals itself by appearing in the temple. There Jesus speaks with the elders, the upholders of the Mosaic Law, astounding them with his wisdom and authority. '*And the Word became flesh and dwelt among us, full of grace and truth . . . the law was given through Moses; grace and truth came through Jesus Christ.*'[34]

Conventional retelling of this event normally focuses our attention on the figure of Jesus, as an illustration of his spiritual wisdom and his knowledge of the Mosaic Law. But a very different meaning becomes apparent when we consider the role of Mary and Joseph in the light of the two gospel sayings: 'Seek and ye shall find' and 'The kingdom of heaven is within you'. For while Jesus personifies our potential nondualistic spiritual consciousness, his earthly parents represent our dualistic man-and-God mind-set: our divided self, which secretly yearns to be reunited with the Source of our being. In this role they illustrate three stages in our own potential spiritual evolution.

At first, like Mary and Joseph who do not realize Jesus has stayed on in Jerusalem, we are blissfully unaware that we are missing something from which we have inadvertently become separated while going about our this-worldly business. When Mary and Joseph awaken to the fact that Jesus is missing, they ask the people they are travelling with, supposing him to be with them. Likewise, when we initially awaken to the predicament of our divided self we begin our search outside ourselves. We ask those who, like us, are journeying along the path of life if they have found what we are looking for. Perhaps we turn to religion, read a mountain of books, or embark on a course of self-improvement. But if we do not find what we are looking for in the outer world, our search to become whole may eventually lead us to our inner world. Like Mary and Joseph, by retracing our steps to the point from where our journey began, to the Source (symbolized here in their return to Jerusalem), we find that what we are looking for lies within ourselves, in the metaphorical temple of the body. The return to the temple therefore marks an important stage in our spiritual evolution: the recognition that the goal of our search – whether we see it in terms of spiritual fulfilment, the knowledge of who we are and where we come from, or the healing of our divided self – lies within us.

In the context of this interpretation, Mary's complaint about the way their son has treated them, causing them to search high and low for him, echoes our own frustration when it dawns on us that in many ways our search also appears to have been unnecessary. As Jesus points out to his parents when they find him, 'Why did you look for me? Did you not know that I must be in my father's house?' As our own search may reveal: where else can the Spirit/ Word possibly be? Are we not each and all the temple or dwelling-place of the incarnate Spirit? But the additional comment that Jesus' parents could not understand what he said to them reflects the fact that we may not yet fully comprehend the true nature of what it is we are looking for. In that respect it is an invitation, even a challenge, to us to reflect on our own understanding.

In one sense the Self-revelation of the Spirit/Word to the world is now complete, but not quite. As the author of Luke makes plain: the Spirit/Word may have made itself heard; the wider implications of its presence in the world have yet to be understood. For the time being he leaves us with a verbal image which on the surface describes the physical appearance of the child in the temple. But beneath this allegorical image he is drawing our attention to the presence of the Spirit within us. In weaving together the strands of his story in this way he presents us with two super-imposed images that correspond to the mind-sets associated with the 'old' and 'new' covenants. The old man-and-God consciousness is personified in the physical temple building; the new spiritual consciousness is embodied in the child within it. The simultaneous coexistence of the two is echoed in the words that conclude the event: '*And Jesus increased in wisdom and in stature, and in favour with God and man.*'[35]

The next time we encounter the child he will be fully grown.

8

BORN OF WATER AND THE SPIRIT

Luke's allegorical account of the progressive Self-revelation of the Spirit/Word has so far taken us from its initial unsung manifestation in the world to a point at which its presence has been acknowledged at one or more levels. It has even spoken for itself in the temple building, symbol of our dualistic man-and-God mode of consciousness. But the Spirit/Word has not yet declared itself openly, from within human consciousness. It is now that John, who has been 'in the wilderness till the day of his manifestation to Israel', reappears on the banks of the Jordan. The paths of the two children with whom the author of Luke began his story are about to cross once more. Now they are fully grown, and in their meeting on the banks of the Jordan the underlying strands of the narrative become woven together more tightly.

Born of water

John's reappearance is heralded in words taken from the Hebrew prophets, those intimates of God who had endeavoured to awaken the people to the knowledge of God within them. John is 'the voice of one crying in the wilderness: "Prepare the way of the Lord",'[1] and his mission is to preach a baptism of repentance for the forgiveness of sins. But the nature of the intimate 'knowledge of God' or 'way of the Lord' announced by John and the prophets is such that the mere telling of it does not of itself bring it into being.

For this reason the words of the prophets may sound like little more than hollow thunderings. Their foretelling of a 'new covenant' was understood according to the beliefs of the old; the new therefore never arrived.

By giving John an identity close to that of the prophets as well as timing his re-emergence from the wilderness to coincide with the beginning of Jesus' ministry, the gospel narratives provide us with an image of the old and new covenants or modes of consciousness side by side. The one is embodied in John the Baptist, the other in Jesus. The essential difference between the two is illustrated in the contrast between the behaviour of their disciples. Those who follow John faithfully observe the statutes of the Law; those who follow Jesus are guided by their Lord (the Spirit) in spontaneous response to the needs of the moment, whatever these may be. In doing so they frequently break social and religious convention. Jesus sheds further light on the difference between the two, and in doing so alludes to the two modes of consciousness/ being personified by John and himself: 'Among those born of women there has risen no one greater than John the Baptist; yet he who is least in the kingdom of heaven is greater than he. From the days of John the Baptist until now the kingdom of heaven has suffered violence, and men of violence take it by force.'[2] But if John the Baptist was preaching a message of repentance and proclaiming the way of the Lord, why is he classed as being less than the least in the kingdom of heaven?

As explained earlier, repentance (*metanoia*) refers to a fundamental change of mind. It is a shift of consciousness, an awakening to Reality prompted by the Spirit within us. The 'John the Baptist' Jesus refers to here is our recognition of the guiding light of the Spirit from a uniquely human viewpoint. However profound that recognition may be, it is not true *metanoia*. It retains a degree of our old man-and-God mind-set. This may manifest itself in the claim that we can know what is or is not the will or work of God, or that the simple recognition of the presence of the Spirit in the world is, of itself, spiritual consciousness.

Genuine spiritual consciousness is not something we can claim for ourselves: there is no longer an egocentric 'I' to make such claims. Our sense of this-worldly authority is replaced by something of a totally different order inspired by the Spirit, embodied here in the Jesus of the gospels. Of those who claim the Spirit's work for themselves, he says: 'All who came before me are thieves and robbers.'[3] Why Jesus should define them thus is clarified by John the Baptist when he describes the transition from the old mode of consciousness to the new – a transition that also involves the demise of the ego: 'No one can receive anything except what is given him from heaven. You yourselves bear me witness, that I said, I am not the Christ, but I have been sent before him. . . He must increase, but I must decrease.'[4] *'John bore witness to him, and proclaimed . . . "This is he of whom I said, 'He who comes after me ranks before me, because he was before me'"'*.[5]

If we turn to the baptism narratives we find how this transition takes place. The account of Jesus' baptism given in Luke differs from those in the other New Testament gospels. Both Matthew and Mark state clearly that Jesus was baptized by John, although in Matthew's version John appears to have some initial reluctance because he recognizes that Jesus' spiritual authority is greater than his own. In John the two men meet on the banks of the river Jordan, but the author does not mention the actual baptism of Jesus. Similarly, the author of Luke does not state in so many words that Jesus is baptized by John. Instead, having informed us about John's preaching of the 'good news', he jumps forward in time to tell us that this was 'just one more thing that Herod held against John', and so 'shut him up in prison'.[6] Following the reference to John's imprisonment we are immediately told that when all the people have been baptized, and Jesus has also been baptized, the heavens open. The Holy Spirit descends upon Jesus in the form of a dove, and a voice from heaven brings the event that unfolds on the banks of the Jordan to a close with the words: *'Thou art my Son, the Beloved, today I have begotten thee.'*[7]

Why does the author of Luke comment on the end of John's activity at this particular juncture, especially when he will refer to him again in later chapters? And why at this stage of the gospel story does he refrain from saying either that Jesus was baptized by John, or that the two actually met by the Jordan? One possible explanation is that he has intentionally condensed events so that John's re-emergence from the wilderness, his preaching of the good news and his consequent incarceration in prison, really do prepare the way of the Lord in that they lead up to the descent of the Holy Spirit and the voice from heaven saying 'today I have begotten thee'. The demise of John is thus presented in such a way that it precedes the first appearance of the adult Jesus, giving narrative form to John's own words: 'He must increase, but I must decrease.' The impression being created in Luke is that John and Jesus are two aspects of one person: the one aspect born of water, the other of the Spirit. In like manner, John's re-emergence from the wilderness and Jesus' baptism by the Spirit seem to be a single event seen from two different perspectives: the one human, the other spiritual. As we shall see shortly, the idea would have been nothing new for Luke's Jewish audience; but first there are some things to clarify concerning baptism, for the act itself has more than one level of interpretation.

We encountered one form of baptism earlier in the traditional mythical journey and the hero's trial(s) by water, which symbolizes a re-emergence from the archetypal 'waters of the deep', the Womb of Life. As such it signifies a rebirth or the transition from one level of being to another. As a symbolic ritual, baptism is usually administered by one person to another as part of an initiatory rite; the initiator is generally someone in a position of greater spiritual authority than the initiate. Perhaps this is one reason why the author of Luke avoids saying that Jesus was baptized by John. To do so would have implied that, at that stage of the story at least, Jesus was the inferior of the two. There is also another reason why he avoids saying so that would have been obvious to a Jewish audience. For this we need to turn to the books of the Old Testament.

Born of the Spirit

Ever since God first breathed the Breath or Spirit into Adam's lifeless physical body in the Genesis creation myth, the procreative power of the Spirit and our spiritual birth have been an integral part of biblical tradition. The first instance we encounter following the creation of Adam is the birth of Eve, for Eve was not created as the result of any human action; she was made by God from one of Adam's ribs.[8] But once the original mythical couple had been created the theme of spiritual birth could no longer be repeated in quite the same way. It would have been too much out of line with everyday human experience: we are not made from one of our parents' ribs. Yet the normal procreation of children would not serve to illustrate the idea of spiritual birth either; it was too close to everyday human experience. Consequently a new and different form of analogy was established: the rivalry between two sons/brothers, with the second-born somehow receiving the birthright or blessing destined for the first. This new analogy, which corresponds with many people's experience of a spiritual awakening or rebirth at some stage in later life, is expressed succinctly by St Paul:

> It is not the spiritual which is first but the physical, and then the spiritual. The first man was from the earth, a man of dust; the second man is from heaven . . . Just as we have borne the image of the man of dust, let us also bear the image of the man of heaven.[9]

Where the stories of two sons/brothers are concerned the first-born is the 'man of dust', our human or physical aspect, while the second personifies the spiritual or heavenly. The uneasy relationship that binds the two together reflects the changes in our own relationship with the Spirit within us.

We meet the new analogy for the first time in Cain and Abel, the sons of Adam and Eve. When Cain, the first-born and 'a tiller of the ground', and Abel, 'a keeper of sheep', make their offerings to God, the acceptance of Abel's offering and the rejection of Cain's leads the latter to kill his younger brother. The this-worldly nature of Cain, the tiller of the ground, is emphasized in the fate that befalls him, for he is condemned to be a 'fugitive and a wanderer on the earth' until such time as he builds the city of Enoch.[10] On the one hand it would appear that the author of Genesis is using the fratricide as a myth of origin to account for the transition from a nomadic to an agrarian way of life and the birth of civilization. On the other it would appear that in Cain's murder of Abel, the one who received God's blessing, the author echoes the separation of our humanity from our spirituality that occurred at the time of the Fall.

The theme appears again when the twins Esau and Jacob struggle with each other while still in the womb of Rebekah, Isaac's wife. On asking God why, he tells her: 'Two nations are in your womb, and two peoples, born of you, shall be divided; the one shall be stronger than the other, the elder shall serve the younger.'[11] Esau is born first, red and hairy, followed by Jacob who has hold of his heel (the name Jacob, a play on the Hebrew word for 'heel', can be translated as 'he takes by the heel', or 'he supplants'). As the two grow up Esau becomes a 'man of the field', while Jacob is a 'quiet man, dwelling in tents'. When Esau is hungry, Jacob buys from him his birthright for the famous 'mess of pottage',[12] and later disguises himself to obtain Isaac's paternal blessing. Told that he will have to serve his younger brother, Esau's anger is such that he plans to kill Jacob, but, warned by his mother, the latter is able to flee and escape from sharing in the fate that befell Abel.[13]

Jacob's fight with the angel conveys a similar idea to the analogy of the two brothers, for it brings about a change of name that reflects the emergence of a new *persona* that has both 'striven with God and men' and seen God face to face. Jacob's new name is *Israel* (Hebrew for *God strives* or *God rules*). It is therefore perhaps no coincidence that the transformation marked by his change of name is immediately followed by a reconciliation with his brother Esau.[14] Our own process of spiritual evolution – the unfolding life of the Spirit within us – has the potential to bring about a similar natural healing of our erstwhile divided self.

The theme takes yet another twist with Jacob/Israel's son Joseph, in the naming of Joseph's two sons by Asenath, an Egyptian woman. Joseph names the first-born Mannaseh (Hebrew: *making to forget*), 'For God has made me forget all my hardship and all my father's house'. The second he names Ephraim (Hebrew: *to be fruitful*), 'For God has made me fruitful in the land of my affliction'.[15] In themselves the two names reflect our human and spiritual natures, but they also echo what appears to our human eyes to be our own two-stage journey through life: first the physical, in which we forget who we are and where we come from, then the spiritual in which we have the possibility to 'bear fruit' by fulfilling our spiritual potential. Later, when Israel is on his deathbed he adopts Joseph's two sons, but at the moment of placing his blessing upon them he switches hands so that Ephraim receives the blessing from Israel's right hand – the traditional hand of power, the hand of transmission – and Mannaseh from the left. In protest Joseph lifts the hand from Ephraim's head, but Israel refuses to be moved. Telling Joseph that the younger brother will be the greater, he blesses them, saying: 'By you Israel [the nation] will pronounce blessings, saying, "God make you as Ephraim and Mannaseh".'[16]

In the same way that the quality associated with the name Israel provides a *persona* first for Jacob and then for the emerging Israelite nation, the qualities associated with Ephraim and Mannaseh also provide *personae* for Joseph's two sons and the two tribes that will later bear the same names. Echoing the way in which the power of symbolic numbers is increased through their multiplication by 10, 100, or 1,000, the power inherent in a name is amplified through its attribution to a person, a tribe, or a nation. Conversely, when the name of a person, tribe or nation is invoked in the Bible, it is the quality or power behind the name that is also being called upon. This leads to frequent double meanings. For instance in the new covenant/virgin Israel chapter from Jeremiah referred to earlier, we find God saying: 'I am a father to Israel [the nation] and Ephraim [the tribe] is my first-born.'[17] At least, that is what he appears to be saying. If we look at the same sentence from a spiritual viewpoint, through God's own eyes so to speak, we find him saying: 'I am a father to whoever strives with me, and fruitfulness is my first-born.'

A similar interpretation can be applied to a further reference to Ephraim in the same chapter – which is essentially about the fruitfulness that will come to Israel through following the 'new covenant' – where we find God again invoking the name Ephraim: 'Is Ephraim my dear son? Is he my darling child?'[18] The implication here is not so much that God has personally conceived either Joseph's son, or the tribe that shared his name, but the fruitfulness that manifests through the name itself. I suggest that a similar interpretation can be applied to the verse in Psalms, where God says of his anointed one (the Messiah): 'You are my son, today I have begotten you.'[19] This same phrase is pronounced by the voice from heaven after Jesus has been baptized. For the myth-makers, God's apparent approval of what he himself has created would seem to be an integral part of the nondualistic Self-revealing, Self-knowing process by which the One Reality acknowledges its own existence.

We are now in a better position to consider the various elements brought together in the event that took place on the banks of the Jordan: an event intended to portray the eternal Spirit alive and unfolding within us, which was itself the genesis of biblical tradition. First we have the two figures of John the Baptist and Jesus, who although no longer the two brothers of Genesis myth are at least related to each other, possibly even cousins. On the one hand is John, the first-born of the two, who embodies some of the characteristics of the first-born cited above. Like Cain he is a tiller of the ground who prepares the way, or ground, for one who will follow. Like Esau he moves in his mother's womb, but now in the joy of recognition rather than struggle. His 'garment of camel's hair'[20] mirrors Esau's hairiness, while his time in the wilderness recalls that Esau was a 'man of the field'. On the other is Jesus, who refers to himself as a shepherd, like Abel. Compared with John, Jesus is a 'quiet man', like Jacob. The latter's flight from Esau's anger has its parallel in Jesus' own departure to Egypt to escape the anger of Herod. It could even be said that Jesus' acquisition of the titular name 'the Christ' bears a strong resemblance to Jacob's transformation into Israel. For the power of their new names is perpetuated in the respective 'nations' to which the two men gave birth. Similarly, in the qualities associated with the names of Joseph's two sons, Mannaseh ('making to forget') and Ephraim ('to be fruitful'), we find the destinies that will befall John and Jesus. In the Baptist's own words, 'he must increase, but I must decrease'. Lastly, the patriarchal transmission of power bestowed upon Ephraim by Israel finds a powerful new expression in the descending dove of the Spirit and the patriarchal blessing bestowed upon Jesus with the words: 'Thou art my Son, my Beloved, today I have begotten thee.' In these words that bring the event on the banks of the Jordan to a conclusion, the spiritual inheritance that has been transmitted physically through generation after generation from Adam to Jesus becomes reunited with the ethereal Spirit of God. In the process the author of Luke presents us with an image that has the potential to bring an end to the separation of our humanity from our spirituality that took place in our minds around the time of the birth of Adam.

It has to be said that reducing the similarities between John and Jesus and the archetypal figures of Genesis to little more than a list of words fails to convey anything of the power associated with either the archetypes or their names, and even less of the power of the oral tradition that would have impressed the ancient myths upon the minds of generations of Israelites. Nonetheless, I suggest that it was from within that same mythical tradition that the gospel writers drew their models for the figures of John the Baptist and Jesus in order to provide a contemporary variation on a theme that would have been instantly recognizable to a Jewish audience whose mythical tradition flowed like the blood in their veins.

From a modern historical perspective, the suggestion that John and Jesus are intended to represent two aspects of one person will sound far-fetched, as will the proposition that John's re-emergence from the wilderness and Jesus' baptism by the Spirit are one and the same event depicted from two different views – the one human, the other spiritual. But the recording of history was not the intention of the gospel writers. What concerned them above all else was the announcement of our potential to experience our original spiritual nature through a nondualistic mode of consciousness, an intimate 'knowledge of God'. In that respect the event that takes place on the banks of the Jordan is an initiation into one of the most profound mysteries of life. But the event is not, as we may at first believe, a symbolic outer gesture in the waters of the Jordan. The baptism is embodied in the composite figure of John and Jesus, with the man born of water making way for a new man born of both water and the Spirit. As for the initiation, it is potentially our own.

Temptation in the Wilderness

Our story has now taken us from the incarnation of the Spirit/Word in an unconscious world to an awakening recognition of its presence. Before his demise John the Baptist actively preached the gospel, the 'good news', concerning the coming of the Spirit/Word in the world. God himself has acknowledged its physical manifestation, not merely somewhere 'out there' in the physical world but living and breathing in our human form. But so far Luke's concluding comments on the progress of the Spirit/Word have come from the outside; the Spirit/Word has still not manifested itself fully at the level of human consciousness, from *within*. This occurs in the event known as the Temptation in the Wilderness.[21]

Why, after the voice of God has just said 'This is my Son, the Beloved, today I have begotten thee,' is Jesus 'led by the Spirit for forty days in the wilderness' during which time he is 'tempted by the devil' three times? A clue lies in the number 40. Traditionally a period of time linked to the number 40 represents a period of probation, trial or initiation signifying the resistance the Spirit encounters as it reveals itself through its manifestation as material or physical form. Without this resistance 'matter' would remain immaterial, for the resistance offered by the material world is nothing other than the process by which the Spirit spontaneously comes into being, manifesting itself as physical form. It is the process by which the One Reality creates the diversity of the natural world without compromising its own unity. As a consequence, our apparent resistance to, or rejection of, the spiritual dimension of our being is a natural part of our own individual spiritual evolution, for without that resistance there is nothing to be either formed or transformed. But in our process of becoming fully human beings there is an additional element that comes into play: the ever-present potential for us to be diverted from our true purpose in life by the desires of our ego.

Traditionally the Temptation is interpreted as an allegory for our potential to be seduced by 'the devil' of our own desires. But there is also a different interpretation that lies just beneath the surface. In revisiting the one, we shall discover the other. As the order of the three temptations itself differs slightly from Matthew to Luke, it is the order in Luke that is followed here.

Having fasted for 40 days Jesus is understandably hungry. So the first temptation involves food. The devil tempts Jesus to use his powers to turn a stone into bread to eat. Jesus responds by saying: 'Man shall not live by bread alone.' The fast Jesus has undergone can be understood as a period of time spent without physical food, but the symbolic wilderness setting infers that it is a period of time without spiritual food. The temptation to turn the stone into physical food is therefore of little interest to Jesus as true sustenance comes from the spiritual Source of our being.

For the second temptation the devil shows Jesus the kingdoms of the entire world, offering him all the this-worldly authority and power they represent, providing that he worships the devil. Our dualistic man-and-God perception tends to separate this second temptation out into time. The inference is that if Jesus worships the devil, power and authority will be given to him afterwards. We can however look at it another way, that our sole devotion to this-worldly concerns *is* to worship the devil. But this is not the devil of popular superstition and fear; the 'devil' merely personifies the actual presence of the temptation. Whether or not we are seduced by the material world to the extent that it becomes our only point of reference is a choice for which we ourselves are entirely responsible. We cannot blame the devil for our own shortcomings; if we do succumb to temptation, we will be emulating those of whom Paul said: 'They exchanged the truth about God for a lie and worshipped and served the creature rather than the Creator.'[22]

The opposite view is expressed in Jesus' reply: 'You shall worship the Lord your God, and him only shall you serve.' If we momentarily visualize the this-worldly power and authority that Jesus has just turned down, we begin to have an idea of the resolve needed to overcome the temptations presented by this-world. By the same token, that power only exists in our dualistic man-and-God perception of the One Reality. From the nondualistic viewpoint embodied in the figure of Jesus, the temptation is not a real one for 'this-world' as a separate entity does not even exist.

The third temptation sees the devil take Jesus up onto a pinnacle of the temple in Jerusalem. There he says to him: 'If you are the Son of God, throw yourself down from here,' for it was written that God's angels would prevent him from coming to harm. Jesus' reply is definitive: 'It is said, "You shall not put the Lord your God to the test".'[23] Of the three temptations this is the final one, but it is also the final temptation in another sense. Having taken us through the different allegorical stages of the progressive Self-revelation of the Spirit, the author of Luke has now brought us to a crucial stage, the stage at which the Spirit manifests itself, from within us, at the level of the conscious mind. As it does it has the potential to transform our old man-and-God mind-set into the spiritual consciousness that marks the mode of consciousness/being set out in the new covenant of Jeremiah, the origins of which can be traced back to the very beginnings of Genesis, when God first breathed the Spirit of Life into Adam, and Man became a living being. When our old dualistic mind-set drops away, any sense of judging, of testing, or of temptation, drops away with it as our egocentric sense of 'I am' becomes integrated into the I AM of the One Reality. With the new nondualistic spiritual consciousness comes what was described earlier as the freedom of no-choice; for where there is no choice there is also no temptation. There is only I AM. In that context it is the words of Jesus' response to the third temptation that conclude this stage of Luke's allegory of the progressive Self-revelation of the Spirit: '*You shall not put the Lord your God to the test.*'[24]

We have now come to a turning-point in our exploration of the gospel narratives. From here on the figure of Jesus is indistinguishable from the archetypal Perfect Man embodied in the Messiah of Jewish myth as he becomes 'Christ the power of God and the wisdom of God'.[25] But the power of such verbal imagery must not overwhelm us. As spiritual beings, our need is to manifest the spiritual wisdom that lies within us waiting to make itself known. In effect, what the figure of Jesus himself personifies is what we have the potential to become – not by doing anything, but by simply *being* who we really are.

9

SPIRITUAL EMPOWERMENT

The events that have taken us from the Annunciation to the Temptation in the Wilderness provide a subtle but powerful allegory for the process of spiritual empowerment. Not to be confused with the self-aggrandizement of our egocentric 'I am', spiritual empowerment is the process by which our original spiritual nature – the I AM – becomes fully integrated with our human nature at all levels of our being, including our conscious mind. As we are shown in the Temptation, the resultant spiritual consciousness brings with it the numinous freedom of knowing who we are and where we come from. And with that freedom come the spiritual power and authority we shall now see embodied in the figure of Jesus, manifesting themselves spontaneously through his words and actions. To provide our dualistic mind-set with a suitable point of comparison, the gospel writers use the reactions of those around him to personify our own potential response when we too come consciously or unconsciously face to face with the spiritual Source of our being.

We rejoin the gospel narratives immediately after the Temptation, with Jesus returning 'in the power of the Spirit' to Galilee where he enters the synagogue at Nazareth on the Sabbath. His earlier childhood appearances in the temple at Jerusalem were used allegorically to illustrate different stages in the progressive Self-revelation of the Spirit, and his appearance in the synagogue follows the same pattern. As the archetype of spiritual empowerment, it is the occasion on which Jesus reads aloud the following passage from Isaiah: 'The Spirit of the Lord is upon me, because he has anointed me to preach good news to the poor. He has sent me to proclaim release to the captives and recovering of sight to the blind, to set at liberty those who are oppressed. . .'[1]

When the reading is over, Jesus says to those in the synagogue: 'Today this scripture has been fulfilled in your hearing.' The people praise him for his eloquence. Jesus responds by saying: 'Doubtless you will quote the proverb "Physician, heal yourself" at me, and tell me to do here, in my own country, the healing work that you have heard I did in Capernaum. But let me tell you, no prophet is welcome in his own country.' He then goes on to give several examples to illustrate his last point. Then as if to fulfil his own prophecy the people turn against him, leading him out of their city to the top of the hill on which the city stands. There they intend to throw him over the precipice, but he mysteriously passes 'through the midst of them' and goes on his way.[2]

With the reading of the prophetic passage from Isaiah, the empowered Spirit expresses in human terms and with human voice its eternal presence in the world. Speaking simultaneously through the prophet Isaiah, the gospel writers, the figure of Jesus and the conscious mind that reads the words, the Spirit yearns to make its infinite and eternal presence known to both you and me, *here and now*. The Spirit is simultaneously the Message and the Messenger who brings it.

But the gospel message is only fulfilled 'in our hearing' – that is, according to our own capacity to understand it. And as the events that unfold afterwards reveal, the message is not understood. It is at once too simple and too subtle for us to understand. If we try to grasp it with our conscious minds, to take it by force, it slips mysteriously through our fingers – in much the same way that Jesus passes mysteriously through the crowd that seeks to do him harm. But then like the wind, the Spirit always 'blows as it wills'. We cannot impose our own will upon it.

As well as being an appropriate setting for the reading of the scriptures, the synagogue also has a further significance in the present context. It once again draws our attention to the distinction between our dualistic and nondualistic modes of consciousness, referred to in biblical language as the 'old' and 'new' covenants. Initially there is no friction between the two, but then as the new covenant/consciousness seeks to emerge from within the old, the old becomes increasingly resistant. Both the sabbatical synagogue setting and the congregation's changing response serve to illustrate this last point. The initial response of the congregation is one of acceptance, even praise, but as the fuller implications of the gospel message are explained the acceptance turns to hostility, then rejection, and finally to thoughts of murder.

Like William Blake's image of Man sealing himself up in his dark cavern, we tend to reject what we cannot understand, often for no other reason than the simple fact that we *cannot* understand it. As a consequence our capacity for understanding is actually diminished rather than increased. Eventually we may arrive at a point where, like the congregation in the synagogue, we no longer have the capacity to understand at all; all we have is a set of increasingly intractable beliefs and opinions. Of course, that does not mean that we need to understand absolutely everything about absolutely everything. The opposite is the case. Where spiritual consciousness is concerned there is nothing for us to understand. Instead there is direct perception. Everything is seen simply and directly, *as it is*.

A man born blind

As for the healing nature of the gospel message proclaimed in the passage read from Isaiah, we have already met with the healing power attributed to Jesus/the Spirit in the healing of the Gerasene demoniac. Many other miracles are open to interpretation in a similar way, as allegories for the potential healing of our divided self. That is to say, as allegories for the process of spiritual evolution which fulfils itself in our becoming fully human. From a human point of view the process appears to work upside down. Our spiritual need to become human is translated into a human need to become spiritual. But the two are not the same thing. To our human eyes 'being spiritual' can mean renouncing the world, or adopting a set of physical and behavioural mannerisms intended to present a 'spiritual' image. But there is nothing genuinely spiritual about either. We do not need to *become* spiritual, we already are. And if we allow ourselves simply to be who we are, we have the *extra*-ordinary potential to become both fully spiritual *and* fully human.

The miracle of a Man Born Blind offers us a valuable insight into this apparently topsy-turvy world in which everything is turned upside down.

One day Jesus passed by a man who had been blind from birth. His disciples asked him, 'Teacher, who sinned, this man or his parents, that he should be born blind?' Jesus answered them, saying, 'This man was born blind neither because of his own sin, nor that of his parents. He was born blind so that the mystery of God's work might reveal itself in him. While it is day we must do the works of him who has sent me. The night will come and then no one can work. As long as I am in the world, I am the light of the world.'

While he was saying this he spat on the ground and made clay from his saliva, and dabbed the clay on the man's eyes, and said to him, "Go and wash in the pool of Siloam" (which means Sent). So the man went away and washed and came back seeing.[3]

At first glance the narrative appears to be relatively simple and straightforward. But the simplicity is deceptive, for the author of John uses the rest of the chapter to expand on the themes he introduces here. For our present purposes, however, we shall focus our attention on the opening verses given above.

The event begins with the disciples giving voice to the popular belief, still held in some quarters today, that suffering is the result of sin in the narrow, moralistic or behavioural sense of the word, and to the idea that our present life is affected either by the sins we have somehow committed pre-natally, or by the sins of our parents. In other words, this life is little more than an atonement for the sins of the past. A similar idea is expressed in Eastern philosophy as the *law of karma*, according to which our present life is affected by the good or bad deeds performed in previous lives, while the good or bad deeds we do in this life will be redeemed in future lives.

We have already encountered the same idea in the parable of the Prodigal Son, where it was suggested that suffering was used as a metaphor to illustrate the dualistic state of mind, or dualistic mode of existence, that characterizes our separation from the spiritual Source of our being. In biblical parlance the word 'sin' refers to much more than mere moral or social behaviour, it denotes a state of being in which we are missing the mark/target/point *vis-à-vis* our true purpose in life. And although in a narrow, moralistic sense our actions may be adjudged good or bad, in a spiritual sense they simply either advance our evolution as spiritual beings or they do not. The moralistic language found in both the Old and New Testaments seeks to identify for us as human beings our place within the unfolding mystery of the universe. But our humanity and our spirituality are not two separate entities. The moralizing pronouncements that appear to be aimed exclusively at our human conduct also serve to instruct us with regard to our spiritual life. Our dilemma lies in not being able to see through the one in order to see the other.

In a spiritual sense we are all born blind; but as the miracle of a Man Born Blind reveals, the 'sin' of blindness to the presence of the Spirit is of a totally different order to the guilt-invoking pronouncements about the sinfulness of mankind to which we have become accustomed. Spiritual blindness is merely a metaphor for a state of spiritual innocence or ignorance, for which there is nothing whatsoever to feel guilty about. It is a natural part of our evolutionary process, as illustrated in the gospels' many references to Jesus calling children to him. In the same way that adults accept a child's innocence or ignorance as a natural stage of his or her evolution – however frustrating or wilful this may at times seem to be – the gospel narratives portray our own spiritual innocence or ignorance in a similar way. At the same time they urge us – as we do our own children – to grow in stature and wisdom. Our part in the process is to acknowledge that whilst physically we may be fully grown, spiritually speaking we are as children still in the nursery.

The miracle of a Man Born Blind also reiterates the idea that we are born of both water and the Spirit. In his account of Jesus spitting on the ground and making the clay which he dabs on the man's eyes, thereby giving him his sight, the author of John provides us with a clear re-enactment of the creation of Adam in Genesis. The image also recalls the analogy of the potter and the clay, with its implication that we are in a constant process of re-creation as the Spirit works to perfect us – transforming us from within until we become fully human – thereby empowering itself through our completion. Needless to say, our human perception of the perfect human being is not the same as the spiritual. The one sees us from the outside only; the other sees us from the inside out.

Our blindness to the Spirit is also illustrated in the earlier analogy of the Gothic cathedral. From the outside of the building the opacity of the stained glass windows prevents us from seeing through them to the interior. When we enter the building it takes a few moments for our eyes to become accustomed to the darkness; but once they do we are able to appreciate the quality of the interior light and the jewel-like effect of the windows when seen from the inside. Our own inner world is also light and jewel-like, except that where we are concerned there is an additional problem. Darkness has become synonymous with the unknown, and our fear of the unknown has invested it with considerable power. As the unknown, darkness has become the realm of the many malevolent dark forces that mirror the unredeemed thought-forms of our personal unconscious, of our own dark side or 'shadow'. Perhaps it is the fear of coming face to face with that particular 'dark' aspect of ourselves that prevents us from exploring our inner world. Nonetheless, if we allow our eyes to grow accustomed to the superficial dark of our personal unconscious, we will be able to see beyond it to the infinite Spirit that is the Light of the world, the eternal Life that is the light of humankind. We will see the Light that shines in the darkness and cannot be overcome by it.[4] In urging us not to hide our own light under a bushel but to let it shine forth,[5] the Sermon on the Mount reminds us that we ourselves are the light of the world.

Empowerment and healing

Letting our light shine out into the world is a natural part of the process of spiritual empowerment, the Self-revelation and Self-empowerment of the Spirit. As a stage in our own process of spiritual evolution, it is important that we *allow* it to happen naturally because the process is not a human one; it is essentially spiritual. It is not something we can force to happen. If we do try to force the process, all we will reveal to the world is the self-aggrandizement of our ego.

The consequences of allowing the ego to take over the process of our spiritual evolution are illustrated in Proverbs. There the folly of men is contrasted with the wisdom of the birds, for even birds avoid the most obvious snares: 'For in vain is a net spread in the sight of any bird; but these men . . . set an ambush for their own lives. Such are the ways of all who get gain by violence; it takes away the life of its possessors.'[6] The alternative is to emulate the disciples and leave behind us the snares of this-world. When they heard Jesus say 'Follow me', they immediately left their nets and followed him.[7] As their example shows, when we hear those words resonate deep inside us there is no dithering or pro-crastination. Instead there is the total freedom of no-choice.

But who are the disciples we read about in the gospel narratives? In the same way that Jesus embodies the Light of the world, the disciples personify the means by which that Light illuminates our darkness. It is here that the number of disciples is important – as 'the twelve' they signify the mysterious outpouring of the life-giving Spirit in the world. In the same way that the twelve tribes of Israel symbolize the dissemination of the *seed* of Abraham, so the twelve disciples of Jesus represent the dissemination or spreading of *the Word*.

To spread the Word or word (the gospel) effectively we must first hear it for ourselves, and that brings us back to the disciples response to the words 'Follow me'. Their instant response illus-trates the degree to which they have heard the word. It has gone straight down into their innermost parts: in hearing it they have received it. This is in stark contrast to the congregation in the synagogue at Nazareth. On hearing the word they rejected it. They would even have killed it but for its mysterious ability to pass through their midst unharmed.

In a wider context the disciples can be likened to the whisperers of the oral tradition: the wise men and women whom Jeremiah refers to as the shepherds who distribute the food of knowledge and understanding.[8] Or again, they can be likened to the fishermen whom God will send to catch the wayward Israelites.[9] Whatever physical form the disciples appear to take, they signify the dissemination of wisdom and knowledge. Their number is essentially symbolic, as becomes apparent when Jesus appoints 'seventy others'.

Traditionally the number 70 symbolizes the Self-revelation of the Spirit. But the sending out of the 70 disciples serves another purpose by illustrating the true nature of spiritual empowerment. When the 70 return they joyfully tell Jesus, 'Lord, even the demons are subject to us in your name!' He responds by telling them that he has given them both the authority and the power to achieve many things; but nevertheless their rejoicing should not arise from what they are able to do, rather from the fact that their names are written in heaven.[10] By boasting of what they have achieved the 70 clearly illustrate what spiritual empowerment does not mean. It is *not* the empowerment of the ego. Nor is spiritual empowerment the conversion of others to this or that particular religious belief.

At a personal level spiritual empowerment is simply to be who we really are. And by being who we are we empower the Spirit to work through us.

The last point is illustrated in an event narrated in Matthew. A certain woman who has had a haemorrhage for twelve years says to herself that if only she could touch Jesus' garment, she would be healed of her condition. Approaching Jesus from behind she touches the edge of his garment, at which he turns around and says to her: 'Your faith has made you whole.' She is instantly healed.[11]

'To haemorrhage' literally means to lose the very blood that keeps us alive, but the inclusion of the symbolic number 12 suggests that we are intended to understand this incident figuratively. The woman personifies the wasting away of spiritual energy that can happen to any one. When it does the only course of action for us is to renew our contact with the spiritual Source of our being. As the embodiment of that Source, Jesus' turning to face the woman when she has touched his garment reveals the nature of true healing. It is not we who go to the Spirit; it is already there, *waiting for us to empower it by responding to its presence.* Faith in its presence is simultaneously the healing and the empowerment.

The slightly longer accounts of the same incident in Mark and Luke inform us that the woman had suffered much at the hands of many doctors, but no one had been able to heal her.[12] In doing so they remind us that in the One Reality there is only One Healer, One Teacher, to whom, as the story of the woman with the haemorrhage reveals, we all have free and instant access.

Feeding the Five Thousand

The miraculous Feeding of the Five Thousand offers further insights into the process of Self-revelation, or the mysterious outpouring of the Spirit in the world. (The use of the phrase '*in* the world' is deliberate, the word *into* would imply that the Spirit is separate from the world. It is not. The separation is in our dualistic perception.)

The significance of John the Baptist was discussed at some length in the previous chapter. I suggested that both he and Jesus are to be understood as two aspects of one person, or rather two modes of consciousness. The reference to John the Baptist's death at the beginning of the present miracle portrays the demise of the old consciousness as concomitant with the empowerment of the new. That empowerment is expressed in narrative form in the Feeding of the Five Thousand. Recounted in all four canonical Gospels, the miracle of the loaves and the fish is one of the best known of the miracles performed by Jesus. As the narratives differ slightly in their detail, the following version combines the principal elements from all four accounts:

> Following the death of John the Baptist, Jesus and the disciples boarded a boat and withdrew to a lonely place. The crowd, learning where they had gone, made its way there on foot and when Jesus disembarked the people were on the shore waiting for him. As evening approached the disciples suggested to Jesus that he sent the crowd of people away to lodge in the nearby towns and villages and to buy food for themselves because there was nothing with which to feed them in that lonely place.
>
> [Here the account in John differs significantly from the other three, with Jesus asking one of the disciples, 'How are we to buy bread so that these people may eat?' This is accompanied by an aside, telling us that he did this to test him, for he himself knew what he would do. The disciple replied that 200 denarii would not buy enough bread to ensure that each of them got a little. Another of the disciples brought forward a young boy who had five barley loaves and two fish.]
>
> Instead of doing as they had suggested Jesus told the disciples to feed the crowd, but all the food they had was five loaves and two fish. As the disciples were at a loss as to how to feed all the people from such a small quantity of food, Jesus instructed them to sit the people down on the grass, in groups of about fifty. When they were all sat down he took the food and, looking up to heaven, he blessed and broke it, and then gave it to the disciples to distribute. Once the people had eaten sufficient to satisfy their hunger, Jesus instructed the disciples to gather up the remains of the meal. When this had been done they found that there was sufficient left over to fill twelve baskets, and about five thousand people had eaten the loaves. Immediately Jesus made his disciples get into the boat and cross to the other side while he dismissed the crowd.[13]

As with other miraculous events related in the gospel narratives the words that express the underlying meaning also have the potential to become a veil between us and the message they seek to convey. To transmit that message the gospel writers had to narratize it, turning it into a story that unfolds itself in the dimensions of time and space. As the meaning, or rather the original message, is itself *beyond* time, it will be helpful to our present exploration to detach the principal elements from the narrative. In doing so we will also be removing them to some degre^ from the dimensions of time and space.

The principal elements of the miracle can be summarized briefly as follows: (1) John the Baptist dies; (2) Jesus and his disciples 'withdraw to a lonely place' in their boat; (3) the crowd follow him and are on the shore awaiting his arrival; (4) as it begins to get dark the disciples suggest Jesus send the people away to get their own food, because there is no food for them in that 'lonely place'; (5) Jesus tells the disciples to feed the crowd; (6) the disciples are at a loss as to how, because the only food available is five loaves and two fish; (7) Jesus tells the people to sit down; (8) he breaks and blesses the food; (9) the disciples distribute the food; (10) everybody gets as much as they need; (11) the disciples gather up twelve baskets of leftovers; (12) the disciples get back in their boat and Jesus dismisses the crowd.

When taken together as a single event seen simultaneously from two different points of view, the death of John the Baptist and Jesus' withdrawal to a lonely place can be interpreted as marking a change in our understanding of our relationship with the Spirit. No longer looked for in the words of others, it is now seen to be more subtle, more withdrawn. It needs to be searched out. Nonetheless, the Spirit is instantly accessible, as is illustrated by the simultaneity of the crowd following Jesus and yet being on the shore when he arrives at the 'lonely place'. The 'lonely place' – which, like the wilderness, signifies a lack of spiritual food – would therefore seem to be where the people have been all the time. The 'lonely place' describes their current state of being.

The approach of evening signals a coming darkness – a further metaphor for the lack of spiritual food. The lack of the latter is confirmed by the absence of physical food – the people are (spiritually) hungry and need to eat/be fed. Genuine spiritual food can only come from one source, the Spirit (embodied here in Jesus), which explains why the disciples are at a loss as to how to feed the people. (The interpolation from John infers that money is incapable of providing the kind of food the people need.) In the event, Jesus/the Spirit takes charge. The people do as he tells them = they hear the Word. The food is distributed = the outpouring of the Spirit. After everybody has eaten the amount left over far exceeds the amount originally distributed = the infinite nature of the spiritual food that is itself the outpouring of the Spirit. The difference in the amounts of (1) the original food, (2) what was eaten by the five thousand, and (3) what was gathered up, can be understood in terms of the 'bearing fruit' that is an integral part of the outpouring of the Spirit.

A more precise indication of what is meant by the term 'spiritual food' is given in John. There Jesus says to his disciples: 'Food to me means to do the will of him who sent me, and to fulfil his work.'[14] Where we are concerned, spiritual food can be understood as simply allowing the Spirit to work through us, to allow ourselves to 'bear fruit', thus bringing its work to fruition. If we now remove the dimensions of time and space altogether, the essential message of the miracle is that the more we bear fruit the more food we receive in order to bear yet more fruit. Such is the nature of spiritual empowerment.

One important aspect of the miracle not yet taken into account is the symbolic role played by numbers to express the spontaneous play or Self-expression of the One Reality. In the process they offer us further insights into the timeless mystery of what – on the surface at least – appear to be events in time. The specific numbers in the Feeding of the Five Thousand are: 5 (the number of loaves); 50 (the size of the groups in which the people sat); 5,000 (the number of people who were fed); as well as 7 (the number given us by the 5 loaves and 2 fishes) and 12 (the number of baskets collected up). The last two numbers (7 and 12) are related to each other in that they are both products of 3 and 4 (7 = 3 + 4; 12 = 3 × 4).

When we examine the numbers connected with the loaves, the size of the groups, and the overall number of people fed, we find a numerical progression based on multiples of 5 – 5 (5 × 1), 50 (5 × 10), 5,000 (50 × 100, 5 × 1,000) – in which the thousandfold multiplication of the original number indicates symbolically the powerful nature of the event we are witnessing. As the number 5 stands for the human microcosm or little universe – a reflection in miniature of the great universe or macrocosm – we begin to get an inkling that the thousandfold multiplication has to do with the relationship between the two. As the physical material transmitted is food, we can deduce that the numbers express the way in which the microcosm is nourished by the macrocosm.

Taking into account the role played by Jesus/the Spirit in instigating the miraculous feeding in the first place, it would appear that the 5 to 5,000 expresses the outpouring of the Spirit in the world in terms of a Self-emanation. The numbers 7 and 12 also tell us something about the spontaneous Self-revelation conveyed by means of a this-worldly narrative. 7 and 12 are both products of 3 and 4, with 3 being the 'heavenly' number while 4 signifies physical existence, or the material or earthly plane. If we look at the numbers 7 and 12 again in the light of their relationship to 3 and 4, we can see that 7 (3 + 4) contains within itself the idea of a heaven and an earth, whereas 12 (3 × 4) denotes the fusion of the two. If we now bring into play the amplification of 5 to 5,000, we can perhaps conclude that the gospel writers sought to express the way in which the apparent dualism of the ethereal and material worlds is a natural consequence of the mysterious Self-revelation of the One Reality. But the dualism is in appearance only. The essential nonduality of the spiritual and material aspects of existence is characterized as the outpouring of the Spirit in the world, which is also the 'food' that binds the two inseparably together.

Walking on water

Numerical symbolism may express something of the mysterious workings of the One Reality, but it is of relatively little practical use in helping us to face the immediate ups and downs of everyday human life. Perhaps for that reason the Feeding of the Five Thousand is immediately followed by a further miracle of a different kind. The following account of the miraculous Walking on Water is a compilation of the three versions narrated in Matthew, Mark and John.

> Immediately after the Feeding of the Five Thousand, Jesus insisted that his disciples get into their boat and make their way ahead of him to the other side, while he stayed behind to dismiss the crowds. After all the people had gone, he went up on the mountain by himself to pray. When darkness fell he was alone on the land, and the boat was some way out on the sea, where it was making little headway, for it was being battered by the waves and the wind was against it.
>
> Just before dawn the disciples saw Jesus walking across the water

towards them. Terrified because they thought he was a ghost, he
called out reassuringly to them, 'It is I; do not be afraid'. Peter called
back in reply, 'Lord, if it really is you, bid me come to you on the
water'. Jesus said, 'Come', and getting out of the boat Peter started
to walk across the water towards him. But when he saw the wind he
became afraid, and began to sink. Jesus immediately stretched out
his hand and caught hold of him, saying, 'O man of little faith, why
did you doubt?' When the two men got back into the boat the wind
dropped, and straight away the boat arrived at its destination. And
the disciples were utterly astonished, for their minds were too dull
to understand the significance of the loaves.[15]

Here as elsewhere in the gospels, the Sea of Galilee can be
understood as a metaphor for the Sea of Life. The boat in which
Jesus and the disciples frequently cross from one side to the other
is a metaphor for ourselves. Our spiritual essence is embodied
in the figure of Jesus while the disciples represent our human
personality, which Jesus is endeavouring to turn into a vehicle for
his work. As with our exploration of the Feeding of the Five
Thousand, it is helpful if we begin by detaching the principal
elements from the narrative to understand more fully the original
'event' that the gospel writers have turned into the story of Jesus
Walking on Water. In this case the story begins by presenting us
with the more or less synchronous occurrence of the following
minor events: (1) the separation of the disciples from Jesus; (2)
the setting out onto the sea; (3) the coming of darkness; (4) the
battering of the boat by the waves and (5) the wind blowing
against it.

Whether taken separately or together, these minor events
provide us with a powerful allegory for our own journey across
the waters of life when, for one reason or another, our human
nature becomes separated from the spiritual dimension of our
being. Our separation from the sure guidance of the latter is
expressed in the figure of Jesus remaining on the land while the
disciples set off to cross the sea on their own. When we do turn our
backs on the guiding light offered by the Spirit our journey is made
into gathering darkness as the purpose of our existence becomes
increasingly obscured from us. The more we lose sight of who we
really are, the more it feels as though we are tossed about willy-
nilly, even subjected to a relentless battering, by the events and
changing circumstances of our everyday lives. The explanation
offered by the narrative for our predicament is that we are going

against the wind – that is, we are travelling in a contrary direction to our true spiritual purpose in life. But if that is the case, how can we turn ourselves around?

The second part of the narrative presents us with a miraculous reversal of the disciples' predicament with: (1) the approach of daylight, which coincides with (2) Jesus appearing to the disciples; (3) Peter's recognition of Jesus; (4) Peter's attempt to walk on the water; (5) Jesus catches hold of Peter and pulls him into the boat; (6) the wind drops, upon which (7) the boat arrives immediately at its destination.

Whereas the storm-tossed boat in the first part of the story conveys a sense of powerlessness, of simply being cast adrift on the sea of life, the second part begins with a glimmer of hope in the imminence of a new dawn, reminding us that the guiding light of the Spirit is never far from us. Sure enough, in their moment of need Jesus appears to his disciples. Likewise, when we ourselves are most in need, when we feel at our most powerless, or when we are at our most fearful, our spiritual essence will endeavour to make its presence known and reassure us that all will be well. But the chances are that, like Peter, we will not recognize it for what it is, so great is our fear.

The words Jesus addresses to the terrified disciples – 'It is I; do not be afraid' – echo the reassuring words spoken by the angel to an apprehensive Mary at the Annunciation. The prefatory 'It is I' reminds us that the figure of Jesus personifies the I AM, the spiritual Source of our being, speaking to us from deep within ourselves. But, as Peter's reply implies, we need some kind of tangible sign, even a miracle, to convince us of its presence. His question recalls the similar question quoted earlier (page 64) from the Gospel of Thomas, where the disciples asked Jesus when he would reveal himself to them. As we saw then, spiritual revelation is a reciprocal process. The Spirit reveals itself to us when we remove the veil we have placed between us and it. Our dilemma seems to lie in not wanting to remove the veil until we know for sure that there is something on the other side. If we were sure, we could pass through the veil as easily as Alice passed through the looking-glass.

The only tangible proof we will ever have of the presence of the Spirit will come from our own experience of life in this world. There therefore comes a point at which we need to have faith. But faith is easily confused with belief. Belief confines itself to the realm of the conscious mind. We believe *in* some thing or another – a concept, an idea, even a word – that may have little bearing on our actual experience of everyday reality. To have faith is simply to have faith. It is to walk with certainty across the waters of life in the unshakeable knowledge that whatever challenges life may present us with, we will not sink beneath the waves. For the wind and the waves that batter us are not caused by the circumstances and events that confront us, they are the powerful stirrings of our own emotions and fears. As Jean-Pierre de Caussade says: 'If only we have the courage to let the thunder, lightning and storm rage, and to walk unfaltering in the path of love and obedience to the duty and demands of the present moment, we are emulating Jesus himself.'[16] Lacking the faith/courage to emulate his Lord, Peter begins to sink. Herein lies the reason why Mark's account of the miraculous Walking on Water concludes by referring to the disciples not having understood the significance of the loaves. Similarly, the author of John follows his version with Jesus' discourse on bread, in which he reminds us of what he personifies with the words 'I am the bread of life'.[17] When we understand about the loaves, we too will walk on water.

Calming the storm

In uncomplicated terms *faith* can be equated with simply being in the here-and-now, experiencing life in its fullness, just as it is, with the whole of our being. A favoured *hadith* (saying) of the Sufis describes it thus: 'Faith is a knowledge in the heart, a voicing with the tongue, and an activity with the limbs.' It also makes the important point, as did de Caussade earlier, that faith is not separate from everyday life. If we believe that faith has no place in even the most mundane of everyday activities, then we are merely reinforcing the dualism of our man-and-God mode of consciousness – at the same time opening ourselves up to the stormy turbulence of our thoughts, our emotions, and our fears.

The last point is expressed in the Calming of the Storm, which shares many of the symbolic details met with in the miraculous Walking on Water. The message of this variation on the theme benefits from the brevity of the narrative.

[Mark begins by telling us that the crossing took place 'when evening had come'.] During the crossing there arose a great storm, with high winds, and the waves crashed into the boat, which began to fill with water. The disciples awoke Jesus, who was sleeping on a cushion in the stern, with the words: 'Save us, we are perishing.' Having been awakened, Jesus rebuked the wind and the waves, saying: 'Peace, be still.' The wind ceased to blow and the sea once more became calm. He then turned to his disciples, saying to them, 'Why are you afraid? Have you no faith?' And the disciples wondered what kind of man this was who even had authority over wind and water.[18]

If we remove the dimension of time completely we find ourselves with an event in which our two modes of consciousness/being are presented to us like the two sides of a coin. On the one side is a great storm; on the other are peace and calm. On the one the men are subject to the battering of the wind and waves; on the other the wind and waves are subject to the authority of a man who, ever since the Temptation in the Wilderness, is 'in the power of the Spirit'. We can reduce the two sides of the coin even further: to the states of disempowerment and empowerment. The one mirrors our dualistic man-and-God mode of consciousness, with its perception of the Spirit as a separate entity; the other corresponds to the nondualistic mode of spiritual consciousness. That the two modes are simply two sides of the same coin – the one human, the other spiritual – is underlined by the entire event unfolding in one place: the boat containing Jesus and the disciples. Removed from the dimensions of time and space, the event is reduced to its essential message: *faith is a fundamental part of our spiritual evolution, for without it we disempower both ourselves and the Spirit.* As in the story, the latter is left to sleep on a cushion in the stern of our boat. Conversely, it could be said that if we have faith we are given the power to sail calmly through even the greatest of storms. But that is not quite true, if we have faith there simply are no storms.

A flask of precious ointment

In the preceding two miracles the Sea of Galilee provided a dynamic image of our relationship with a world in which we appear to be at the mercy of outside circumstances. But beneath the ripples and waves on the surface of our mind lie deeper levels of consciousness that make up our inner world. Here we find the peace that remains undisturbed by the roughest of storms. It is into this world that the next event takes us.

Accounts of Jesus' being anointed by a woman with a flask of precious ointment appear in a different form in all four canonical Gospels. The version that is of greatest interest to us is the one in Luke. Here the woman is described as a 'woman of the city . . . a sinner', which is frequently interpreted to mean she was a prostitute. Conventional interpretations therefore tend to use the 'fallen woman' approach to emphasize that the unconditional nature of Jesus' love extends even to those whom society regards as morally sinful. But the real moral of the story is very much closer to home. The Pharisee's house in which the incident takes place is our own inner space; the people in the house represent different aspects of ourselves:

A certain Pharisee invited Jesus to eat with him, and so Jesus went into the Pharisee's house where he took his place at table. A woman of the city, who was a sinner, heard that Jesus was in the house and brought an alabaster flask of ointment and came and stood weeping at Jesus' feet, bathing them with her tears, and drying them with her hair. Then she kissed his feet, and anointed them with the ointment.

When Jesus' host saw what was happening, he said to himself, 'If this man were really a prophet, he would have known what kind of woman was touching him and recognized her to be a sinner.' Jesus turned to him, saying, 'Simon, I have something to tell you.' Simon replied, 'What is it, teacher?'

'A creditor once had two debtors. The one owed him five hundred denarii, and the other fifty. As neither of them were able to pay, he forgave both of them their debts. Now, which of the two debtors will have the greatest respect for the creditor?' 'The one to whom he forgave the most, I assume,' replied Simon. 'You are right,' said Jesus.

Then turning to the woman he said to Simon, 'You see this woman? Now, when I entered your house you gave me no water to wash my feet, but she bathed my feet with her tears, and dried them with her hair. You gave me no welcoming embrace, but ever since she came in she has not ceased from kissing my feet. You did not anoint my head with oil, but she has anointed my feet with ointment. For this, her many sins are forgiven, because she showed

great love and respect. But one who is forgiven little, shows little
of either.'

Then Jesus said to the woman, 'Your sins are forgiven.' But the
other guests talked amongst themselves, saying, 'Who does he think
he is, that he even forgives sins?' And Jesus said to the woman,
'Your faith has saved you. Go in peace.'[19]

The anointing of Jesus uses the figures of the Pharisee and the
woman to illustrate our potential attitude towards the spiritual
dimension of our being. Numerical symbolism has a small part to
play too, although this is confined to the parable Jesus tells Simon.
As the parable is crucial to a fuller understanding of the event, that
is where we shall begin – noting as we do that the parable is told in
response to the Pharisee's criticism of the woman who has wept at
Jesus' feet.

The parable Jesus tells Simon is not really about money at all. As
we saw in the Feeding of the Five Thousand, the number five
stands for the human microcosm as a reflection in miniature of the
macrocosm, for the relationship between life and Life itself. In
the overall context of the story I suggest that the number five,
amplified here tenfold and a hundredfold, is used to convey the
idea of the debt we owe to the Life within us for our existence. Of
course, a debt of that kind is so hypothetical that we barely give it
a second thought. Who is there to 'forgive the debt' anyway?
Nobody. It is simply the parable's way of telling us that the debts
are never even called in. There is no one to whom we have to
account for either our life, or what we do with it.

As the 'debtors' in the parable, it is entirely up to us both how
much we value our life, and the extent to which we feel indebted to
our creditor, the Source of Life within us. The more indebted we
feel, the greater the love and respect we have for it. It is these
qualities of love and respect that are represented by the sums of
'denarii', with the debtor who owes 50 denarii displaying
relatively little of either in comparison with the debtor who owes
500. In effect, the parable provides us with the entire incident in
miniature, for the debtors and their sums of denarii are personified
by the Pharisee and the woman with the flask of ointment in their
respective attitudes towards the figure of Jesus.

As the embodiment of the Spirit, the latter is the creditor who
himself describes for us the differing degrees of value and respect
shown to him by the man and the woman. The attitudes they
display are also potentially our own, for the house is our own

inner space. On the one hand is the Pharisee, a householder who, in both his attitude and comments, reveals that he has very little respect for (and even less knowledge of) the Source of Life within him. On the other is the woman 'who was a sinner'. Metaphorically speaking she has been a woman *of* the world. Now we are witnesses to her conversion, her *metanoia*. Turning within herself to the spiritual Source of her being, she gives living form to St Paul's words, 'You are a temple of the Holy Spirit within you . . . So glorify God [the Spirit] in your body.'[20]

In anointing Jesus – the personification of the Messiah/Christ, the Anointed One – from her flask of ointment the woman exemplifies the moment of spiritual fulfilment and completion expressed in the gospels as 'entering the kingdom of heaven'. Her profound self-realization means that she is no longer missing the mark *vis-à-vis* her true purpose in life, consequently her 'sin' – her 'missing the mark' – is no more; it is forgiven. She is at peace within herself.

Our exploration of the Flask of Precious Ointment has come to a point at which words have taken us as far as they can, for words are merely the physical means the gospel writers have used to transmit the gospel message. When we explore the allegorical meaning of the words themselves in the way we have just done, the symbolic meaning of the words may possibly become a bit clearer but that does not necessarily mean to say we are anywhere nearer the message, because the meaning on its own is *not* the message.

To get closer to the message we now need to put to one side the symbolic meaning of the events examined in this chapter and allow the imagery stirred up in our minds by the narrative to do its work. If we are able to relive these events in our inner world, they may take on meaning for us in relation to our own individual experience of life. We will then be hearing the stories afresh, in the way the gospel writers originally intended us to do.

10

IN TWO MINDS

For centuries it has been the custom for writers to satirize public figures of any profession or social rank where a position of authority can be exploited, either for selfish gain or for the abuse and manipulation of others. In some cases a playwright or satirist creates fictitious individuals who are held up for ridicule, either through their portrayal as incompetent fools or by the lampooning of their empty posturing, offering us a trenchant mirror for our own devious wiles and artifices. The gospel writers are no exception, for many of the characters who appear in their narratives share a similarly censorious fate.

Two groups in particular are dealt with in this way: the crowd or multitude, whose sheep-like behaviour we have already encountered in the congregation in the synagogue at Nazareth; and the religious authorities, comprising the scribes, Pharisees, Sadducees, chief priests, lawyers and elders. The latter's attempts to get the better of Jesus over points of religious law frequently bring about their own humiliation and embarrassment. The scribes and Pharisees in particular are denounced publicly for their hypocrisy and double standards, as well as for the many ways in which they lead astray those for whom they purport to act as religious guides and mentors.

Whilst the significance of the exchanges between the Jesus of the gospels and the religious authorities of his day may appear to confine itself to a specific historical setting, if we look on them solely as examples of Jesus outwitting those opposed to his ministry and teaching we will have completely missed the point. The relevance of these exchanges is both timeless and universal: they characterize the dilemma that faces us when our mind comes into confrontation with itself. That is to say, they illustrate the friction that occurs when our old dualistic man-and-God mind-set comes face to face with the new, nondualistic consciousness inspired by the Spirit within us. These exchanges also highlight the contrast between outer and inner authority, with the various religious leaders embodying the former, the figure of Jesus the latter. In doing so they also bring to our attention the dichotomous relationship between religion and spirituality.

Traditionally the function of religious leaders is to nurture our spiritual evolution and well-being, educating us in matters both human and spiritual so that we may learn to dwell in harmony with ourselves, our fellow beings and the One Reality within which we live. At the same time religious leaders and teachers are also obliged to uphold the doctrines, laws and rituals of their particular religion in order for the religious institution itself to survive and fulfil its function as just described. The theological point the gospel writers are really making with their exchanges between Jesus and the religious authorities who oppose him is that the Spirit is neither subject to nor dependent upon religion and/or religious laws and doctrine.

Not my will, but thine

One of the primary functions of religion is to turn our minds away from this-worldly things in order to remind us of our original spiritual nature. Yet religion has been and still is freely exploited by some as a means to achieve purely selfish, non-religious or this-worldly ends. The mere assertion that one is a member of this or that religion, or that one is simply 'doing the Will of God', is often used as a thinly-disguised pretext for imposing our own will or opinions on others. Occasionally the same assertions are even used as a veil to hide our real motives from ourselves. However, such an attitude is nothing new, nor is it exclusively Western. We find traces of it the world over wherever the 'will of man' becomes confused with the 'Will of God'.

Learning to make the distinction between these two 'wills', or motivating forces, as well as the two modes of consciousness/being that correspond to them is a key phase in the process of spiritual empowerment. It is also a primary theme of both Old and New

Testaments. Both remind us constantly of the supreme intelligence – the Divine Will, Wisdom, the Spirit, the Word or *Logos*, or whatever else we like to call it – that permeates the cosmos, giving it both form and life, as well as of our own participation as spiritual beings in the unfolding mystery of the universe. Where the gospel narratives are concerned, the distinction between the two 'wills' is perhaps most powerfully expressed during the Agony in the Garden immediately preceding the arrest of Jesus. Knowing that he faces certain death, Jesus utters the words: 'Not my will, but thine, be done.'[1] In doing so he gives voice to the unspoken words at the heart of all religious and spiritual traditions.

True religion (from the Latin *religare*, 'to bind') is founded on the principle that the ultimate authority in human and spiritual affairs is the Spirit, or Divine Will. The fundamental purpose of any religious or spiritual tradition is to lead us towards a point at which our humanity bonds with our spirituality in such a way that we become simultaneously one with, and a vehicle for, the spiritual Source within us. When we do realize our spiritual potential and become fully human beings it could be said that we transcend the doctrine, laws and rituals, whose very purpose is to bring us to that point in the first place. The externals of religious law are then superseded by the inner authority of the Spirit working through us, freely and spontaneously, as it wills. As St Augustine said: 'Let him no longer use the Law as a means of arrival when he has arrived.'[2]

As the gospel narratives ably illustrate, whenever religious leaders come to regard their authority as an end in itself rather than as a means to an end, they contradict the very principle on which any religion is founded. For religion then becomes dogmatic rather than liberating, exclusive rather than inclusive. It is at this point that the potential for conflict between religious and spiritual authority may become a reality. In going on to explore the gospel writers' portrayal of what is essentially a clash between the man-and-God mind-set of the old covenant and the spiritual consciousness of the new, we need to bear in mind that the gospel writers' observations extend far beyond the realms of religion and religious leaders. They offer us a mirror image of the various polarized attitudes and qualities – arrogance/humility, hypocrisy/honesty, folly/wisdom, ignorance/insight, – we ourselves manifest in both the everyday and spiritual aspects of our lives. Ultimately, the various confrontations and debates between Jesus and the religious leaders give us glimpses into the true nature of spiritual wisdom and authority, for it is through the words attributed to Jesus that the authors of the gospels give voice to the insight and understanding that come from the spiritual Source of Life itself.

The bread of life

The exchanges between Jesus and the religious leaders cover a wide range of issues. We shall begin with one that sheds further light on the Feeding of the Five Thousand. Following a brief debate with the Pharisees and Sadducees, we are told that the disciples 'reach the other side' but that they have 'forgotten to bring any bread'. Jesus then warns them: 'Take heed and beware of the leaven of the Pharisees and the Sadducees.' But the disciples, who are frequently portrayed as failing to understand what Jesus says to them, talk amongst themselves, saying 'We brought no bread'. Jesus reprimands them for being 'men of little faith', and then asks them: 'Why are you discussing among yourselves the fact that you have no bread? Have you not understood?' Reminding them of the five loaves that fed the five thousand and the baskets of food that were gathered up afterwards, he asks them how it is they failed to understand that when he had said 'Beware of the leaven of the Pharisees and Sadducees' he was not referring to bread, but to their teaching.[3]

The disclosure that *loaves* are a synonym for the teaching of Jesus explains why he scolded the disciples for being men of little faith. Their complaint that they have no bread is used to illustrate our own lack of awareness of the guidance that comes from the Spirit within us, whose presence is embodied there with the disciples in the person of Jesus. But as we saw in the Feeding of the Five Thousand, the 'teaching' or 'loaves' of Jesus is no ordinary teaching. It is synonymous with the outpouring of the Spirit in the world. As Jesus says of himself elsewhere in the gospels: 'I am the bread of life . . . I am the living bread which came down from heaven; if any one eats of this bread, he will live for ever.'[4]

A focus for many of the confrontational debates between Jesus and the authorities is the subject of religious law. For example, in their duty to uphold the Law the scribes and Pharisees frequently accuse Jesus and his disciples of deliberately flouting the sabbath which, according to Mosaic Law, is a day dedicated entirely to worship and rest, unsullied by the need to work or engage in menial tasks.

On one occasion the Pharisees rebuke Jesus' disciples for breaking the laws of the sabbath by eating ears of corn as they pass through a cornfield. Jesus responds to their accusation with a question:

> Have you not read that when David was hungry he and his followers had gone into the house of God, and had taken the shewbread, the loaves of the Presence, which according to the law could only be eaten by the priests, and distributed it, and they had all eaten it?

He concludes by saying to them: 'The Son of man is lord of the sabbath.'[5] The implication of Jesus' words is that spiritual food or teaching – both symbolic (the loaves of the Presence) and actual (the Spirit itself) – have come to be regarded as the exclusive domain of the priesthood. In quoting the example of David helping himself to the shewbread, he not only questions this exclusive right of the priesthood. He also makes the point that if any of us are in need of spiritual food we are able to help ourselves to what we need to assuage our hunger. Of course, the analogy of David going into the temple to help himself to the loaves of the Presence does not mean literally going into a temple or church and helping ourselves to the sacraments. It alludes to the body, the temple of the Spirit. According to the principle of 'ask and you will receive', spiritual food is freely available to us all from within ourselves.

The issue of spiritual food is raised on another occasion narrated in Luke. There Jesus calls Levi, a tax-collector, to join him as a disciple. At the words, 'Follow me,' Levi leaves everything and follows him. During the ensuing feast that Levi gives in Jesus' honour, the scribes and Pharisees accusingly ask Jesus' disciples, 'Why do you eat and drink with tax-collectors and sinners?' Jesus replies for them, saying: 'It is not the healthy who need a doctor, but those who are sick. I have not come to call the righteous to repent, but sinners.'[6] Bearing in mind the allegorical meaning of the different elements of this event – the house, the meal, the sinners, and the call to repent – we can sense the ambiguity of

Jesus' answer, in which for 'righteous' we can also read 'self-righteous'. At one level the answer illustrates the self-righteous point of view of the scribes and Pharisees: considering themselves to be 'healthy' they have no need for the healing offered by Jesus. At another, the 'sick' are those 'tax-collectors and sinners' who, like Levi, have awakened to their spiritual infirmity and promptly turned to the Spirit to be made whole.

During the same feast at Levi's house, the scribes and Pharisees ask Jesus why it is that John's disciples fast and pray often, as do the disciples of the Pharisees, whereas Jesus' disciples eat and drink freely. He answers with a question: 'Can you oblige wedding guests to fast while the bridegroom is with them?' He also answers the question for them, saying that the day will come when the bridegroom will be taken away from them, and then they will fast.[7] This second answer provides us with a further example of the way in which, through simple plays on words, the gospel narratives convey multiple layers of meaning. The Pharisees' initial comment criticizes Jesus' disciples for eating and drinking freely and not following religious tradition by undertaking ritual fasting and prayer. Jesus' response turns this criticism around on to those who made it. The 'wedding guests' are those who, like the disciples of Jesus, share company with the bridegroom/the Spirit. To insist they fast – refrain from taking (spiritual) food – in their situation is asking them to do the impossible. By expressing the inspired nature of spiritual consciousness, Jesus infers that the ritual fasting undertaken by the followers of John and the Pharisees is more in the nature of spiritual deprivation: it merely reinforces our man-and-God mode of consciousness.

As for the comment about the disciples fasting when the bridegroom is taken away from them. Are we to understand from this that the 'disciples' will be deprived of spiritual food when Jesus/the Spirit is no longer with them? Or, as the Spirit is always with us, are we to understand that ritual fasting only makes sense once we comprehend the true nature of spiritual food?

The meal at Levi's house concludes with two parables that clarify the relationship between our modes of consciousness/being: the parable of the Patched Garment and the parable of New Wine:

No one tears a piece from a new garment and puts it upon an old garment; if he does, he will tear the new, and the piece from the new will not match the old. And no one puts new wine into old wineskins; if he does, the new wine will burst the skins and it will be spilled, and the skins will be destroyed. But new wine must be put into fresh wineskins. And no one after drinking old wine desires new; for he says, 'The old is good.'[8]

In the parable of the Patched Garment the old and new garments stand for the old and new 'covenants', our dualistic man-and-God mind-set and spiritual consciousness. It demonstrates the inherent incompatibility of the two. If we take a little bit of the new and try to make it fit onto the old, our understanding of the new will be incomplete. Even though they may appear to be of the same stuff, the two simply do not go together.

The second parable takes up the theme of the first using the synonym of new wine for spiritual consciousness. On the one hand, if we attempt to understand spiritual consciousness from within the framework of our old man-and-God mind-set, not only will the old wineskin of the latter be destroyed but the essence of the new will be lost as well. The final statement sums up the predicament facing those of us who cling to the dualism of our old man-and-God mode of consciousness. If that is what we are used to, why should we wish to change it? St Augustine answers the question for us: 'You must be emptied of that with which you are full, so that you may be filled with that of which you are empty.'[9]

The leaven of the Pharisees

Where Mark tells us that Jesus uses the expression 'the leaven of the Pharisees' to refer to their teaching, the author of Luke is more direct. According to him Jesus says: 'Beware of the leaven of the Pharisees, which is hypocrisy.'[10] From this we can deduce that the hypocrisy of the Pharisees (and Sadducees) lies in their preaching one thing and doing another. That is to say, they instruct the people to follow the precepts of the Law and the scriptures whilst they themselves do not. But there is possibly a more subtle aspect to their hypocrisy: their man-and-God mind-set prevents them from seeing for themselves the deeper significance of what they are teaching others. It is in that sense also that the Pharisees and Sadducees preach one thing and do another. That their hypocrisy derives from ignorance as much as wilfulness becomes apparent in the subtle shift that occurs in the nature of the confrontations between Jesus and the Pharisees. From simply commenting on the way in which Jesus and his disciples disregard the Mosaic Law, they begin to take on a more active role: either testing him with their questions, or waiting to catch him *in flagrante delicto*.

On one occasion the scribes and Pharisees are watching to see whether Jesus will heal a man with a withered hand in the synagogue on the sabbath. If he does, they can accuse him of breaking the sabbath law. Knowing what is in their minds, he asks them a question: 'I will ask you one thing: Is it lawful on the sabbath day to do good, or to do harm? to save life, or to destroy it?' Then, in the full view of his accusers, he proceeds to heal the man's hand. Frustrated and infuriated, the Pharisees discuss amongst themselves what they can do about him.[11]

As part of the plot unfolding within the gospel narratives as a whole, the incident illustrates the emerging discontent that will culminate in the powers that be deciding the only way to deal with Jesus and the threat he poses to their authority is to have him put to death. But the healing in this incident is not solely an external, physical event. As with the miraculous healing of the Gerasene demoniac, true healing takes place at an inner, spiritual level. It is a natural process of transformation, of being made whole. Like the distribution of spiritual food, healing is not subject to man-made laws, for the Spirit is a law unto itself.

One of the gospels' definitive statements concerning the external authority of the Law is to be found in Mark, in the often quoted words: 'The sabbath was made for man, not man for the sabbath.'[12] Religious laws are intended to provide us with a structure, a religious or spiritual framework, from within which we may be guided towards the profound self-knowledge which is knowledge of God. When the original purpose of these same laws becomes obscured they no longer fulfil their function. If anything, they do the opposite by reinforcing our dualistic sense of separation. One of the accusations Jesus levels at those who insist on the strict observance of religious law is that they have 'taken away the key of knowledge'. Worse than that, not only do they not enter the kingdom of heaven themselves; they also hinder those who would enter from doing so.[13]

But the confrontations between Jesus and the religious authorities do not confine themselves to matters of written law.

The author of Mark tells us that the Jews observe many 'traditions of the elders', amongst which is the tradition of washing their hands before eating. When Jesus' disciples are seen to eat without first washing their hands, the Pharisees and scribes ask him why it is that his disciples ignore the tradition and eat with unwashed hands. He answers that Isaiah had prophesied their hypocrisy. Quoting the prophet's words, he says: 'This people honours me with their lips, but their heart is far from me; in vain do they worship me, teaching as doctrines the precepts of men.' Jesus continues: 'You neglect God's commandment and cling to the tradition of men . . . thus making void the word of God through the tradition you pass on.'[14]

This last incident illustrates one of the principal points underlying the protracted dispute between Jesus and the scribes and Pharisees: a religious tradition – indeed any tradition – is only as good as those who hand it down. In this instance the gospel writers use the scribes' and Pharisees' petty concerns for traditional ritual as an example of the way they have replaced the essence of their tradition – which is knowledge of God – with doctrines formulated by human interests. But this subterfuge is not necessarily deliberate. Because 'their heart is far from God' the ritual has become all-important. Yet ritual is merely the symbolic re-enactment at the outer, physical level of an inner, spiritual event. When it loses sight of its original meaning it becomes little more than a hollow gesture. At a behavioural level, washing our hands before eating fulfils a useful hygienic function. At a ritual level the gesture of washing our hands becomes a purification, a washing away of this-worldly concerns, in preparation for receiving the food the Spirit provides for us. Because of the directness of their relationship with Jesus/the Spirit the disciples have no need for such symbolic gestures.

The author of Matthew devotes almost an entire chapter (Chapter 23) to a series of accusations against the scribes and Pharisees. The comments in the first part are addressed simultaneously to the crowd and the disciples. From one of Jesus' opening remarks it would seem that the phenomenon of religious guilt is nothing new, for he accuses the scribes and Pharisees of placing heavy burdens on the people without themselves lifting a finger to help remove them. He also accuses them of self-importance, of loving the honours and respect that go with their position, because they 'do all their deeds to be seen by men'. The first part of the chapter comes to a close with the disciples being advised against allowing themselves to be called teachers, for they have one teacher, the Christ.

Jesus now turns his attention on the scribes and Pharisees themselves, addressing them as 'hypocrites' and 'blind fools' because they concern themselves with petty details and ignore matters of real substance. As an example he cites the tithes they impose on mint, dill, cumin and other herbs, while failing to instruct the people in the more important issues of justice, mercy and faith. (In a similar passage the author of Luke adds that they also neglect the issue of love of God.[15]) Jesus concludes his denunciation of their petty-mindedness by accusing them of being blind guides, who in their blindness strain out a gnat and swallow down a camel.[16] But the essence of his comments is not restricted to its apparent historical context. Its timelessness extends to all of us who become so involved in the minutiae of our own everyday lives that we ignore the more important issues, including our purpose in being here.

The accusations in Matthew continue with a reference to the dualism of our man-and-God mode of thinking. Jesus accuses the scribes and Pharisees of cleaning the outside of the cup and plate, while inside they are full of extortion and greed. Again accusing them of blindness, Jesus tells them to first cleanse the inside of the cup and of the plate, so that the outside may also be clean.[17] The last part of this admonition regarding our inner and outer worlds also expresses the nonduality of spiritual consciousness. Where the latter is concerned there is only one, indivisible world.

Jesus next addresses the spiritual poverty generated by the dualism of our man-and-God mode of consciousness. He tells the scribes and Pharisees that they are like whitewashed tombs: they appear beautiful from the outside, but within are full of dead men's bones.[18] The fate that befalls people who follow those who are spiritually dead is made clear elsewhere in Matthew. Jesus warns against becoming disciples of the Pharisees, saying: 'Have nothing to do with them. They are blind guides for blind people. And if a blind man guides another blind man, they will both fall into the ditch.'[19] His warning is relevant to our own time too. A fear of condemnation and/or rejection can often prevent us from asking our own religious or spiritual guides where they think they are taking us.

Fear of any sort is a powerful obstacle to our spiritual evolution. But the fear of rejection is perhaps our most common fear – especially where institutionalized religions or religious cults are concerned – as it stems from our deep-seated human need for approval, to know we belong. The author of John points to this in what appears little more than an aside: 'Many of the religious leaders believed in him [Jesus], but they did not openly admit it for fear of the Pharisees, in case they should be excommunicated; for they loved the praise of men more than the praise of God.'[20] The word-play in the last sentence draws attention to the conflicting motives of our ego and our spirituality. Whilst we may be told in Proverbs that 'the fear of God is the beginning of understanding,'[21] the fear of our fellow beings or of what they may think of us is itself an obstacle to understanding, if not the end of it.

It is fear that eventually motivates the scribes and chief priests to silence Jesus: the fear that their authority is being undermined. But it is fear of a different kind – fear of the people – that leads them to send out spies to lay traps for him with their questions. Pretending to be wise men, the latter ask Jesus if it is lawful for them to pay taxes to Caesar. Whether he answers 'yes' or 'no', he will lay himself open to criticism. If 'yes', he will be seen to be siding *with* the Romans; 'no', he can be charged with treason *against* Rome. But the inspired answer he gives rises above the pettiness of the question. He tells them to show him a coin, and then asks them whose head is on it. When they reply 'Caesar's', he simply tells them to: 'Render to Caesar the things that are Caesar's, and to God the things that are God's.'[22] Between them the question and the answer provide us with a glimpse of our two potential modes of consciousness in action.

The One Teacher

In its simplicity and straightforwardness, Jesus' response to the two-sided question about the coin typifies the direct perception of spiritual consciousness. There is no choice between 'yes' and 'no'. There are no 'ifs' or 'buts'; no 'either–or'. The reality of any situation is perceived directly and simply, as it is. But the nature of such perception is beyond the ego-centred mind that dominates our man-and-God mode of consciousness. It is inspired.

The essential nonduality of Jesus' teaching reminds us that the confrontational debates between himself and the religious authorities are about much more than points of law. Between them the protagonists present us with a concrete image of the gulf that separates two entirely different understandings of our relationship with the One Reality. In doing so they also draw attention to a particular stage in our own spiritual evolution, which Jesus reveals to a gathering of his disciples: 'You are not to be called rabbi [teacher], for you have one teacher, and you are all brethren. And call no man your father on earth, for you have one Father, who is in heaven. Neither be called masters, for you have one master, the Christ.'[23]

Our dilemma is that we tend to understand such statements in accordance with our dualistic man-and-God mind-set rather than see that they endeavour to take us beyond it. The predicament in which we find ourselves *vis-à-vis* the One Teacher is given voice in a conversation between Jesus and the disciples when they are sitting on the Mount of Olives. The disciples ask Jesus about the Last Times and the signs that will announce the coming of the One Teacher. Jesus answers:

> Take heed that no one leads you astray. For many will come in my name, saying 'I am the Christ', and they will lead many astray . . . If any one says to you, 'Lo, here is the Christ!' or 'There he is!' do not believe it. For false Christs and prophets will arise and show great signs and wonders, so as to lead you astray . . . So, if they say to you, 'Lo, he is in the wilderness,' do not go out; if they say, 'Lo, he is in the inner rooms,' do not believe it. For as the lightning comes from the east and shines as far as the west, so will be the coming of the Son of man.[24]

The One Teacher is neither *this*, nor *that*. It is a process of unlearning. Then, when we have cleared away our concepts and expectations, there may come a moment of inspired revelation, of direct experience of the One Reality, which is itself the One Teacher.

11

A MARRIAGE MADE IN HEAVEN

From our current dualistic Western perspective it is perhaps difficult to understand what is meant by nonduality: a state of being in which Reality is experienced firsthand, directly and numinously, as it is. As such it can only be alluded to indirectly. If we feel inclined to describe it, we can only do so in dualistic terminology, which involves words, and words are not the same as experience. In the end they are an inadequate way to express the fullness of being, the fullness with which life is experienced, when we are in a state of nonduality – that is to say, when we experience fully and directly, for ourselves, what it really means to be a human being. And their inadequacy is reflected in the fact that although an infinite number of words have been both spoken and written about our potential to experience being fully human, they seem to have had very little impact. Instead the words themselves have been studied, as though the secret of direct experience lies concealed within them. It doesn't. The secret lies concealed within ourselves.

What is direct experience? It arises naturally, of itself, when life is experienced with no interference from our personal desires, thoughts, or emotions; when there is no sense of 'I am experiencing this' or 'I am doing that'; when we are not distracted by events that do not concern us. It is a state of being in which life is lived spontaneously, without hesitation; or as Zen Buddhists say, without even 'a hair's breadth' between ourselves and Reality. That is also all that separates our two potential modes of being from each other: a hair's breadth. But a hair's breadth can at times seem like a million miles.

Essentially, nonduality refers to our natural state of being, which is one with Reality. It is experienced as a numinous oneness with our fellow creatures and the rest of creation. It is the state in which we originally come into this world. But as we progress further and further into our earthly life, the worries and concerns of everyday living lead us to forget the profound spiritual nature of our innate relationship with both the rest of the universe and the Spirit, the Source of our being. Our primordial nondualistic state is related in Genesis as the creation of man and woman from one breath (the Spirit) and one flesh. These same words also express the inherent unity of our spirituality and our humanity. But the insight they give us into our original nature has subsequently become obscured from us by the moral emphasis placed on the Fall and Expulsion from Paradise. Furthermore, the doctrine of Original Sin has instilled in us the belief that, as human beings, we are all subject to some kind of curse – a fatal flaw – that has been transmitted like a genetic mutation from generation to generation since the time of Adam.

Whereas the separation portrayed in the mythical Fall and Expulsion sought to express our genuine sense of unease at seemingly being left alone in the world to fend for ourselves, the dogmatic teaching that we are all flawed and inherently sinful has merely served to reinforce our unnatural sense of separation from the One Reality. In clearly stating the nature of our human dilemma the former is a profoundly compassionate psycho-spiritual observation rather than the simplistic but eternally damning judgement that we have turned it into. But then things were very different two to three thousand years ago. Then expressions such as 'sin', 'loose living' and 'repentance' were understood in a context that was at once psychophysical and psychospiritual, unlike the narrowest sphere of moral and/or social behaviour to which we confine them today.

The moralistic language found in both the Old and New Testaments seeks to identify for us our place within the unfolding mystery of the universe. In the sense of 'as above, so below' – that our humanity and our spirituality are not two separate conditions – the moralizing pronouncements that appear to be aimed exclusively at our human behaviour also serve to instruct us with regard to our spiritual conduct. Against that background the image of God as our husband seeks to express the true nature of our relationship with the One Reality in terms of marriage or union, thereby suggesting that the purpose of our errant life on this planet lies in the consummation of that union. As the following words from Isaiah suggest, the realization of our oneness with God brings an end to our sense of unease at being left alone and forsaken in the world: 'Fear not . . . For your Maker is your husband . . . For the Lord has called you like a wife forsaken and grieved in spirit.'[1]

A similar idea is expressed in the gospel narratives in a number of parables and events with a marital theme. But there seems to be a slight shift in the understanding of our relationship with the One Reality. It is no longer regarded as an automatic right. Our oneness with God now needs to be consummated – by us. Because of this the emphasis is now on the *potential* nature of our relationship with the One Reality. The metaphor of God as our husband is replaced by another. The Spirit as *bridegroom* appears in the first example we shall explore: an invitation to a marriage feast. As we shall see, the invitation is addressed to us. The marriage is our own.

The parable of the Marriage Feast

The parable of the Marriage Feast is told in Matthew,[2] but as it shares much in common with the parable of the Great Banquet in Luke,[3] the version that follows is an amalgamation of the two.

> The kingdom of heaven may be compared to a king who gave a marriage feast for his son. When the time for the feast came he sent his servants to call those who had been invited, but they refused to come. He sent out more servants, saying: 'Tell those who are invited that I have prepared the banquet, and everything is ready. Come to the marriage feast.' But those who were invited mocked the servants. Some of them gave excuses why they would not come. One said, 'I have bought a field, and I must go and attend to it.' A second said, 'I have bought five yoke of oxen, and I must go and examine them.' And another said, 'I have married a wife, and therefore I cannot come.' Yet others took hold of his servants, manhandled them and then killed them.
>
> In his anger the king sent his troops to destroy the murderers and

burn their city. Then he said to his servants: 'The wedding is ready, but those who were invited are not worthy. Go out into the city and invite the poor, the maimed, the blind and the lame.' When the servants had done this, there was still room at the feast. And so the king said: 'Go out to the highways and byways, and summon everyone you can find.' The servants went out into the country and gathered together everyone they found, both bad and good, so that the wedding hall was filled with guests.

When the king came in to see his guests, he caught sight of a man who had no wedding garment. 'My friend,' said the king, 'how did you get in here without a wedding garment?' The man was unable to answer, and so the king said to the attendants, 'Bind this man hand and foot, and throw him out.'

Both parables conclude with Jesus summing up their meaning for the benefit of his audience. At the conclusion of the Marriage Feast in Matthew, he says: 'For many are called, but few are chosen.' At the end of the Great Banquet he adds: 'For I tell you, none of those men who were invited shall taste of my banquet.'

As suggested, the parable is an invitation to our own wedding. It is an allegory for the spontaneous call we all receive to awaken to our original spiritual nature and consummate our relationship with the One Reality within which 'we live and move and have our being'. From the opening reference to the kingdom of heaven it is evident that, like the father in the parable of the Prodigal Son, 'the king' personifies God, the Spirit, the One, or whichever other term we personally use to designate That which is ultimately beyond words. By the same token, our own *potential* response to the call to awaken is represented by the different responses of the various people invited to the wedding.

I stress the word 'potential' because the primary purpose of the parable is to awaken us to the possibility of receiving just such a call in the first place. But the use of the word 'call' can lead to a profound misunderstanding. Our ego can run away with the idea that we are being singled out to fulfil some special purpose. We may believe we have been 'called by God', or have somehow even 'got God'. That is why the invitation comes with the following warning.

In what can be regarded as a preface to the parable of the Great Banquet in Luke, we are told that Jesus is dining at the house of a Pharisee. When he sees how the guests all head for the most prestigious seats, he relates a short parable. He ends it by telling his audience: 'Every one who exalts himself will be humbled, and he who humbles himself will be exalted.'[4] Once again, our attention is drawn to our potential for two modes of existence: the one motivated by our egocentric 'I'; the other by something far greater, which has the capacity to 'exalt us', to lift us up, to transform us. Jesus' words are both forceful and ambivalent: they are addressed to an audience whose hearts are hardened and whose ears are deaf. The delivery of the message may therefore appear strident, akin to the thunderings of the Hebrew prophets. Even so, the central message is simple and full of compassion.

Jesus' prefatory remark to the parable of the Great Banquet holds the key to the parable of the Marriage Feast: humility. Not false humility; nor the hypocritical kind of humility that manifests itself in a display of ingratiating self-humiliation; but the artless state of being humble, of quite simply being who we are, without thought or pretension as to what that might be. In that naturally ego-less state there is no longer even an ego to say '"I" am humble'. There is only I AM. In humbling ourselves we will have been exalted.

The converse – the humbling of those who exalt themselves – is illustrated with the help of the original invitees to the marriage feast. Their self-exaltation consists of being too busy fulfilling the whims and desires of the ego to have the time to acknowledge that there may be another purpose to our existence. Like the first invitee we may perhaps have invested too much in our own 'field' – that is to say, in the ego-centred illusion that it is 'we' who 'do' – whereas our purpose is to become 'God's field,'[5] the ego-less vehicles through whom things are done. Or, like the second, we may have acquired the 'five yoke of oxen' that stand for both the human microcosm and the five physical senses, indicating that we have become 'yoked' – attached – to the physical/material dimension of our being to a degree that ignores our relationship with the macrocosm. Again, like the third, we may have 'married a wife', which is to say we have 'married the world'. But the belief that the sole object of this life is material fulfilment is to ignore our real purpose. Finally, there are those who respond by man-handling and killing the king's servants, thus bringing about their own destruction. How do their actions apply to us? Whilst the king's destruction of the murderers and their city reiterates the familiar theme of Divine Retribution, it also reminds us of the saying from the Gospel of Thomas: 'If you bring forth what is within you, what you bring forth will save you. If you do not bring forth what is within you, what you do not bring forth will destroy you.'[6] In its own way this brief passage expresses the same idea as Jesus' comment about the humbled and the exalted. Our purpose is to become what we are capable of becoming, not to limit ourselves to being who we think we already are.

In contrast to the original guests are the recipients of the second invitation. Described as the 'poor, the maimed, the blind and the lame', these correspond to those of us who inwardly yearn for healing and wholeness of being. It is an invitation we cannot refuse. The third time the servants are sent out affirms the universal nature of the invitation at the heart of the gospels. We are all invited to consummate our inherent oneness with Reality. But, as the fate of the man who had no wedding garment reveals, we need to prepare ourselves for the occasion.

Knowingly or not, we are all involved in our own process of self-realization, of spiritual expansion, *all of the time*. As the parable points out, however, some of us have better things to do than get involved in our own individual evolutionary process. And while others may yearn intensely for spiritual completion, there are yet others who have no inclination either way. None the less, the 'many who are called' applies to all of us. Those who respond freely and without pretension are the few. In becoming self-less vehicles for the universal I AM, they are no longer in a position to say 'I am one of the chosen'. They have become those who are chosen. For as the in-dwelling Spirit reminds us: 'You did not choose me, but I chose you and appointed you that you should go and bear fruit.'[7]

The parable of the Bridegroom

From the way in which the man who had no wedding garment is thrown out of the marriage feast it becomes obvious that the potential consummation of our inherent oneness with Reality requires some form of preparation on our part for it to become reality. The gospels make it quite clear that the simple observance of religious law and ceremony is not enough. But what else can we do? One possible answer is given in the parable of the Bridegroom (also known as the parable of the Wise and Foolish Virgins), related in Matthew.

> The kingdom of heaven may be compared to ten maidens, who took their lamps and went to meet the bridegroom. Five of them were foolish and five were wise. The foolish ones took their lamps, but no oil, whereas the wise took containers of oil with their lamps. When the arrival of the bridegroom was delayed, they all dozed off and fell asleep. But in the middle of the night there was a shout, 'The bridegroom is coming! Go out to meet him.'
>
> The maidens all got up and trimmed their lamps, and the foolish ones said to the wise, 'Give us some of your oil, for our lamps are going out.' But the wise replied, 'We cannot, for there might not be enough for the both of us. Better still, go to the merchant and buy some for yourselves.'
>
> While the foolish maidens were away buying oil the bridegroom came, and those who were ready went in with him to the marriage feast, and the doors were shut. After a while the other maidens arrived, and said, 'Lord, lord, let us in!' But he replied, 'I tell you truly, I do not know you.'
>
> Jesus ends the parable by addressing his audience with the words: 'Watch therefore, for you know neither the hour nor the day.'[8]

Where the parable of the Marriage Feast presented us with several examples of our possible response to the invitation to consummate our relationship with the One Reality, the parable of the Bridegroom confines it to two. The directness of the parable is also reflected in the manner of its telling.

Jesus (who relates the parable) and the bridegroom (its central figure) are both personifications of the Spirit. The arrival of the bridegroom therefore represents our inherent potential for spiritual awakening; our potential for two modes of being is embodied in the maidens' contrasting states of preparedness. On the one hand we have five foolish maidens: when the bridegroom does finally arrive they are simply 'not here'. They may appear to be awake, but metaphorically speaking they are still fast asleep. On the other, we have five wise maidens. When the bridegroom comes, not only are they awake, they are also totally 'here' for him. As a result they go in with him to the marriage feast and the doors (to the kingdom of heaven) are shut behind them. Contrary to appearances, the bridegroom's response to the entreaties of the late arrivals is not a rejection. The gospels are quite clear concerning our entry to the metaphorical kingdom of heaven: it is for every one. Rather it is we who exclude ourselves. Jesus' concluding comment that we 'watch' infers that a permanent state of *watch-fulness* is what is required. In the parable it is the preparation or 'inner work' symbolized by the containers of oil the wise maidens took with their lamps.

What exactly is watchfulness? In simple terms it means being totally here, in the present moment. In Reality we are never anywhere else but in the present; there is nowhere else to be. But in everyday reality, like the foolish maidens, we are rarely ever here. Either our thoughts are somewhere on the other side of the world, or in a café down the street, or anywhere else where we are not. Or our memories have taken us off into the past, or our hopes and fears have taken us off into the future. But, as we are told in the Sermon on the Mount: 'Do not be anxious about tomorrow, for tomorrow will be anxious for itself. Let the day's own trouble be sufficient for the day.'[9]

Watchfulness entails collecting up those parts of us that are scattered through time and space so that all our attention is focused on where we are, and on whatever requires our attention in the moment. Like the path of humility – the artless state of being humble – we encountered in the parable of the Marriage Feast, watchfulness offers us a practical tool by which we may learn to live intuitively, in the moment. Watchfulness, or mindfulness as it is also known, is not a passive state. Comparable to the *wu-wei* of the Taoists – which can be translated as 'emptiness', 'being without doing', 'effortless effort' – and the 'surrender' or 'dynamic submission' of the Sufis,[10] watchfulness can be described as a state of heightened awareness. It is a state in which, by endeavouring to be totally awake to the very least of our actions as well as to everything around us – both inside and outside ourselves – there is no room left in which to arise the thoughts of our egocentric 'I'. By simply *being* in the present we will become as one with the Source of our being.

A wedding at Cana

Those with the greatest spiritual wisdom are often to be found leading the least complicated of lives. Living spontaneously in the present and simply taking responsibility for whatever arises in the moment, they have neither the inclination nor the desire to interfere with the Source of Life at work within them. For the majority of us, however, things are very different. We are so used to *doing* that we *have* to know what is going on; we *have* to be in control, even where the mysterious workings of the Spirit are concerned. Perhaps it was to assuage our curiosity that the author of John wrote about the miraculous transformation of water into wine. The first of Jesus' miracles, it offers us a timeless insight into the invisible miracle taking place within us – the transformation of human consciousness into spiritual consciousness:

> On the third day there was a wedding at Cana in Galilee, and the mother of Jesus was there. Jesus and his disciples had also been invited to the wedding. When the wine ran out, Jesus' mother said to him, 'They have no wine.' In response he said, 'Woman, what have your concerns to do with me? My time has not yet come.' And his mother said to the servants, 'Do whatever he tells you.'
>
> Now it so happened that six stone vessels for the Jewish rites of purification were standing there, each holding twenty or thirty gallons, and Jesus instructed the servants to fill them with water. When the vessels were filled to the brim, he said, 'Now draw some out, and take it to the steward of the feast.'
>
> They did as he had told them and the steward of the feast tasted the water turned to wine. Not knowing where the wine had come from – although the servants knew, for they had drawn the water – the steward called the bridegroom over and said to him, 'People usually serve the good wine first and then, when everyone has drunk freely, they serve an inferior wine. But you have kept the good wine until now.'[11]

Why does Mary's simple statement 'they have no wine' elicit such a seemingly brusque response from Jesus? A clue lies in the words 'wine' and 'bridegroom', both of which are synonyms for the Spirit, embodied here in the figure of Jesus. The guests 'have no Spirit'. But the Spirit reveals itself spontaneously, in its own time, conforming neither to human expectations nor to human will. The distinction made here by Jesus between 'your concerns' and 'my time' recalls a saying found elsewhere in John: 'My time has not yet come, but your time is always here.'[12] As if to underline the divergence between the spiritual and human viewpoints, Mary turns to the servants instructing them to 'Do whatever he tells you,' so that Jesus/the Spirit may reveal himself in his own time, and in his own way.

The author of John now turns our attention to the 'six stone vessels for the Jewish rites of purification'. In the interpretation of this miracle in his book *The New Man*, the psychologist Maurice Nicoll points out that '*stone* represents the most external and literal form of esoteric Truth'.[13] But in the context of this present book it feels more appropriate to suggest that stone represents a literal *understanding* of Truth. This initial, literal level of understanding is a necessary prerequisite for deeper understanding. It is the bedrock on which faith is built, for within it lie further levels of understanding, and further levels of consciousness. The stone jars can therefore be equated with our literal, man-and-God mode of understanding the way things are. The pouring of water into the stone jars marks the beginning of the transformation process. We are filled with a new, living understanding. If we already know the outcome of the event, we could even say that the wine in the jars now stands for spiritual consciousness. In one way it does, but the wine has not yet been tasted.

It is now that Jesus instructs the servants to draw out some of the wine and take it to the steward of the feast for tasting. Surprised by its fine quality, the steward calls the bridegroom over to compliment him, because he has 'kept the good wine until now'. With this the figure of Jesus takes on additional significance. Not only is he the embodiment of the Spirit; but as the Spirit he is also personified in the figure of the bridegroom. As such it is the Spirit that both initiates the transformation and acknowledges its fruitful outcome.

The human perspective is enacted for us through the words and actions of the steward. Initially he has no idea where the wine he has just tasted has come from, but knows that it is better than he was expecting. In calling the bridegroom/Spirit to him he comes face to face with the Source of the 'good wine' of spiritual consciousness. The transformation is complete. More importantly, the wedding has now taken place. But whose wedding is it? In one sense it is the steward's. For he is the one who, on tasting the new wine, has come face to face with the Source of his being. In another sense the wedding is ours. When we too recognize simultaneously the Spirit without and the Spirit within, we will consummate our relationship with the One Reality.

A marital problem

As human experience has taught us, marriages do not always run smoothly. Whenever two people are joined together there is always the possibility that they may grow apart, no matter how strongly they are bonded together. The moment at which the process of separation begins is often difficult to pinpoint with precision. Opinions will differ because the process is invariably a gradual one. Perhaps there was an inbuilt incompatibility from the start, or else consummation of the bond may have taken place at the simplest of physical levels, and no deeper. Alternatively there may not have been enough communication between the two parties, culminating in an insurmountable barrier of misunderstanding being built between them. Then again, perhaps the gradual erosion that led to separation was ignited from the outside by a third party, to be fuelled either from without or from within by unfounded suspicion or rumour until such time as the mis-perception of reality itself became real. Once an actual separation has taken place it is very difficult to bring about a reconciliation, as any one who has ever experienced the breakup of a relationship will know.

The relationship between our humanity and our spirituality is no different, except perhaps that we are not aware the two have become separated. Indeed, we may not even be aware that such a relationship exists at all, because we have acquired the belief that the spiritual dimension has more to do with an after-life than life in the here-and-now. But such a belief is erroneous, as the gospel writers endeavour to point out to us. In their narratives they go further still, using the confrontational debates between Jesus and various religious leaders to demonstrate that beliefs have very little to do with reality – whether spelt with an 'r' or an 'R'. Such debates often present us with a mind-bending dilemma similar to that posed by Magritte's apple, for the gospel writers' intention is identical to that of the painter. At root, the debates between Jesus and the religious authorities of his time have more to do with confronting the mind with itself, than they do with matters of religion. As the following example shows, the confrontation is essentially between two modes of thinking, or two modes of consciousness.

> Some Sadducees, who say there is no resurrection, asked Jesus a question, saying: 'Teacher, according to Moses if a man dies

childless, his brother must marry the widow and raise children for his dead brother. Now, we know of a case where there were seven brothers. The first one married and when he died childless his wife passed to his brother. The same happened to the second and third brothers, and likewise down to the seventh. Last of all, the woman died. Whose wife will she be at the resurrection, because they all had her as a wife?'

Jesus replied, 'The sons of this age marry and are given away in marriage; but the sons of that age neither marry nor are given away in marriage. Having been raised from the dead they cannot die any more, because they are like angels. Being sons of the resurrection, they are sons of God.'[14]

The incident begins by drawing our attention to the paradoxical nature of beliefs that concern themselves with issues beyond the realms of human experience. Using the voice of the Sadducees, the gospel writers demonstrate that when we say we do not believe in something we also give credence to the very thing in which we say we do not believe. Conversely, when we say we do believe in something, our statement of belief carries with it the implication that the thing in which we say we believe may not actually exist. Therein lies the distinction between belief and faith. The tenuous nature of the former is reflected by the fact that our beliefs have to be stated, debated, and proven. Faith, wisdom, and true knowledge have no need to be stated or proven in quite the same way. Approved, amended or rejected they may be, but their nature is such that they are never open to debate. The difference between the two becomes apparent when we compare the Sadducees' question with the authority of Jesus' response.

The Sadducees' question concerns the Final Resurrection that will precede the Last Judgement. Jesus picks up the idiomatic language of the Last Times in his answer, making it clear that such questions only concern the sons of 'this age'. For the sons of 'that age' the questions do not even exist. But the question-and-answer format adopted here by the gospel writers is subtle enough for the point they are really making to escape us. If we look more closely we see that because the question about the resurrection is one that is of immediate concern to the Sadducees, the reply Jesus gives them infers that the Sadducees themselves are 'sons of this age'; whereas Jesus, for whom such questions appear not to exist, is evidently a 'son of that age'. It would appear that where Jesus is concerned, the resurrection has already taken place.

This brings us to a crucial question about the resurrection. Are we meant to understand the raising from the dead literally or figuratively? We have already seen that the allegorical language of the gospels uses words such as 'death' and 'dead' to refer to those who, spiritually speaking, have no life in them. Similarly, we have met with the idea of spiritual rebirth, of metaphorically being 'raised from the dead'. Is it possible that the gospel writers are here trying to correct an erroneous belief? In other words, the resurrection refers to neither an historical nor a physical event. Instead it marks a profound change of consciousness: the spiritual consciousness portrayed in both the Temptation in the Wilderness and the Wedding at Cana. For where the dualistic man-and-God mode of consciousness perceives things in terms of life and death, spiritual consciousness sees only Life. That this is the point the gospel writers are trying to get across would seem to be borne out by the words with which Jesus closes this brief debate: 'As for the resurrection of the dead, have you not read the word of God, "I am the God of Abraham, and the God of Isaac, and the God of Jacob"? He is not God of the dead, but of the living.'[15]

12

The Path of Return

We now come to the events that mark the dramatic conclusion of the gospel story. But it is hard to come to them with a fresh mind. We have possibly heard the story so many times before that our understanding of the events from Palm Sunday to Pentecost has become indelibly coloured by one particular interpretation or another. And yet it is more important here than with any other part of the story that we endeavour to come with a fresh mind. For the events unfolding are the re-enactment of the gospels' central message – a message that has already been expressed either openly or by allusion through the teachings, parables, miracles and seemingly more mundane events of Jesus' life. But the roots of the gospel message go further back in time, to the Torah and the Hebrew prophets. Weaving together the past, present and future into one seamless garment, the gospel writers drew on this older tradition so that their story would be seen to fulfil the prophecies spoken by the prophets concerning a 'new' covenant, a new understanding of our relationship with the One Reality. The new covenant of the prophets had proclaimed a direct knowledge of God – a knowledge that came from within rather than without – which was experienced as a new, spiritual consciousness; a new, nondualistic mode of being. Now the gospel writers were to give the prophets' message a powerful new voice. It was given literary form in the gospel narratives.

Thus far we have explored some of the ways in which the gospel writers expressed their central message. As with many previous events, those we are to witness are open to simultaneous interpretation from both the human and spiritual viewpoints. But to set out these viewpoints side by side would not only be over-repetitious; it would also detract from the subtle drama being played out within the events themselves. Our exploration therefore takes a slightly different form: a minor change of vocabulary has been adopted.

At this stage in our homeward journey our humanity and spirituality, our personality and essence, have joined company and are travelling in the same direction. From here on the words 'self' and 'Self' will frequently be used to refer to these two dimensions of our being. They are used in the context of this book to convey the principle that the self (the individual human being) is merely an aspect of a greater Self (the Spirit or universal I AM). In that particular sense the self is both an expression of and a vehicle for the Self. Our human dilemma is that, unaware of the underlying purpose for our existence, we find a purpose for ourselves. We become what was described earlier as a *divided self*, for our true purpose continues to unfold within us. In effect, the self is influenced simultaneously by two 'wills': the human ('I am') and the Divine (the I AM).

At times it may seem as though these two wills are in opposition to each other; but without our human will our experience of the physical world would be incomplete. Indeed, it is generally through our experience in the everyday physical world that we are awakened to the presence of the Spirit and the greater Will working through us. That awakening (*metanoia*) may be sudden, or it may take place over a prolonged period of time. In either case it instigates a change of 'will', whereby the will of the self cooperates willingly – consciously or unconsciously, and to a lesser or greater degree – with the Will of the Self.

This change-over of will is the transformative process referred to earlier as spiritual expansion and integration, or spiritual empowerment. The process completes itself when the will of the self *becomes* the Will of the Self. At that point in our spiritual evolution we experience for ourselves what it means to be fully human. That is to say, we experience everything (including ourselves) in the fullness of its being.

It is this process of transformation which now unfolds in the events that take place between Palm Sunday and the Ascension of Jesus into heaven. We rejoin the gospel narratives at the transformative point where the self is awakened to the presence of the Self and the two begin to travel (more or less) harmoniously in the same direction. This turning-point is represented by Jesus' decision to return to Jerusalem for the Passover.

When the gospel narratives were compiled Jerusalem was literally, symbolically and spiritually the heart of the Jewish nation. Collectively and individually, it was also the heart of the Jewish people. It is in the latter sense that we shall approach both the return of Jesus to Jerusalem and the events that unfold there. That is to say, as an allegory for our own journey home.

Riding on a donkey

The gospel accounts of the return to Jerusalem share a common imagery, with Jesus instructing his disciples to fetch a donkey or an ass from a nearby village. His entrance to the city is to fulfil the prophecy in Zechariah, that Jerusalem's king is coming to her, 'humble and riding on an ass'.[1]

> And when the disciples returned with the donkey they threw their garments over its back, and Jesus sat upon it. As he rode towards the city many people spread their garments on the road, and others spread branches they had cut from the trees. And those who went ahead of him and those who came behind him, shouted, 'Blessed is he who comes in the name of the Lord!'[2]

As with the other events we have explored, the Entry to Jerusalem reflects the reciprocal nature of the transformation process by which we become fully human beings. This becomes apparent when we recall the symbolism of 'garments' – in particular the passage from the Gospel of Thomas where Jesus tells the disciples he will reveal himself to them when they 'disrobe without being ashamed' and place their garments under their feet 'and tread on them' (*see* Chapter 5, page 64). Jesus' conscious decision to return to Jerusalem in response to the decision of the self to follow the Self, is acted out symbolically by the disciples and the crowd taking off their garments. They either throw them over the back of the donkey for Jesus to sit on or strew them along the road for him to ride over. This disrobing is without shame. In fact it is a moment of joyous celebration in which the cries of 'Lord' give voice to their recognition. Like the return of a king to reclaim his kingdom, the recognition of the Self removes our garments for us and metaphorically rides a donkey over them in the process.

The metaphor of *riding on a donkey* is not unique to the gospel story. For St Francis, the physical body was 'poor Brother Donkey', the faithful beast of burden that carries the soul on its earthly journey. 'Riding the donkey' means bridling the whims and desires of the self so that neither rider (Self) nor donkey (self) are distracted from the common purpose of their journey. As the author of the Letter of James says: 'If we put bits into the mouths of horses that they may obey us, we guide their whole bodies.'[3] But as Jesus demonstrates, this is no heavy-handed bridling. It arises naturally, through the combination of humility and grace – of no-willing and no-forcing – that correspond to our natural state of being. In that context 'riding the donkey' or 'mastering one's self' simply mean that we become a vehicle for the Self.

The archetypal image of a king entering the capital of his kingdom by riding humbly on a donkey also expresses one of the fundamental teachings common to all the world's religious and spiritual traditions. Addressed to all of us who may find ourselves in a position of power or authority over our fellow beings, the teaching urges us to recognize that the ultimate Source of Power bestowed that position upon us in order for us to serve. But it would seem that few of those in positions of power today – whatever their realm of influence – are aware of the chaotic effect a misuse of that position can have on the subtle interconnectedness of all life. Like the king riding on a donkey, a person who really understands the nature of power is one who has the humility and wisdom to know that by serving others we also serve the Source of Power itself.

Cleaning the temple

Unlike the synoptic gospels, the author of John places his account of Jesus driving the traders from the temple before the triumphal return to Jerusalem. Of the three synoptic gospels, Matthew and Luke place it immediately after Jesus enters the capital. Mark also has him go straight to the temple, but says he simply 'looked round at everything [and then] as it was already late, he went out to Bethany with the twelve'.[4] On his way back to Jerusalem the next morning Jesus does something that provides us with an allegorical parallel for what is about to take place in the temple. Mark begins by telling us that Jesus 'was hungry'. Seeing a fig tree in leaf in the distance he went over to it to see if there was anything on it to eat. Not being the season for figs, he found only leaves, and so said to it: 'May no one ever eat fruit from you again.'[5] We shall come back to the fig tree when Jesus returns that way later in the day. For the moment we rejoin him as he enters the temple.

> When Jesus went into the temple he found money-changers, and people selling oxen, sheep and pigeons. Making an impromptu whip he drove the people and animals out of the temple, scattered the money-changers' coins across the floor and overturned their tables. And he said to those in the temple, 'Is it not written, "My house shall be called a house of prayer for all peoples"? But you have turned it into a den of thieves.' The Jews asked him, 'What sign have you to show us for doing this?' Jesus replied, 'Destroy this temple, and in three days I will raise it up.' The Jews then said, 'It has taken forty-six years to build this temple, and will you raise it up in three days?' But he spoke of the temple of his body. And when he was raised from the dead, his disciples remembered what he had said.[6]

At a literal level the Cleaning of the Temple can be explained as the simple condemnation of the buying and selling of goods within the precincts of the temple building. Or again it may have been that the temple stall-holders took advantage of their prestigious position to charge exorbitant prices for the goods they sold. However, the aside (which comes from John) reminds us the temple is a metaphor for the human body, so the event can also be understood as signifying a point in our spiritual evolution when we perhaps realize that we are not in this world solely for material gain. This does not necessarily mean we have to become an ascetic, totally renouncing this-worldly things. As Ali, the companion of the Prophet Mohammed, said: 'Asceticism is not that you should not own anything, but that nothing should own you.'[7]

The conclusion to the fig tree episode provides us with a commentary on what has taken place in the temple. Mark tells us that on his way back to Bethany Jesus and the disciples again pass the fig tree, now 'withered away to its roots'. On the way to the temple Jesus had gone to the tree in search of (spiritual) food, but found nothing to eat as there was no fruit on it. Yet the tree was covered in leaves and apparently healthy. As Mark has told us, however, the fig tree is barren because it is not the season for figs. Likewise, the temple appears to be thriving as the house of God, but it too is barren. Instead of real spiritual food, all Jesus finds are the sacrificial animals used in the ritual practices of the old, dualistic man-and-God consciousness. At this point Jesus accuses those in the temple of turning it into a 'den of thieves', which echoes what he says elsewhere in John: 'All who came before me [Jesus] are thieves and robbers.'[8] And so Jesus (the Spirit) drives them out in a symbolic gesture by which he reclaims the 'house of prayer' or temple (the body in which the spirit dwells) from the unfruitful dualism of our man-and-God mind-set. In that context, *cleaning the temple* can be understood as an allegory for a further stage in the empowerment of the Spirit, or as the re-dedication of the self to the Self.

Jesus' closing comment about the destruction and 'raising up' of the body in three days derives from the book of Hosea. There Israel talks of returning to the Lord, saying: 'For he has torn, that he may heal us; he has stricken, and he will bind us up. After two days he will revive us; on the third he will raise us up . . . Let us know, let us press on to know the Lord.'[9] The connection made by Hosea between the healing – being made whole, or completion – of Israel and the knowledge or *gnosis* of God is an important one. For the figure of Jesus personifies the new spiritual consciousness, the direct knowledge of God, that is the salvation of Israel and all people. He also embodies the Will of the Self. In making his announcement he indicates the transformative nature of the events to which we are witness. We shall encounter the theme of being raised up on the third day, again, when we come to the Crucifixion and Resurrection.

In an upper room

Of all the events narrated in the gospel narratives, the two that are no doubt most difficult to come to with a fresh mind are the Last Supper and the Crucifixion. Not only has our understanding of the two events been coloured by almost two thousand years of theological and doctrinal overlay. The two have also been dove-tailed together in the liturgy of the Mass or Eucharist. The blessing and sharing of the bread and wine is now inseparable from the physical body and blood of the Jesus who was crucified and died on the cross. The resultant image of a sacrificial death, by which a historical Jesus literally died on the cross to save us from our sins, has impressed itself on our collective psyche to an extent that it has become impossible to understand these two events in any other way. In addition, the re-enactment of the sacrificial death in the daily offices of the Church and its myriad portrayals across the centuries in the visual and performing arts[10] have invested the symbol of the cross with an emotive power that is unique in world history. To come to the gospel account of the Last Supper afresh, we need to put all of the above to one side. We also need to remind ourselves that it was not the gospel writers' intention to found a new religion. That came later on. For our present purposes we shall continue to focus our attention on those particular elements that shed further light on the myth of Being at the heart of the gospel narratives.

The accounts given in the four canonical Gospels of the meal celebrated by Jesus and his disciples vary considerably, both in detail and length. They range from the nine verses of Matthew to the five chapters (122 verses) of John.[11]

> As they were eating, Jesus took bread, and blessed, and broke it, and gave it to the disciples, saying, 'Take, eat; this is my body which is given for you.' And he took a cup, and when he had given thanks he gave it to them, saying, 'Drink of it, all of you; for this is my blood of the new covenant, which is poured out for many for the forgiveness of sins.'[12]

In timing the evening meal shared by Jesus and the disciples to coincide with the traditional Passover meal, the gospel writers portray one of the levels – the literal – on which the new non-dualistic spiritual consciousness will supersede the old. For the focus of the meal, the consecration and sharing of the symbolic bread and wine, replaces the animal sacrifices of the old man-and-God mind-set. But the meal itself is merely part of an extended sequence of symbolic events that together mark the progressive establishment of the new consciousness. First we had the allegory of the king entering his kingdom, riding humbly on a donkey, signifying the union of self and Self in a common purpose. Then we witnessed the Cleaning of the Temple. There the themes of spiritual food, transformation and prayer marked the re-dedication of the self to the Self. It also paved the way for the meal in a 'large upper room'.[13]

The symbolic setting of the upper room itself recalls the instruction Jesus gives to the disciples regarding prayer, related in Matthew: 'When you pray, go into your room and shut the door and pray to your Father who is in secret; and your Father who sees in secret will reward you.'[14] In both that and the present contexts, I suggest *prayer* signifies a state of being corresponding to faith, profound contemplation or meditation. What transpires when in that state of being is acted out in Jesus' distribution of bread and wine in the upper room.

Bread and wine are mentioned innumerable times in the Bible, but two examples are particularly relevant in the present context. The first occurs in Proverbs. Recalling the invitation sent out in the parable of the Marriage Feast, we there find Wisdom inviting us to the banquet she has prepared for us. This banquet also represents a new way of life: 'Come, eat of my bread and drink of the wine I have mixed. Leave simple ones, and live, and walk in the way of insight.'[15] The idea that bread and wine are synonyms for life is met with again in Lamentations: 'They cry to their mothers, "Where is bread and wine?" as they faint like wounded men in the streets of the city, as their life is poured out on their mother's bosom.'[16]

The gospel writers' own use of bread as a metaphor for spiritual teaching, and wine as a synonym for the Spirit, suggests that the two together signify the spiritual teaching that comes directly from the Source of our being. There are also other metaphors to be considered in the present context: the presence of Jesus (the Spirit) and the twelve disciples (its dissemination) in a room (a place of prayer). Taking these elements together with the two preceding events – the divesting of our garments and the cleaning of our temple – I suggest the communal meal of bread and wine is an allegory for the inner event of prayer, of true meditation, in which the self communes with the Self. In other words, we are witnessing the establishment of the 'new covenant' according to which true knowledge, or *gnosis*, emanates from the Source of Life itself.

The account of the meal in John differs from the synoptic gospels in that there is no similar consecration of bread and wine. Instead the same event is portrayed in a distinctive and enlightening way, with Jesus washing the disciples' feet.

Jesus rose from supper, and laying aside his garments he tied a towel round himself. He then poured water into a basin and began to wash the disciples' feet, and to dry them with the towel that was round him. When he came to Simon Peter, Peter said, 'Master, are *you* going to wash my feet?' Jesus replied, 'What I am doing you do not understand now, but later you will understand.' Peter said, 'You shall never wash my feet.' Jesus answered him, 'If I do not wash you, you have nothing to do with me.' 'In that case, Master,' said Simon Peter, 'Do not just wash my feet, but my hands and head as well.' Jesus said to him, 'He who has bathed only needs his feet to be washed for him to be completely clean. And you are clean, but not every one of you.'

When he had washed their feet and put on his garments, Jesus took his seat and said to them, 'Do you know what I have done to you? You call me Teacher and Master, and you are right, for so I am. Therefore if I, your Teacher and Master, have washed your feet, you ought to wash each other's feet. I have set you an example, so that you should also do as I have done to you.'[17]

As a symbolic gesture the washing of the disciples' feet is related to a number of themes we have already encountered: baptism, Cleaning the Temple, and the comment Jesus made to the Pharisees about cleaning the cup and the platter (*see* page 155). The role adopted by Jesus in washing the disciples' feet can also be linked to the humility he demonstrated by entering Jerusalem riding on a donkey, as well as to the teaching that the more authority one has, the more one attends to the needs of one's fellow beings. But the more subtle aspects of the incident require closer examination, for again it is an allegory of an inner event. Or rather, a potential inner event.

The laying aside of Jesus' garments suggests that we are witnessing a moment of spiritual revelation. But Peter is possibly the last person to understand the subtle and spontaneous workings of the Spirit. In the same way that he later denies three times that he knows Jesus – a threefold denial signifies a total denial – his misunderstanding of what is happening here is also reiterated three times. Rather than allowing Jesus/the Spirit to do 'as it wills', he tries to take charge. He tells Jesus what he will or will not allow him to do. First, when Jesus comes to wash his feet, Peter questions him, 'Master, are *you* going to wash my feet?' Second, when Jesus says, 'What I am doing you do not understand now,' Peter's reply shows that he really does not understand: '*You* shall never wash my feet.' Third, when Jesus says to him, 'If I do not wash you, you have nothing to do with me,' Peter now responds by asking to have the whole of himself washed. Again Jesus has to correct him, saying 'just the feet will do'.

When Jesus puts his garments back on the moment of revelation is over. He now explains to the twelve what has taken place. But if, like Peter, they have not understood what was revealed to them, they will be none the wiser as to what it is they are told they should do. We may even ask ourselves, have we understood what has been revealed? Or, like Peter, have we imposed our own under-standing on what is taking place before it has even had time to happen? In fact we have been given a subtle insight into the nature of spiritual revelation. And in Peter's response we have been given a not so subtle insight into our own human reaction. If we approach life in a similar way to Peter, full of expectation or prejudice, we will never perceive the subtle workings of the Spirit that permeates all things. For spiritual revelation occurs when we are in the receptive state of being, or state of prayer, embodied in the shared meal in the upper room.

The extended length of John's account is due to the teaching Jesus addresses to his disciples, much of which concerns itself with explaining the mystery of his person. The comment he makes to Peter in the above episode regarding present ignorance and future wisdom – 'What I am doing you do not understand now, but later you will understand.' – is a recurring theme in the chapters that follow. But the revelatory nature of what transpires in the room is never far beneath the surface of the words. We shall bring this chapter to a close with the author of John revealing the trans-formation in understanding that comes when our conscious mind is inspired through its communion with the Spirit:

> 'And I will pray the Father, and he will give you another Counsellor, to be with you for ever, even the Spirit of truth, whom the world cannot receive, because it neither sees him nor knows him; you know him, for he dwells with you, and will be in you.'[18]

> 'I have yet many things to say to you, but you cannot bear them now. When the Spirit of truth comes, he will guide you into all the truth . . .'[19]

13

THE END OF MEANING

It was suggested earlier that the evolution of spiritual consciousness is a natural process – a process that we can assist, but which we cannot bring about for ourselves. We can assist it by un-learning, by abandoning our expectations and prejudices, and by un-doing the hold exerted upon us by the this-worldly whims and desires of our ego. In other words, we simply go about our business without giving too much thought to the process taking place naturally within us. Our dilemma lies in the fact that the more thought we give to the process and what we can do to speed it up, the more our thoughts turn to 'me', and the more we feed the dualism that is generated by our egocentric sense of 'I am'. As the Sufi Abu Yazid al-Bistami said: 'For thirty years I went in search of God, and when I opened my eyes at the end of this time, I discovered that it was really He who sought for me.'[1] What we are looking for is what is looking.

For the naturals who are blessed with spiritual consciousness from an early age, life simply is as it is. Their experience of the world is very different to those who perceive life in dualistic terms, as a conflict of opposites. For the latter even the natural process of spiritual evolution is experienced as a conflict between the ego and the Spirit, or as a time of intense psychological and emotional suffering characterized as the 'dark night of the soul'. The intensity of that inner suffering now becomes part of the gospel story.

Agony in the Garden

The word 'agony' derives from the Greek *agon*, 'contest', and refers to the suffering or struggle that precedes death.[2] As the oil that was most commonly used for anointing and healing was the oil of the olive, it is fitting that the agony of the Messiah/Christ, the Anointed One, is set on the Mount of Olives at 'a place called Gethsemane'.[3] The name *Gethsemane* means 'olive press'.[4] For the olive to yield up its precious essence it needs to be taken to just such a press and crushed. The essence is then released, the pulp discarded.

The Agony in the Garden illustrates our experience of transformation as one of profound emotional and psychological suffering. It is a process during which it sometimes feels as though we are being turned upside down, or inside out. The apparency of suffering is due to the resistance mounted by the will of the self – with all its whimsical desires and beliefs – to its transformation. It may even feel as though we are ourselves being reduced to nought. But if we knew why we suffered, we would not suffer. This is not a negative or nihilistic 'nought'. It is only our psychological and emotional garments that are being discarded. Our original nature is being released.

The synoptic gospels offer us three different accounts of the suffering that takes place at Gethsemane. The version that follows is compiled from all three.

> Then they went to a place called Gethsemane, and Jesus said to his disciples, 'Stay here while I go and pray.' And he took Peter, James and John with him. Jesus then became greatly troubled and filled with sorrow, and he said to them: 'My soul is very sad, even to death. Stay here and keep watch.' And going a bit further on, he fell on his knees and prayed, saying: 'Father, to thee all things are possible. Let this cup pass from me; yet not my will, but thine, be done.'
>
> When he came back to the disciples and found them sleeping, he said to Peter: 'Simon, are you asleep? Could you not stay awake for one hour? Be watchful and pray, in case you are put to the test. The spirit indeed is willing, but the flesh is weak.'
>
> Jesus went away a second time and prayed the same prayer. Coming back to the disciples he again found them asleep, for their eyes were heavy. A third time he went away and repeated the same prayer. When he came back to them he said, 'Are you still sleeping and not awake? It is enough; the time has come. The Son of man is

betrayed into the hands of sinners. Come, let us be going. My betrayer approaches.'[5]

As we come closer to the turning-point marked by the death on the cross, the increasing tension underlying the events brings about a polarization in the attitudes manifested by Jesus (the Self) and the disciples and other protagonists (the self). On the one hand we have the figure of Jesus proceeding knowingly towards the death on the cross; on the other we have those who are seemingly conspiring towards the same end but for different reasons. Somewhere in between the two are the disciples.

The profound state of *being* represented by the meal in the upper room moves to a further level in the Agony in the Garden. Like the room before it, the garden setting also provides an inner landscape within which Jesus and the three disciples portray our own process of transformation. The weakening resolve of the self to follow the Self is apparent in the contrast between Jesus' praying while the disciples fall asleep, in spite of his request that they remain awake and watchful. As we saw earlier, to be awake and watchful is a state of being in which we are totally *here*. (*See* the parable of the Bridegroom, page 164.) But the three disciples are most definitely not 'here'. They are fast asleep – both to the will of their Master who asked them to remain awake and to the suffering he endures on their behalf a step or two away from them.

In essence the Agony in the Garden is a test of will between the will of the self and the Will of the Self. It reveals how the Self is at work within us, urging the self to continue along its path to completion, even when we are asleep to its presence. To remind us of the distinction between the two wills, numerical symbolism is used to underline the extent to which (a) the Self is willing us to stay awake, and (b) the self is weakening in its resolve. Three times Jesus repeats the prayer that concludes with the words: 'not my will, but thine, be done.' Three times the disciples are put to the test, and three times they are unable to remain awake. They are totally asleep. It is no coincidence that Judas arrives while they slumber.

Judas

The popular image of Judas Iscariot is that of the traitor, the one who betrays Jesus. For it is Judas who delivered Jesus into the hands of those who sought to kill him. Yet in the context of the gospel story it has to be said that without Judas' betrayal there would be no Crucifixion, and no Resurrection. His role is therefore a crucial one that needs to be seen from more than one point of view. As with some of the other incidents we have examined, numerical symbolism holds a key to understanding the underlying 'meaning' of Judas.

The author of John provides us with some useful background information about Judas in his version of the anointing of Jesus. The setting is the house of Lazarus, Mary and Martha, in Bethany, where Jesus has supper six days before the Passover.

> Mary then took a pound of the most expensive spikenard and anointed the feet of Jesus, and then wiped his feet with her hair, and the whole house was filled with the fragrance of the ointment. Then Judas Iscariot said, 'Why was this ointment not sold for three hundred denarii and the money given to the poor?' He said this not out of concern for the poor, but because he was a thief, and as he had the alms-box he took for himself whatever was put into it. Jesus said: 'Leave her alone, for she had kept it for the day of my burial. You have the poor with you always, but you will not always have me.'[6]

Judas' remark draws our attention to the value of the precious ointment. At the time the denarius was a day's wage, so the ointment represents almost a year's earnings.[7] But we shall see that Judas' concern for money is essentially symbolic. The value of three hundred denarii he places on the ointment has a significance of its own. Its real value is to be found in the letter-number code of the Qabala, where the number 300 expresses the universal *Sheen*, the Spirit or Breath of God.[8] But spiritual matters are of little interest to Judas. It appears to be money that concerns him. And money also appears to have been his motive for betraying Jesus. We are told that he went to the chief priests and asked them what they would give him if he betrayed Jesus to them. They gave him 30 pieces of silver.[9]

In the numerical symbolism associated with the progressive Self-revelation of the Spirit, Judas stops short at 30. That is, he does not bear fruit. He remains a simple physical manifestation of the Spirit in human form. Like the three disciples who fell asleep three times, he is either unaware of, or does not fully understand, the spiritual dimension of our existence. This is why Judas appears on the scene at the precise moment that the weakened resolve of the self (embodied in the disciples) fails the test. But in spite of their failure the disciples remain followers of Jesus (the Self). Judas is different. He personifies the self which, through ignorance, material greed or self-interest chooses to follow its own will rather than empower the Spirit within. Metaphorically speaking Judas 'steals' the outpouring of the Spirit, symbolized here as the 'alms-box of the twelve' from which money was distributed to the poor. His betrayal is consequently as much of his own completion as it is of Jesus. But even though (metaphorically speaking) we may 'betray' the Spirit, we remain in essence spiritual beings. As such we still have a part to play, consciously or unconsciously, in the unfolding of the Spirit. There is even a role for Judas, as is revealed during the meal in the upper room, where his innermost thoughts are translated into action:

> When it was evening Jesus sat at table with the twelve, and as they were eating he said, 'Truly, I say to you, one of you will betray me.' The disciples were deeply distressed, and said to him one after another, 'Is it I, Master?' He answered, 'It is one of the twelve dipping his hand in the dish with me. The Son of man is going as it is written of him, but woe to that man by whom the Son of man is betrayed. It would have been better for him that he had never been born.' When Judas said, 'Is it I, Master?' Jesus said to him, 'You have said so. What you are going to do, do quickly.' Now no one at the table knew why he said this to him. Some of them thought that because Judas had the alms-box Jesus was telling him to buy something for the feast, or that he should give something to the poor. And Judas immediately went out, and it was night.[10]

The gospel writers' skill in weaving together the different threads of their narrative is evident in the aftermath of Jesus' announcement that he will be betrayed. They know that at a literal level the different allegorical themes need to appear logical and consistent. So in keeping with his own role Jesus has to be seen to know not only that he will be betrayed, but also the identity of his betrayer. For his part, Judas has to know that his victim knows of his betrayal for us to understand that his (Judas') decision to act as he does is a fully conscious one. He also needs a reason for leaving the meal without arousing the suspicion of the other disciples. As for the disciples, they are informed of the betrayal without becoming aware of the identity of the betrayer. Finally, we are presented with the human and spiritual views of the same event. On the one hand we see Jesus betrayed by Judas. On the other, the words 'the Son of man is going as it is written of him' remind us that the destiny of Jesus is in the hands of something greater than the human will of Judas. The author of John verbalizes the spiritual darkness that coincides with us turning our back on the Source of our being. The departure of Judas is followed with the ominous words, 'and it was night'.

Later, when Judas sees that Jesus is condemned, we are told he repents. That is, he awakens to the reality of what he has done. He takes the 30 pieces of silver back to the chief priests and elders, saying: 'I have sinned in betraying innocent blood.' But they merely say to him: 'How does that concern us? It is your problem.' At which Judas throws down the 30 pieces of silver and goes and hangs himself.[11]

A dramatic end indeed. Yet it is really no different to the fate that befell the guests who killed the servants in the parable of the Marriage Feast. Moreover, it is in the nature of teaching stories to use dramatic 'shocks' of this kind to awaken us from our own state of sleep: a state embodied in the slumber of the three disciples at Gethsemane that coincided with Judas' kiss of betrayal. It is up to us whether we take such shocks simply at their face value, or as an opportunity to awaken.

We find a clue to the connection between Judas and our own spiritual evolution in the Temptation in the Wilderness, which Luke tells us Jesus was subjected to at the symbolic age of 30. Judas undergoes a temptation that is numerically similar. In his case, however, the number 30 is expressed in pieces of silver rather than years. For Jesus there was no temptation. As a vehicle for the Divine Will, there was no-choice. But for the 'Judas' (the will of the self) in us, on the surface there appears to be a choice. The nature of that choice becomes apparent when we realize that we are all – at least, in the numerical symbolism of the gospel narratives – the number 30. That is to say, as physical manifestations of the Spirit we carry within us the potential for spiritual evolution and fulfilment. The numerical expression of that potential goes far back into Jewish tradition: it was at the symbolic age of 30 that the pre-Messianic figure of Joseph became governor of this-worldly Egypt, and David united the divided kingdoms of Israel and Judah.[12] In the gospel narratives that same potential for spiritual evolution is embodied in the figure of Jesus, who at the age of 30 dismisses the will of the self to serve the Divine Will.

Peter

We rejoin the gospel story where we left it, with the arrival of Judas at Gethsemane. All four Gospel accounts of the ensuing arrest of Jesus relate an incident in which one of those with him draws his sword and strikes the high priest's servant, cutting off his ear. The author of John is alone in naming the man with the sword as Simon Peter. Jesus tells Peter to put his sword back in its sheath, adding, 'Shall I not drink the cup which the Father has given me?'[13] This is not the first time Peter's impetuosity has earned him a rebuke from his Master. In an earlier incident Peter is reprimanded after having first received unqualified praise, even been given the keys of the kingdom of heaven:

> Jesus said to the disciples, 'Who do you say that I am?' Simon Peter replied, 'You are the Christ.' And Jesus said, 'Blessed are you, Simon Bar-Jona! For no mortal revealed this to you; it was my Father who is in heaven. And I tell you, you are Peter, and upon this rock I will found my community [church], and the powers of death shall not prevail against it. I will give you the keys of the kingdom of heaven . . .'
> And Jesus began to teach them that he must go to Jerusalem and suffer many things at the hands of the elders, chief priests and scribes, and be killed and rise again on the third day. Peter caught hold of him and objected strongly, saying, 'God forbid, Master! Nothing of the sort shall happen to you!' But Jesus turned and rebuked Peter, saying to him, 'Follow me, *satan*! Yours is the human point of view, not God's.'[14]

The incident makes the point that spiritual truths are self-revealing. We can no more uncover them for ourselves than we can influence the timing of their revelation. At the same time the incident also provides us with a clear picture of the two sides the gospel writers have intentionally given to Simon Peter's character. He embodies the tussle we experience between the two 'wills' in the course of our own spiritual transformation. One moment Jesus calls him 'blessed'; the next, he rebukes him for his all-too-human point of view. One moment Jesus says, 'You are

Peter (Aramaic, *Kepha*), and upon this rock (Aramaic, *kepha*)[15] I will build my community', and promises him the keys of the kingdom of heaven; the next he calls him *satan* and commands him to 'Follow me!'. The reference to Peter's human point of view in conjunction with the word *satan* – which originally simply meant 'adversary' rather than the demonic embodiment of evil the figure of 'Satan' has now become[16] – underlines the opposition of the will of the self to the Will of the Self. Jesus, the Spirit within, calls to order our errant human will with the command 'Follow me!'.

The contrast between the two sides of Simon Peter's character is an important part of the gospel story. It gives us an insight into our own ambivalent attitude towards our inherent spiritual nature. Whereas Peter understands something of the nature of the in-dwelling Spirit – 'You are the Christ' – the incomplete nature of his understanding is demonstrated by his impetuous defence of Jesus: both in the statement 'God forbid, Master!' and in the wielding of his sword to prevent the arrest at Gethsemane. He may be totally devoted to his Master, but as we saw earlier in the episodes of Walking on the Water and the Washing of the Disciples' Feet his impetuous human will is an obstacle to any deeper understanding of the true relationship between self and Self. In this respect Simon Peter personifies the human devotion of the old man-and-God consciousness. Jesus embodies the unconditional love that is an essential characteristic of spiritual consciousness.

Devotion is dualistic. Single-pointed in its focus, we reserve it exclusively for the person or cause to which we are devoted. Unconditional love is nondualistic. Like the Spirit from which it emanates, it is all-embracing, open-hearted and freely given. The contrast between Jesus' unconditional spiritual love and Peter's human devotion is illustrated by the author of John. In a conversation that takes place after Judas has left the symbolic meal in the upper room Jesus gives his disciples a new commandment that is central to our understanding of spiritual consciousness:

> And Jesus said to them: 'Children, I shall be with you for only a little while longer. You will look for me, but as I said to the Jews so I now say to you, "Where I am going you cannot come." I give you a new commandment, to love one another. As I have loved you, so you must love one another. If you love one another, every one will recognize that you are my disciples.'

'Master, where are you going?' asked Simon Peter. Jesus

answered, saying, 'Where I am going you cannot follow me now; but you will follow later on.' Peter said, 'Master, why cannot I follow you now? I will give my life for you.' Jesus replied, 'You will give your life for me? I tell you truly, you will deny me three times before the cock crows.'[17]

The significance of Jesus' closing reference to the cock crowing is encountered in a passage from Mark. There we are advised to stay awake, 'for you do not know when the master of the house will come, in the evening, or at midnight, or at cockcrow . . . in case he comes suddenly and finds you asleep'.[18] The fulfilment of Jesus' prophetic remark that Peter will deny him three times before the cock crows is narrated in all four canonical Gospels. After Jesus' arrest, Peter follows his Master to the house of Caiaphas, the high priest, where he warms himself by a fire in the courtyard:

A maid came up to him [Peter] and said, 'You also were with that Nazarene, Jesus.' But Peter denied it, saying, 'I do not know him.' He withdrew to the outer court, where another maid saw him and said to the bystanders, 'This man was with Jesus the Nazarene.' Again Peter denied it, 'I do not know the man.' Shortly afterwards the bystanders said to Peter, 'Of course you're one of them. Your Galilean accent gives you away.' But Peter said, 'I do not know the man you're talking about.' Immediately the cock crowed. And, remembering how Jesus had said to him, 'You will deny me three times before the cock crows,' Peter broke down and wept.[19]

The fact that Peter denies his Master three times represents the extent of his denial. It is total. Once again when put to the test, Peter – the man who tried to walk on water and sank; who was told to stay awake at Gethsemane, and fell asleep – appears to have failed. But has he? Whereas the gospel writers portray Judas' betrayal as the result of a conscious decision, Peter's denial of his Master is unconscious. As the passage from Mark quoted above points out, the sound of the cock crowing is a sign that he is asleep. With that in mind, Peter's denial can be seen as an affirmation, an affirmation that he has awakened to two facts of which he was not previously aware: the fact that he has been asleep, and the fact that his devotion has not prevented him from denying knowledge of the Master for whom he had sworn to lay down his life. And so for Peter the cockcrow is a moment of profound and painful self-revelation. That is why he breaks down and weeps. When put to the test, his devotion had been found wanting. But as we shall see later on, however much Peter may sink when he tries to walk on water, metaphorically speaking the man himself is unsinkable.

A matter of choice

In the figures of Judas and Peter the gospel writers characterize two of the many potential ways we may respond to our relationship with the spiritual Source of our being. Of the two Peter remains a follower of his Master. We shall be returning to him in the final chapter. For now, we shall consider briefly the responses characterized by those figures who condemned Jesus to death – Caiaphas and the Sanhedrin, Pilate and the crowd. In the context of the gospel narratives these have never been followers of Jesus, nor are they ever likely to be. Hence their condemnation of him. But in their condemnation they too have a role to play within the unfolding gospel story.

CAIAPHAS AND THE SANHEDRIN

Following his arrest at Gethsemane Jesus is taken before the high priest and the Jewish supreme court. There we are told the latter sought false evidence that would enable them to condemn Jesus to death. But they could establish none because the witnesses could not agree on their testimony. Finally the high priest stands up and says to Jesus: 'Tell us if you are the Messiah, the Son of God.' Jesus replies, 'You have said so.' At this the high priest tears his robes. Turning to the council, he says: 'He has blasphemed. Why do we still need witnesses? You have heard his blasphemy. What is your judgement?' They answered: 'He deserves to die.'[20]

The appearance of Jesus before the Sanhedrin illustrates the gulf that separates our two modes of consciousness. Like the parables of the Patched Garment and New Wine, the two are essentially incompatible. This is perhaps why Jesus is shown as remaining silent when confronted by his accusers. He knows their judgement is prejudiced against him. When the accusation of blasphemy does come it is based more on what the high priest himself has said than on Jesus' response. But that is enough for sentence to be passed.

Claiming to be the Messiah, the King of the Jews, was a capital crime under Roman, not Jewish, law as it was treason against Caesar.[21] So Jesus was taken before the Roman governor for the death sentence to be executed lawfully. This turn of events provided the author of John with an opportunity to place a slightly different slant on the Sanhedrin's condemnation. He relates that after Pilate had examined Jesus he asked the question, 'Shall I crucify your King?' The chief priests' answer, 'We have no king but Caesar,'[22] contains an underlying truism. When our dualistic man-and-God mind-set is faced with a choice between spiritual and this-worldly authority it inevitably chooses the latter. From a nondualistic viewpoint there is no such choice.

PILATE

When Jesus is brought before Pilate, the latter asks, 'Are you the King of the Jews?' Echoing his reply to the high priest, Jesus says: 'You have said so.'[23] The author of John gives us a slightly different account of the interview between Jesus and Pilate. In his reply Jesus makes the distinction between this-worldly and spiritual authority: 'My kingdom is not of this world. Had my kingdom been of this world my followers would have fought to prevent me from being handed over to the Jews. However, my kingdom is not from a worldly source.' Pilate says, 'So you *are* a king?' Jesus answers: 'As you say, I am a king. The reason I was born and came into the world was to testify to the truth. Every one who is of the truth hears my voice.' Pilate appears to be confused, not quite sure what to make of the man before him. But he is an embodiment of this-worldly authority. Seeming to epitomize the voices of both the 'real world' and political expediency, Pilate asks in reply, 'What is truth?'[24] In doing so he provides us with a contrast between the human and spiritual views of truth. Where the former is concerned, truth is very much a matter of individual perception. And that perception may well vary according to circumstance. For the latter, there is only the One Truth – 'After the Truth what is there save error?'[25]

THE CROWD

When we recall the crowds that had followed Jesus wherever he went, seeking both his teaching and his healing, as well as the crowds who had recently given him such a favourable reception when he had entered Jerusalem, it is difficult to understand why there were no dissenting voices in the mob that gathered that night. The explanation provided by the gospel narratives is that the chief priests had persuaded the crowd to ask for the release of Bar-Abbas. If we look more closely at Bar-Abbas, we understand why. We are told that Bar-Abbas had been imprisoned for insurrection and murder,[26] and that he was a robber.[27] More importantly, *Bar-Abbas* means 'the son of the father'. Given the choice between Bar-Abbas and Jesus, the 'Son of the Father', the crowd that has been primed by the chief priests chooses the former.[28]

The choice that faces the crowd reflects our own dilemma. For the figures of Bar-Abbas and Jesus personify respectively the two 'wills' of our humanity and spirituality, the self and the Self. The contrast between their two characters is forcefully made – the one a convicted criminal, the other the innocent victim of an unfair trial. In choosing freedom for the former we condemn the latter.

The end of meaning

Jesus forewarned the disciples several times about the destiny that lay ahead of him. One such occasion followed Simon Peter's recognition of him as the Messiah/Christ. Then he had told the disciples that: 'the Son of man must suffer many things, and be rejected by the elders and chief priests and scribes, and be killed, and on the third day be raised.'[29] In the often obscure allegorical language of the gospel writers, he was describing the natural process of transformation and spiritual empowerment from the point of view of common human experience: a process of suffering, rejection, death and rebirth. He then describes the process from another point of view, revealing that we are not victims of fate or destiny. Already perfect in essence, we have a positive role to play in our own process of transformation. As the embodiment of the Spirit, he explains to the disciples:

> If any man would come after me, let him deny himself and take up
> his cross daily and follow me. For whoever would save his life will
> lose it; and whoever loses his life for my sake, he will save it. For

what does it profit a man if he gains the whole world and loses or forfeits himself?[30] For what can a man give in return for his life?[31]

Christmas Humphreys, founder of the Buddhist Society, offers a variation on the last question: 'How much do we want Enlightenment, and how much are we prepared to pay for it? A trifle of our income and convenience, or life, the life of the self itself?'[32] We find the same idea of self-abandonment expressed in an event related in Mark and Luke, following the Cleaning of the Temple.

> Jesus was in the temple and he sat down opposite the treasury, and watched the rich people putting in their offerings. Then along came a poor widow who put in two small copper coins. Turning to his disciples, he said, 'Truly, I say to you that this poor widow has put in more than all of them. For they contributed out of their abundance, but in her poverty she put in everything she had, her entire means of existence.'[33]

The setting of this little incident represents the heart or soul (the treasury) in the symbolic temple of the body. The significance of the rich people and the widow becomes apparent when we remember the saying given elsewhere in the gospels: 'Do not lay up for yourselves treasures on earth . . . but lay up for yourselves treasures in heaven. . . . For where your treasure is, there will your heart be also.'[34] By giving little, the rich define themselves as those who have little concern for spiritual matters. If we recall that to have 'no husband' denotes a state in which one lacks knowledge of God, we see that the poor widow gives everything she possesses in order to have the one thing she has not got. Compared to the 'rich people', her self-abandonment is total. She gives the whole of her life.

The timeless theme of abandoning ourselves to life so that we might become alive is exemplified in the death on the cross. As part of an intensely personal inner drama acted out on a public stage, the author of John tells us that 'when the soldiers had crucified Jesus they took his garments and made four parts, one for each soldier; also his tunic. But the tunic was without seam, woven from top to bottom,' and so they cast lots for it.[35] Here he draws on an older source, according to which 'a company of evildoers encircle me; they have pierced my hands and feet . . . they stare and gloat over me; they divide my garments among them, and for my raiment they cast lots.'[36]

The division of Jesus' garments is an analogy for what we do to the Spirit when we exploit its physical aspect – its garments – solely for material gain. By the same token the seamless tunic represents the nonduality of the One Reality. In essence indivisible, it is beyond human possession and yet in our ignorance we cast lots for it among ourselves. Yet where the Spirit is concerned there is neither judgement nor blame. As Jesus looks down from the cross, he simply says: 'Father, forgive them; for they do not know what they are doing.'[37] Nevertheless, the possibility that we will awaken is an ever present reality.

Our moment of awakening coincides with the passing of our dualistic man-and-God mind-set. The moment is itself symbolized by the tearing of the temple curtain 'in two, from top to bottom,'[38] at the moment of Jesus' death. This curtain separated the Holy of Holies from the main body of the temple building; its destruction signifies the moment of revelation that removes the veil of our mind and heals our divided self.

That moment of revelation is represented numerically by the three hours of darkness that fell 'over the whole earth' from the sixth hour until the ninth. The revelation itself occurs at the ninth hour, when 'Jesus cried with a loud voice, "*Eloi, Eloi, lama sabachthani?*" which means "My God, my God, why hast thou forsaken me?"'[39] Does he cry out because of his suffering? Or does his dying cry express the death of an illusory and distant God? For when the veil of the mind falls away it is revealed that there is no separation between us and God; with that the perception of a distant 'God in his heaven' falls away too in the realization that All is One. Our search for meaning may come to an end in the direct knowledge of God, but that knowledge comes at a price. It requires the total surrender of the self to the Self, a surrender that is given voice in the final words from the Cross: 'Father, into thy hands I commit my spirit!'[40]

14

FOLLOW ME!

The night-time conversation between Jesus and Nicodemus on the subject of spiritual rebirth (*see* page 68) concludes with Jesus telling his visitor that the Son of man must be 'lifted up', as Moses had lifted up the serpent in the wilderness, so that 'all who believe in him might have eternal life'. The story of Moses, the Israelites and the bronze serpent in the wilderness provided the people with a compelling metaphor for the almighty 'power of God'.[1] But with sacred myths that seek to make known the mysterious, all-pervading power of the Spirit, that same power can easily become attributed exclusively to the very symbols used to express its presence. Eventually this false attribution may culminate in idolatry: the adoration and/or worship of the symbol itself, while the true Source of power goes unrecognized. Such is the fate that seems to have befallen Moses' bronze serpent, for the power over life and death appears to have become attributed to the symbolic serpent on the pole. In a sequel to the wilderness incident we are told that the serpent was destroyed by King Hezekiah, because the people of Israel had named it Nehushtan and taken to burning incense to it.[2]

Did a similar fate befall both the cross and the Son of man, the heavenly archetype of the gospel narratives when Jesus was proclaimed God at Nicaea in 325 CE? According to Hugh Schonfield that is the case where many Christians are concerned. For if the deity of Jesus is taken away 'their faith in God is imperilled or destroyed'. Explaining why, he says Christianity is 'still much too close to the paganism over which it scored a technical victory to be happy with a faith in God as pure Spirit'. The need remains 'for a human embodiment of deity'.[3] As we come to the concluding stages of our journey, Schonfield's comments serve to remind us that where the original gospel message is concerned, those who announced the new covenant or consciousness advocated direct knowledge of God, the Spirit, *without an intermediary*.

The empty tomb

On the third day, Jesus' followers went to the tomb in which he had been laid following the Crucifixion. They found that the stone placed across the entrance had been rolled away. Apart from agreeing on these two points the gospel writers differ in their accounts of who arrived first and what they found when they got there. According to the author of Matthew, an angel spoke to Mary Magdalene and 'the other Mary', whereas the author of Mark tells us that a young man spoke to three women, Mary Magdalene, Mary the mother of James, and Salome. The words spoken by the angel and the young man to the women are almost identical: 'He is not here; for he has risen, as he said. Come, see the place where he lay. Then go quickly and tell his disciples that he is going before you to Galilee; there you will see him, as he told you.'[4] In Luke the women are named as Mary Magdalene, Joanna, Mary the mother of James, and 'the other women with them', and the two men at the tomb asked them, 'Why do you seek the living among the dead?'[5] The account in John tells us that Mary Magdalene arrived at the tomb while it was still dark, saw that the stone had been rolled away, and went to tell Simon Peter and the 'other disciple, the one whom Jesus loved'. Having run to the tomb and found it empty, the two men returned to their homes while Mary remained outside the tomb, weeping. When she looked inside she saw two angels, who asked her, 'Why are you weeping?' Having explained to them why, she turned and saw Jesus standing by, but did not recognize him. He also asked her, 'Why are you weeping?' Initially she supposed him to be the gardener, but when he addressed her by name she immediately knew who it was. Turning to him again, she exclaimed, '*Rabboni*' (Hebrew for 'teacher'). He replied: 'Do not cling to me, for I have not yet ascended to the Father,' and instructed her to go and tell the others that he was 'ascending to my Father and your Father'.[6]

The empty tomb is part of the sequence of events that begins with Jesus entering Jerusalem riding on a donkey. Since then we have been witnesses to the re-dedication of the self in the Cleaning of the Temple; the communion between self and Self in the Upper Room; the suffering caused by the struggle of the wills of the self and Self in the Agony in the Garden; and finally the 'death' or abandonment of the self on the Cross. From our human point of view the mere idea of abandoning the self, of dropping the ego, is enough to conjure up thoughts of a gaping void.

Like the events that precede it, the empty tomb is a further step on our journey home. It symbolizes the potential void that faces us when the self drops away. It presents us with a powerful image of a virgin state of being, of the conscious mind as a slate wiped clean. As such the empty tomb corresponds to a return to the primordial state of innocence that existed before the Fall, before our dualistic mode of consciousness caused us to experience life as little more than a process of birth, suffering, and death. Now, following the abandonment of the self and the falling away of the ego symbolized by the death on the Cross, we find there is nothing left to suffer or die. By surrendering ourselves to Life itself we have been 'raised up to eternal life', for the empty tomb reveals that *there is no death. There is only Life.*

In his story of *Esarhaddon, King of Assyria*, Leo Tolstoy offers us an insight into what that means. There he relates what was revealed to King Esarhaddon when he too transcended the apparent finality of death:

> 'Do you understand?' the old man continued, 'I have drawn aside the veil of delusion . . . For life there is neither time nor space. The life of a moment and the life of thousands of years, your life and the lives of all creatures seen and unseen, is one. To destroy life, even to alter it, is impossible, for life alone exists. All else seems to be.'[7]

The gospel narratives express the same idea when the men by the tomb ask the question 'Why do you seek the living among the dead?' For the gospel writers 'the dead' are those who are spiritually asleep – that is, asleep to the Spirit of Life within themselves. To be 'raised from the dead' means to become a living vehicle for the Spirit within. Likewise, as the quotation from Hosea revealed earlier, being 'raised up on the third day' refers to the transformative nature of spiritual consciousness, to the direct knowledge of God that comes with the empowerment of the Spirit. As a consequence, I suggest the gospel writers used the

Crucifixion, the enigma of the empty tomb, and the reappearance of a living and 'risen' Jesus to portray the final stages of our own evolution and fulfilment as spiritual beings.

Our dilemma is that centuries of emphasis on the uniqueness of Jesus' resurrection from the dead has impressed itself on our collective psyche to such a degree that we have either lost sight of, or are no longer able to comprehend, the fact that Life alone exists. Somewhat paradoxically, the Church's requirement that its members believe in a miraculous physical resurrection has given both power and substance to a widespread belief in the finality of physical death. And yet, if Life alone exists there is no death. The 'death' of our physical body is simply the moment when the spiritual dimension of our being sheds the particular material garment it has worn during 'our' lifetime and reunites with the Source of Life from which it comes. From a spiritual point of view, the terms 'resurrection from the dead' and 'spiritual rebirth' refer to our potential to reunite consciously with the Source of our being *during* this lifetime, not just at the end of it.

Letting go

When Mary Magdalene sees Jesus in the garden by the empty tomb he enquires why she is weeping. He then says: 'Do not cling to me, for I have not yet ascended to the Father.'[8] These words are also addressed to us, for it is equally important that *we* do not cling to the Jesus of the gospel narratives. If we do, we automatically fill the void in our minds created by the empty tomb. Furthermore, the Spirit embodied in Jesus by the authors of the gospels is unable to ascend into heaven and come again.

With the mysterious Ascension of Jesus into heaven the gospel narratives bring us back to the beginning of our journey through life. Compared to the accounts of the Incarnation, however, the gospel writers say little about Jesus' ascent into heaven. Neither Matthew nor John mention it. Mark contains one verse: 'So then the Lord Jesus, after he had spoken to them, was taken up into heaven, and sat down at the right hand of God.'[9] Luke contains two: 'Then he led them out as far as Bethany, and lifting up his hands he blessed them. While he blessed them, he parted from them, and was carried up into heaven.'[10] The lengthiest account is in the Acts of the Apostles – which is considered to be a continuation of Luke. In the opening chapter we are told that Jesus appears to those he has appointed to be his apostles during a period that lasts a symbolic forty days. He also instructs the twelve to stay in Jerusalem for they are soon to be baptized by the Holy Spirit. Asking him if at that time he would restore the kingdom to Israel, Jesus replies:

> 'It is not for you to know times or seasons which the Father has fixed by his own authority. But you shall receive power when the Holy Spirit has come upon you and you shall be my witnesses in Jerusalem and in all Judea and Samaria and to the end of the earth.' And when he had said this, as they were looking on, he was lifted up, and a cloud took him out of their sight. And while they were gazing up into heaven as he went, behold, two men stood by them in white robes, and said, 'Men of Galilee, why do you stand looking into heaven? This Jesus, who was taken up from you into heaven, will come in the same way as you saw him go into heaven.'[11]

The concluding words have a profound ring of truth to them. For the way in which we ourselves perceive Jesus to have ascended into heaven is the way in which we will anticipate his return. If we perceive him to have ascended physically into the clouds, then that is how we will await his second coming. In doing so we will be reinforcing the old dualistic man-and-distant-God mind-set that the gospel writers seek to dispel. That is why it is important for us to let go of the Jesus of the gospels. By allowing him to return to that 'cloud of unknowing' that lies beyond the comprehension of our conscious subjective mind, the way is prepared for us to receive the promised 'Counsellor, the Spirit of truth', who will guide us from within (*see* 'In an upper room', pages 176–80).

Having timed the Crucifixion and Resurrection (which celebrated freedom from death) to coincide with the Passover (which celebrated freedom from slavery), it is no accident that the gospel writers timed the consummation of the new covenant/consciousness to occur at the Jewish festival of *Shavuot*, the day of Pentecost. For this is the festival that celebrates the giving of the Law to Moses on Mount Sinai – an appropriate time for the fulfilment of a new covenant that lies in the dissemination of the Spirit rather than the written code of the Law. In the same way that the once-and-for-all-time sacrificial death on the cross supplants all other forms of sacrifice, now the inner authority of the Spirit renders obsolete the external authority of the Law. Combining a number of traditional similes for the Spirit – wind, fire, and the word – the event is related in the Acts of the Apostles as follows:

> When the day of Pentecost had come, they [the twelve] were all together in one place. And suddenly a sound came from heaven like the rush of a mighty wind, and it filled all the house where they were sitting. And there appeared to them tongues as of fire, distributed and resting on each one of them. And they were all filled with the Holy Spirit and began to speak in other tongues, as the Spirit gave them utterance.[12]

The account continues by telling us that the sound attracts to it 'Jews, devout men from every nation under heaven', who are dwelling in Jerusalem. In a scene that is a symbolic reversal of the confusion of tongues that followed the attempt to reach heaven by building the Tower of Babel, each of those present hears the words spoken by the twelve in their own native tongue. Bewildered, they ask among themselves, 'What does this mean?' Others mockingly remark: 'They are filled with new wine.'[13] Indeed, they are. For like the steward at the wedding at Cana they have been filled with and transformed by the wine of the Spirit, the new wine that needs new wineskins.

In response to the accusation that they are drunk, Peter stands up. Quoting a passage from the prophet Joel, he explains that the Last Times are here: 'And in the last days it shall be, God declares, that I will pour out my Spirit upon all flesh. . . '[14] Bearing in mind the numerical significance of the 'twelve disciples' – the number twelve itself symbolizing the outpouring or dissemination of the Spirit – Peter's words serve to confirm what the event itself reveals. The new covenant/consciousness of the Spirit is for everyone who is able to receive it. Rather, it is always present *here and now* for everyone who is able to awaken to it.

The outpouring of the Spirit is not only represented symbolically through the event of Pentecost. It is also symbolized numerically, through the 'heavenly' or 'spiritual' number three which is repeated at various levels of amplification in the gospel accounts of the life of Jesus. Among its most significant occurrences are the 30 years of age at which Jesus begins his ministry. This traditionally lasts for three years, culminating in the three days and nights in the tomb and the three hours of darkness that follow the death on the cross.

There are the flask of precious ointment valued at 300 denarii and Judas' 30 pieces of silver. There are also the occasions on which Peter either questions, denies, or misunderstands his Master a symbolic three times. Now with the establishment of the new spiritual covenant we find an amplification of the number three similar to that which we met with in the Feeding of the Five Thousand. For the 3,000 who are baptized on the day of Pentecost[15] symbolize numerically the infinite power of the Spirit to transform and heal and raise us up to a new nondualistic mode of being that consummates our oneness with the Source of Life itself.

A tale of two fishermen

In their accounts of the discovery of the empty tomb, Matthew and Mark record that the heavenly messengers tell the women that Jesus will be going before the disciples to Galilee. On an earlier occasion Jesus has himself told his disciples: 'After I am raised up, I will go before you to Galilee.'[16] John is alone in recording the meeting between Jesus and the twelve that takes place on the shores of the Sea of Galilee.

Traditionally the meeting has been interpreted as the moment when Jesus commissioned Peter to take care of his flock (the Church). But if we dig beneath the surface of the words we find a timeless teaching story that not only summarizes the myth of Being at the heart of the gospels. It also leaves us with profound insights into our relationship with the spiritual dimension of our being. The symbolic imagery draws on the gospel narratives as a whole, weaving together a number of familiar themes taken from the synoptic gospels as well as from the earlier chapters of John, to present us with a fitting dénouement to the gospel story. The two central figures are Simon Peter and Jesus, who are respectively the embodiment of our humanity and our spirituality and the two 'wills' associated with them. The meeting itself is divided naturally into two parts – a fishing expedition and a conversation between Jesus and Simon Peter. We shall examine the two separately.

A number of the disciples were by the Sea of Galilee. Simon Peter said to them, 'I am going fishing.' 'We will come with you,' said the disciples. So they went and boarded their boat; but that night they caught nothing.

As day was breaking Jesus appeared on the shore, but the disciples did not recognize him. He called out to them, 'Do you have anything to eat with you?' When they answered, 'No,' Jesus told them: 'Cast your net on the right side of the boat, and you will find some fish.' So they cast their net, and now it was so full that they were unable to haul it in. The disciple whom Jesus loved said to Peter, 'It is the Lord!' When Simon Peter heard this he put on his clothes, for he was naked, and jumped into the sea. But the other disciples made for the shore in the boat, dragging the net full of fish with them.

When they came ashore they saw a charcoal fire, with fish and bread baking on it. Jesus said to them, 'Bring some of the fish you have just caught.' So Simon Peter went on board and hauled the net ashore, full of one hundred and fifty-three large fish; and although there were so many, the net was not broken. Jesus said to them: 'Come and breakfast.' None of the disciples dared ask him, 'Who are you?' since they knew it was the Master. Jesus then came and took the bread, and gave it to them with the fish.[17]

The narrative contains several allegorical elements that are instantly recognizable – the disciples' boat, the night, the coincidence of daybreak and the appearance of Jesus, food and eating, garments and nakedness, and a meal of bread and fish. As the setting for the event, the Sea of Galilee is a metaphor for the sea of life, on the shores of which we find the disciples without their Master. In the absence of Jesus, Simon Peter appears to become their natural leader. When he announces 'I am going fishing', they follow him and board their boat. What happens next recalls the miraculous Walking on Water and the Calming of the Storm. The disciples putting out to sea without Jesus is again associated with darkness, for we are told that '*that night* they caught nothing'. Similarly, the appearance of Jesus on the shore coincides with the darkness giving way to light.

The fishing trip led by Peter is unsuccessful. So when Jesus asks the disciples if they have anything to eat with them, their answer of 'no' seems logical enough. But when the gospel writers mention food they refer to food of a non-material kind. The implication is that without Jesus/the Spirit they are unable to provide themselves with spiritual food. What then follows bears a striking resemblance to another fishing trip, related in Luke. On that occasion Jesus had also told them to cast their nets after an unsuccessful night's fishing and their nets had been filled. That fishing trip had ended with Peter leaving everything to follow Jesus.[18] The net full of fish also recalls the parable of the Net, which likens the kingdom of heaven to 'a net that was thrown into the sea and gathered fish of every kind'.[19] With these other references in mind, the present fishing trip would appear to be an intentional reminder of both the original calling of Peter to follow Jesus and the spontaneous manifestation of the 'kingdom of heaven'.

What happens next reveals the very human character of Peter. In spite of the re-enactment of his first fishing trip with Jesus he has not yet recognized his Master. Instead of 'seeing' for himself, he 'hears' the news from the enigmatic 'disciple whom Jesus loved'. Peter then does the strangest of things: he puts on his clothes and jumps into the sea. Of course, it could be said that Peter does this to cover his naked body out of respect for his Master. But there is another possible explanation. He may have 'heard', but he has still not understood. Rather than 'disrobing without being ashamed' when the presence of Jesus/the Spirit is revealed, Peter puts on his 'garments'. His subsequent leap into the water serves as a blunt reminder of his earlier unsuccessful attempt to walk on it. His character is thoroughly human – not only in his impulsive behaviour, but also in the way he constantly seems to get things wrong in spite of his good intentions. As elsewhere in the gospel narratives, it seems that every time Peter is presented with an opportunity for spiritual awakening his humanity somehow ends up getting in the way.

Safely on shore again, Jesus invites the disciples to breakfast with him. The sharing of a meal of loaves and fish appears to be a symbolic re-enactment of two earlier incidents from the gospel story: the meal in the upper room and the Feeding of the Five Thousand. If we now remove the dimensions of time and space, we are left with two 'fishermen' – Peter and Jesus. In the contrast between these two figures and what they accomplish that day on the Sea of Galilee, the author of John presents us with an image of the two aspects of our being. He leaves us to choose which of the two we follow on our own journey across the sea of life.

Follow me!

The following version of the conversation between Jesus and Simon Peter on the shores of the Sea of Galilee differs from many translations on a couple of points. The first is the use of the word 'love', both in Jesus' questions and Peter's answers to them. In the original Greek two different words were used, denoting two kinds or degrees of love: the distinction is here made between the two by using the words 'love' and 'devotion'.[20] The second concerns the name by which Jesus calls Simon Peter. In many translations this is given as 'Simon, son of John,' with 'John' being the English rendition of the Greek *Joanes*. However, in an earlier incident in Matthew we find the Aramaic '*Bar-Jona*' being used,[21] and this is the formula adopted here.

> Jesus said to Simon Peter, 'Simon Bar-Jona, do you love me more than these others?' 'Yes, Master,' he replied, 'you know that I am devoted to you.' Jesus said, 'Feed my lambs.' He then asked him a second time, 'Simon Bar-Jona, do you love me?' 'Yes, Master,' he replied, 'you know I am devoted to you.' 'Shepherd my sheep,' said Jesus, and then he asked him for a third time, 'Simon Bar-Jona, are you devoted to me?' Peter was aggrieved that he asked for a third time, 'Are you devoted to me?' And he said to him: 'Master, because you know everything, you must know that I am devoted to you.' Jesus said to him, 'Feed my sheep. To tell you a truth, when you were young, you girded yourself and went wherever you willed. But when you are old, you will stretch out your hands, and another will gird you and carry you against your will.' (He said this to show by what kind of death he would glorify God.) And when he had finished speaking, he said to him, 'Follow me.'[22]

The significance of names has been discussed earlier (*see* pages 33–4 and 119–20). It is sufficient to recall here that a name either fitted the *persona* an individual had already taken on, or provided them with one *in potentia* to grow into. In the gospel narratives we run into the problem that some names retain their original Hebrew or Aramaic form, others have been anglicized, and yet others have been translated into their English equivalent. The problem is aggravated by the fact that the process of modifying names began when the gospels were originally written down in Greek. We therefore end up with the anomaly whereby Matthew gives Simon Peter the name *Bar-Jona* – Aramaic for 'son of Jonah' – whereas in John he is called 'son of John'. The instances when Jesus addresses Simon Peter as *Bar-Jona* are few, but there is a common factor that gives the use of this name an added significance.

The appendage 'son of' either indicates a person's physical paternity, or relates them by name to a prestigious historical figure, thereby furnishing them with a model *persona* for them to fulfil. It is therefore not only Simon's nickname of *Kepha* (Aramaic for both 'Peter', and 'rock' or 'stone') that has a bearing on his character, but his additional name of *Bar-Jona*, or 'son of Jonah', also tells us something important about the role he has to play in the gospel narratives. He has the potential to emulate Jonah.

The passage from Matthew in which Jesus calls Peter 'Simon Bar-Jona' is quoted in full in a previous chapter (*see* page 187). It marks Peter's inspired recognition of Jesus as the Messiah/Christ. On its own the use of the name in that context means very little, but a few verses earlier the Pharisees and Sadducees had asked Jesus for a 'sign from heaven'. He replied: 'An evil and adulterous generation seeks for a sign, but no sign shall be given to it except *the sign of Jonah*.'[23] The author of Matthew had used the same phrase in a previous chapter, where he qualified it by adding: 'For as Jonah was three days and three nights in the belly of the whale, so will the Son of man be three days and three nights in the heart of the earth.'[24] Now, we can either understand this qualifying phrase narrowly, as referring to the 'three days' Jesus would spend in the tomb. Or we can understand it in the a wider sense, as indicating the process of transformation and revelation symbolized in the 'three days and nights of darkness' that Jonah and Jesus spend respectively in the belly of the great fish and the tomb before their reappearance. In effect, Jesus responds to the Pharisees' and Sadducees' question about a sign by telling them that the only sign they can expect is a revelation. Would this be a spiritual revelation of the kind experienced by Simon 'son of Jonah', when he said to Jesus 'You are the Christ,' to which Jesus had replied that such a revelation could only have come from the Source itself?[25]

Before returning to the conversation between Jesus and Simon Peter, we go briefly to the opening chapter of John, where Jesus meets Simon for the first time. Here we are told that Andrew, who had already met Jesus, went and found his brother Simon and 'brought him to Jesus. Jesus looked at him, and said, "You are Simon, the son of Jonah. You shall be called Peter".'[26] It would appear that the author of John turns the meeting into a naming ceremony. Simon is given two new names – 'rock' or 'stone', and 'son of Jonah'. The first name describes his present *persona*, the second alludes to his potential. Between them these two names correspond to the two sides of Peter's character – the human and the spiritual – which reveal themselves through his words and his actions.

The underlying significance of the conversation that takes place on the shores of the Sea of Galilee now begins to emerge. The real setting, however, is our own inner space. Following the very human behaviour Peter displayed during the fishing expedition, Jesus takes him to one side in a profound initiation ceremony akin to the transformation we witnessed in the wedding at Cana. In an attempt to transform the rock/stone of Peter's human nature, Jesus addresses his spiritual nature by name at the beginning of each question. The contrast between the unconditional and all-embracing nature of spiritual love and the narrower focus of human devotion outlined in Chapter 13 (*see* page 118) now comes into play.

Jesus' first question – 'Simon, son of Jonah, do you love me more than these others?' – is effectively a test. Has Peter taken to heart the new commandment Jesus gave the twelve, instructing them to love one another, or not? Peter's reply, 'Yes, Master, you know I am devoted to you,' seems to miss the point of the question. As if encouraging him to be less single-pointed in his outlook, Jesus says to Peter, 'Feed my lambs'. Again he asks, 'Simon, son of Jonah, do you love me?' And again the same answer comes back: 'Yes, Master, you know I am devoted to you.' Willing him to make the shift from human devotion to unconditional love, Jesus says, 'Shepherd my sheep,' and then puts his question slightly differently, 'Simon, son of Jonah, are you devoted to me?' As when Jesus tried to wash his feet, Peter has not understood the deeper significance of what is going on; but then he has not heard the question as it was asked. For him devotion is the same as love, and so he is understandably exasperated when it appears that Jesus asks him a third time if he is devoted to him. Peter replies: 'Master, because you know everything, you must know that I am devoted to you.' Jesus does know. He says a last 'Feed my sheep' to encourage Peter to make the transition from his unbending human devotion into the free-flowing unconditional love of the Spirit. But he remains as solid as a rock. Once again the threefold formula has been used to show that, when put to the test, Peter's spiritual evolution is not yet complete.

Jesus now describes Peter's (and our) potential transformation in straightforward terms. With perhaps deliberate irony, the analogy reminds us of how a few moments earlier Peter had put on his clothes when he had seen his Master on the shore. Jesus effectively says: 'When you were spiritually immature you wore your own garments and followed your own will. But when you are spiritually mature you will stretch out your hands and wear the garments of another who will lead you against *your* will.' The statement that follows – 'He said this as a sign of the kind of death by which he would glorify God' – is generally interpreted in line with the tradition that Peter was crucified upside-down. But the stretching out of one's hands, palms upwards, was the receptive gesture adopted for prayer. It signified an openness of mind and heart to the Spirit. (Praying with the palms of the hands placed together is a later tradition.) Instead, the kind of death by which Peter will glorify God is the 'death' by which we come alive: the 'death' of spiritual rebirth. Rather than wearing our own 'garments' we become a garment, a vehicle for the empowered Spirit. We are then open to being led wherever the Spirit wills, even against the will of the self.

The final instruction – 'Follow me' – is addressed to us as much as to Peter. The latter's unsinkable human devotion to the Spirit is an example for us to follow on our own path of spiritual evolution. It is the rock on which to build a human 'community of the Spirit', a community governed by the enlightenment and wisdom that come from the Source of Life itself rather than the man-made laws that are the product of our dualistic mode of consciousness. But the community of the Spirit will not be found by looking for it with our man-and-God eyes. Those eyes are conditioned to searching for a distant God in some ethereal realm in the heavens. As Alan Watts explains in his book *Behold the Spirit*, there are two ways of getting to what he calls 'the house next door': 'One is to travel all the way round the globe; the other is to walk a few feet. One is to journey upwards and upwards in quest of an ever-receding firmament; the other is to realize that here on earth you are already in the heavens.'[27]

For far too long we have tried to reach a distant heaven with the Babel-like tower of our human concepts and belief systems. Instead the time is ripe to realize our true purpose in this life. By simply *being* who and what we really are the original gospel message – the hidden teaching of Jesus – will make itself known.

NOTES

Quotations from the Jewish and Christian scriptures are taken from the *Authorized* or *King James Version* (KJ), the *Revised Standard Version* (RSV) of the Bible, or *The Original New Testament*, translated by Hugh J Schonfield, London 1985 (ONT).

Grateful acknowledgement is made to the following for permission to reprint previously published material:

National Council of the Churches of Christ in the USA: Scripture quotations marked (RSV) in the endnotes are from the Revised Standard Version of the Bible, copyright 1946, 1952, 1971 by the Division of Christian Education of the National Council of the Churches of Christ in the USA. Used by permission.

Hugh McGregor Ross: Excerpts from *The Gospel of Thomas*, William Sessions Ltd, The Ebor Press, York 1987. © Hugh McGregor Ross 1987. Used by permission.

Introduction

1 The literary genre known as the *gospels* appeared in the first century CE. Of the many gospels produced around this time only four were included in the New Testament – the gospels attributed to Matthew, Mark, Luke and John – when the 'canon' (list) of scriptures to be included in the Christian Bible was established by the Church in the second century.

2 The Council of Nicaea (325 CE) was called in response to the spread of Arianism (a doctrine that took its name from Arius, an Alexandrian priest), according to which God was one person, the Father, and Jesus, although the Son of God, was deemed to be fully human, and therefore less than God. The Council reasserted the doctrine of the Trinity and the divinity of Jesus, declaring that in Jesus God had really appeared on Earth as the person of the Son. Nicaea's definitive pronouncement that Jesus was/is God inspired

further controversy concerning the Incarnation and the relationship between Jesus' divinity and his humanity, necessitating the calling of a further council at Ephesus (431 CE). The two principal camps involved were those who favoured the view promoted by Nestorius, patriarch of Constantinople (that there were two persons in Jesus, one human and one divine) and those who favoured the one promoted by St Cyril, patriarch of Alexandria (that there was only one person). The outcome of the debate was apparently settled when the Western bishops (who were mainly supporters of St Cyril) arrived first and locked the doors against their opponents. In the event the Council proclaimed that, in spite of the difference between divine and human nature, there was only one person in Jesus. The declaration of Jesus' divinity at Nicaea and his unity at Ephesus precipitated yet further debate: to what extent was he human, to what extent divine? Some Christians, such as the Monophysites, proclaimed that Jesus had only one nature, the divine, but this also carried with it the implication that God had not really manifested in human form after all. It was in order to safeguard Jesus' humanity from the threat posed by this new belief that the Council of Chalcedon (451 CE) declared that Jesus, whilst being one in person, had two natures, the human and the divine, each of which existed in him in its entirety.

Chapter 1

1 Anonymous, *The Cloud of Unknowing*, in *The Cloud of Unknowing and Other Works*, *trans* Clifton Wolters, Penguin Books, Harmondsworth, 1978, p 136

2 Mâle, Emile, *The Gothic Image*, *trans* Dora Nussey, Collins/Fontana, London, 1961. p 29

3 At its simplest level – a roadsign – a sign is an instantly recognizable visual or verbal indicator with a clearly defined message. The tangible outer form of a symbol may equally be instantly recognizable, but its underlying message lies on or beyond the boundaries of normal, rational comprehension. For example, a mountain is instantly recognizable as a mountain. As a symbol, however, it is often used to represent the meeting place of the human and the divine, or a higher plane of consciousness.

4 Proverbs 18:8 (RSV)

5 Jaynes, Julian, *The Origins of Consciousness in the Breakdown of the Bicameral Mind*, Houghton Mifflin, Boston, 1976, 1990

6 ibid p 119

7 ibid pp 106f

 8 ibid p 111
 9 ibid p 84
10 ibid pp 117–18
11 ibid pp 202–203
12 ibid p 93
13 ibid pp 208–209
14 ibid p 226
15 Matthew 13:13–15 (RSV)
16 Mark 4:11, 24–25, 33–34 (RSV). Emphasis added
17 Matthew 13:34–35 (RSV)
18 Luke 8:17 (RSV)
19 Proverbs 8:22–27 (RSV)
20 Proverbs 4:7. Author's adaptation
21 Baruch 3:14 (RSV)
22 Proverbs 16:22 (RSV)

Chapter 2

 1 Genesis 11:1–9
 2 Genesis 1:1–3 (RSV)
 3 Genesis 2:5–7 (RSV)
 4 Cooper, J C, *An Illustrated Encyclopaedia of Traditional Symbols*, Thames & Hudson, London 1978, p 188
 5 Isaiah 64:8 (KJ)
 6 Jeremiah 18:1–6 (RSV)
 7 Psalm 139:7–9, 13, 15–16 (RSV)
 8 Deuteronomy 30:11–14 (RSV)
 9 1 Corinthians 6:19 (RSV)
10 Luke 17:21 (KJ)

Chapter 3

 1 For readers unfamiliar with the ancient Greek myth of Narcissus, versions of it can be found in most mythology anthologies, although they may differ in the minor details of the story. A longer version is contained in Ovid's *Metamorphoses*, of which several editions are available.
 2 Romans 12:2 (RSV)
 3 Coomaraswamy, Ananda, 'On being in one's right mind', *The Review of Religion*, Columbia University Press, November 1942,

p 32. Quoted in Perry, Whitall N, *A Treasury of Traditional Wisdom*, Perennial Books, Bedfont, 1971, p 479

4 Ephesians 4:22–24 (RSV)
5 Dante Alighieri, *Il Convito*, II. 2–5
6 Dante Alighieri, *The Divine Comedy*, *trans* Dorothy L Sayers, Penguin Books, Harmondsworth, 1949, p 14. I am indebted to Ann Edwards for drawing my attention to this quotation.
7 Blake, William, *Auguries of Innocence* (many editions available)
8 Luke 15:11–32
9 Matthew 20:20–22; Mark 10:35–38
10 Matthew 7:7–8 (RSV)

Chapter 4

1 Acts 17:28
2 Genesis 2:17 (RSV)
3 Proverbs 3:19–20; 8:22–36
4 John 1:9–11 (RSV). Emphasis added
5 Mark 6:4–6 (RSV)
6 Proverbs 1:7
7 Proverbs 3:11–12 (RSV)
8 Romans 6:23
9 Romans 5:12 (RSV)
10 Romans 7:6
11 Romans 6:23
12 Bertschinger, Richard, *The Secret of Everlasting Life*, Element Books, Shaftesbury, 1994. Opening quotation, from a 1564 Preface to the Taoist text *Can Tong Qi*.
13 Dhiravamsa, *The Way of Non-Attachment*, Turnstone Books, 1975. Quoted in Ann Bancroft, *The Spiritual Journey*, Element Books, Shaftesbury, 1991, p 63.
14 Matthew 8:28–34; Mark 5:1–20; Luke 8:26–39
15 The 'synoptic gospels' is the collective name given to the gospels of Matthew, Mark and Luke, because when 'seen together' – Greek, *syn-optikos* – the many close similarities in their contents mean that all three appear to present the life and teachings of Jesus from a common point of view.

Chapter 5

1 Kristeller, Paul Oskar, *The Philosophy of Marsilio Ficino*, trans Virginia Conant, Columbia University Press, New York, 1943, p 293. Quoted in Perry, Whitall N, *A Treasury of Traditional Wisdom*, Perennial Books, Bedfont, 1971, p 489

2 de Caussade, Jean-Pierre, *The Sacrament of the Present Moment*, trans Kitty Muggeridge, Collins Fount Paperbacks, London, 1981, p 82

3 1 Corinthians 13:12 (KJ)

4 Blake, William, *A Memorable Fancy*, pl 14

5 Matthew 5:15 (RSV)

6 Mark 4:22 (RSV)

7 Matthew 10:26; Luke 12:2

8 Zechariah 3:3–5 (RSV)

9 Matthew 17:2

10 Revelation 7:9

11 Revelation 22:14 (RSV)

12 Luke 5:36 (RSV)

13 Genesis 3:7

14 The Gospel of Thomas is one of the 52 ancient texts discovered at Nag Hammadi, Egypt, in 1945. Unlike the canonical gospels, it takes the form of a collection of short sayings attributed to Jesus, as well as brief dialogues between him and his disciples.

15 Wilson, Ian, *Jesus: The Evidence*, Pan Books, London, 1985, p 25

16 Bancroft, Anne, *The Spiritual Journey*, Element Books, Shaftesbury, 1991, pp 52–3

17 Gospel of Thomas 22. From *The Gospel of Thomas*, presented by Hugh McGregor Ross, Ebor Press, York, 1987, p 24

18 ibid, 3, p 11

19 1 Corinthians 13:9–12 (KJ)

20 John 3:1–13. Author's adaptation

21 John 6:63

22 Genesis 28:12

23 Schonfield, Hugh, *The Passover Plot*, Element Books, Shaftesbury, 1985. p 223 ff

24 ibid, pp 225–6

25 Carroll, Lewis, *Alice's Adventures in Wonderland*, and *Through the Looking Glass*, Penguin Books, Harmondsworth, 1962, p 195

26 St Augustine, *De lib. arb* II, 41. From Chapman, *St Augustine's Philosophy of Beauty*, Sheed & Ward, New York 1939. p 24. Quoted in Perry, Whitall N, *A Treasury of Traditional Wisdom*, Perennial Books, Bedfont, 1971, p 309

27 Panofsky, E, *Abbot Suger, on the Abbey Church of St Denis,*

Princeton, 1946. Quoted in Gilmore Holt, E, *A Documentary History of Art,* Vol 1, Doubleday Anchor, New York, 1957, p 25

Chapter 6

1 The Pentateuch – literally, 'the five scrolls' – comprises the five books of Genesis, Exodus, Leviticus, Numbers and Deuteronomy. In Jewish tradition these 'five books of Moses' are known as the Law or Torah.
2 Gospel of Thomas 45:29–33, in *The Nag Hammadi Library*, New York, 1977, p 126. Quoted in Pagels, Elaine, *The Gnostic Gospels*, Penguin Books, Harmondsworth, 1982, p 15
3 Genesis 2:7 (RSV)
4 Genesis 2:9, 16–17, 3:1–24
5 Genesis 3:5
6 Jaynes, Julian, *The Origins of Consciousness in the Breakdown of the Bicameral Mind*, Houghton Miffin, Boston, 1976, 1990, p 299
7 ibid, p 444
8 Genesis 9:1–17
9 Genesis 15; 17:1–14
10 The covenant between God and the people of Israel was delivered to Moses during the theophany on Mount Sinai. Beginning in Chapter 19 of Exodus it continues through Leviticus and Numbers into Deuteronomy. The consequences of transgressing the conditions of the covenant are outlined in an escalating sequence of threats in Leviticus 26:14, 18, 21, 23, 27, et seq
11 Ezekiel 7
12 Daniel 12
13 Revelation 6
14 Daniel 7:9–14
15 Revelation 20:12
16 The conjoined themes of the Final Resurrection and Last Judgement were often used to decorate the semi-circular tympanum above the west door. Among the better known examples are those in France at Ste Foy, Conques; Abbey Church of St Pierre, Moissac; Abbey Church of Ste Marie Madeleine, Vézelay; St Lazare, Autun; Notre-Dame de Chartres (south door); St Etienne, Bourges; Notre-Dame de Paris, etc. Important examples outside France include the cathedrals at Bamburg (Germany) and Leon (Spain).
17 *See* Leviticus 26
18 Jeremiah 31:31, 33–34 (RSV). Emphasis added
19 Ezekiel 37:1–14

20 Luke 17:20
21 Matthew 16:1–4
22 Luke 12:54–56
23 Mark 13:33
24 Luke 12:40
25 Matthew 24:36
26 Matthew 25:31–46
27 Matthew 25:34–40 (RSV)
28 Matthew 7:1–2 (RSV)
29 John 8:15
30 John 14:20 (RSV)
31 Mark 13:31 (KJ)
32 Revelation 22:13 (KJ)
33 The French art historian Emile Mâle discusses the iconography of this theme in his book *The Gothic Image*, where he refers to examples at Strasbourg, Bordeaux, Paris, Reims. (Mâle, Emile, *The Gothic Image*, *trans* Dora Nussey, Collins/Fontana, London 1961, pp 188–93)
34 2 Corinthians 3:6–8, 14–18 (RSV)
35 I am indebted to Paul Cash for his suggestion that the figures of the two women also provide an image of the classical being/becoming duality.
36 Plato, *Gorgias*, 481 C
37 Psalm 46:10

Chapter 7

1 John 8:14
2 *The Original New Testament*, *trans* Hugh J Schonfield, Firethorn Press, London, 1985, p 479
3 John 1:1–18
4 Genesis 1:3
5 The Koran 36:81, *trans* N J Dawood, Penguin Books, Harmondsworth, 1974 (4th rev. edn.), p 178
6 John 1:4 (RSV)
7 John 1:9 (RSV)
8 John 1:14 (RSV)
9 Luke 1:1–4
10 *The New Oxford Annotated Bible with the Apocrypha*, Oxford University Press, New York, 1977, says of Theophilus that he was 'an unknown Christian, perhaps of social prominence' (p 1240), while according to the *Bible Handbook and A–Z Bible Encyclopedia*, Lion

Publishing, Oxford, 1990, he was 'an otherwise unknown Roman, who had at least some interest in Christianity' (p 147)

11 John 1:6 (RSV)
12 Luke 1:24 (KJ)
13 Matthew 1:23 (RSV); Isaiah 7:14
14 Luke 1:34 (RSV)
15 Jeremiah 31, in particular verses 4–5
16 *The New Oxford Annotated Bible with the Apocrypha*, Oxford University Press, New York, 1977, p 1172
17 Luke 1:35 (RSV)
18 Luke 1:38 (KJ)
19 Psalm 46:10 (RSV). Emphasis added
20 John 1:7 (RSV)
21 Luke 1:80 (RSV)
22 John 1:9–11 (RSV)
23 John 1:5 (RSV)
24 Luke 2:13–14 (RSV)
25 Luke 2:22–39
26 Exodus 13:2; Leviticus 12:2–8
27 Genesis 29:33
28 Job 42:5 (RSV)
29 Luke 2:36–38
30 John 1:12 (RSV)
31 Luke 2:40 (RSV)
32 Luke 2:41–50. Author's adaptation
33 Schonfield, Hugh, *The Passover Plot*, Element Books, Shaftesbury, 1985, pp 54–5, 253
34 John 1:14, 17 (RSV)
35 Luke 2:52 (RSV)

Chapter 8

1 Luke 3:4; Isaiah 40:3
2 Matthew 11:11–12 (RSV)
3 John 10:8
4 John 3:27–28, 30 (RSV)
5 John 1:15. Author's adaptation
6 Luke 3:18–20
7 Luke 3:22 (RSV)
8 Genesis 2:21–24
9 1 Corinthians 15:46 (RSV)
10 Genesis 4:1–17

11 Genesis 25:23 (RSV)
12 Genesis 25:27–34
13 Genesis 27:1–45
14 Genesis 32:24–33:4
15 Genesis 41:51–52
16 Genesis 48:1–20
17 Jeremiah 31:9 (RSV)
18 Jeremiah 31:20 (RSV)
19 Psalm 2:7
20 Matthew 3:4
21 Matthew 4:1–11; Mark 1:12–13; Luke 4:1–13
22 Romans 1:25 (RSV)
23 *See* Deuteronomy 6:16
24 Luke 4:12
25 1 Corinthians 1:24

Chapter 9

1 Luke 4:18 (RSV)
2 Luke 4:20–30
3 John 9:1–7. Author's adaptation
4 John 1:5
5 Matthew 5:14–16
6 Proverbs 1:17–19 (RSV)
7 Matthew 4:20
8 Jeremiah 3:15
9 Jeremiah 16:16
10 Luke 10:1, 17–20
11 Matthew 9:20–22
12 Mark 5:24–34; Luke 8:43–48
13 Matthew 14:13–21; Mark 6:30–44; Luke 9:10–17; John 6:1–14.
Author's adaptation
14 John 4:34
15 Matthew 14:22–33; Mark 6:45–52; John 6:16–21. Author's adaptation
16 de Caussade, Jean-Pierre, *The Sacrament of the Present Moment*, *trans* Kitty Muggeridge, Collins Fount Paperbacks, London, 1981, p 71
17 John 6:35
18 Matthew 8:23–27; Mark 4:35–41; Luke 8:22–25. Author's adaptation
19 Luke 7:36–50. Author's adaptation
20 1 Corinthians 6:19–20 (RSV)

Chapter 10

1 Luke 22:42 (KJ)
2 St Augustine, *De spir et lit*, 16. Quoted in Whitall N. Perry, *A Treasury of Traditional Wisdom*, Perennial Books, Bedfont, 1971, p 300
3 Matthew 16:5–12
4 John 6:48, 51 (RSV)
5 Luke 6:1–5
6 Luke 5:27–32
7 Luke 5:33–35
8 Luke 5:36–39 (RSV)
9 St Augustine, *In Ps. CXXXVI*; *Synth* no 71. Quoted in Perry, Whitall N, *A Treasury of Traditional Wisdom*, Perennial Books, Bedfont, 1971, p 490
10 Luke 12:1
11 Luke 6:6–11
12 Mark 2:27 (RSV). Together verses 27 and 28 read: 'The sabbath was made for man, not man for the sabbath; so the Son of man is lord even of the sabbath.' The authors of both Matthew and Luke, who drew on Mark as a source, only use the last part, 'The Son of man is lord of the sabbath.'
13 Luke 11:52
14 Mark 7:1–13
15 Luke 11:42
16 Matthew 23:23–24
17 Matthew 23:25–26
18 Matthew 23:27
19 Matthew 15:14. Author's adaptation
20 John 12:42–43. Author's adaptation
21 Proverbs 1:7
22 Luke 20:19–25
23 Matthew 23:8–10 (RSV)
24 Matthew 24:3–5, 23–27 (RSV)

Chapter 11

1 Isaiah 54:4–6 (RSV)
2 Matthew 22:2–14
3 Luke 14:15–24
4 Luke 14:11 (RSV)
5 1 Corinthians 3:9

6 Gospel of Thomas 45:29–33, in *The Nag Hammadi Library* (New York, 1977) p 126. Quoted in Pagels, Elaine, *The Gnostic Gospels*, Penguin Books, Harmondsworth, 1982, p 15

7 John 15:16 (RSV)

8 Matthew 25:1–13. Author's adaptation

9 Matthew 6:34 (RSV)

10 Shaykh Fadhlalla Haeri, *Beginning's End*, KPI in association with Zahra Publications, London 1987, pp 14–15

11 John 2:1–11. Author's adaptation

12 John 7:6 (RSV)

13 Nicoll, Maurice, *The New Man*, Shambhala, Boulder, 1981, p 9

14 Matthew 22:23–30; Mark 12:18–25; Luke 20:27–36. Author's adaptation

15 Matthew 22:31–32; Mark 12:26–27; Luke 20:37–38

Chapter 12

1 Zechariah 9:9

2 Matthew 21:7–9; Mark 11:7–9; Luke 19:35–38; John 12:12–13. Author's adaptation

3 James 3:3 (RSV)

4 Mark 11:11

5 Mark 11:12–14, 20–23. In Matthew the fig tree episode is recounted as occurring the morning after the Cleaning of the Temple. In Luke the same idea is expressed in the parable of the Barren Fig Tree. The image of the barren fig tree may derive from Haggai 2:18–19; there the prophet asks 'Since the day that the foundation of the Lord's temple was laid, consider: . . . [Does] the fig tree . . . still yield nothing?'

6 Matthew 21:12–13; Mark 11:15–17; Luke 19:45–46; John 2:13–22. Author's adaptation

7 Shaykh Fadhlalla Haeri, *The Elements of Islam*, Element Books, Shaftesbury, 1993, in association with Zahra Publications, p 55

8 John 10:8 (RSV)

9 Hosea 6:1–3 (RSV)

10 Examples of the Passion in the performing arts include the cycles of medieval Mystery plays, the Passion Play at Oberammergau in Bavaria, Handel's *Messiah*, Bach's *St Matthew Passion*, Mozart's *Requiem*.

11 Matthew 26:20–29; Mark 14:17–31; Luke 22:14–38; John 13:1–17

12 Matthew 26:26–28; Mark 14:22–24; Luke 22:19–20. Author's adaptation

13 Only two of the Gospels describe the room in these terms, they are Mark (14:15) and Luke (22:12)
14 Matthew 6:6 (RSV)
15 Proverbs 9:5–6 (RSV)
16 Lamentations 2:12 (RSV)
17 John 13:4–15. Author's adaptation
18 John 14:16–17 (RSV)
19 John 16:12–13 (RSV)

Chapter 13

1 Abu Yazid al-Bistami, from Nicholson, R A, *Translations of Eastern Poetry and Prose*, Cambridge University Press, Cambridge, 1922
2 *Collins English Dictionary and Thesaurus*, HarperCollins, Glasgow, 1993
3 Matthew 26:36; Mark 14:32
4 *Brewer's Dictionary of Phrase and Fable*, centenary edition, Cassell & Company, London, 1977
5 Matthew 26:36–46; Mark 14:32–42; Luke 22:40–46. Author's adaptation
6 John 12:1–8. Author's adaptation
7 The denarius is given as a day's wage in the parable of the Labourers in the Vineyard. Matthew 20:1–16
8 Suarès, Carlo, *The Cipher of Genesis*, Stuart and Watkins, London, 1970, p 64
9 Matthew 26:14–16
10 Matthew 26:20–25; Mark 14:17–21; Luke 22:14–22; John 13:21–30. Author's adaptation
11 Matthew 27:3–5
12 For Joseph, *see* Genesis 41:46. For David, *see* 2 Samuel 5:4
13 John 18:10–11
14 Matthew 16:15–23; Mark 8:29–33. Author's adaptation
15 *The New Oxford Annotated Bible with the Apocrypha*, p 1193
16 ibid, p 518
17 John 13:33–38. Author's adaptation
18 Mark 13:35–36
19 Matthew 26:69–75; Mark 14:66–72; Luke 22:56–62; John 18:17, 25–27. Author's adaptation
20 Matthew 26:59–66; Mark 14:55–64; Luke 22:66–71
21 Schonfield, Hugh, *The Original New Testament*, p 44, *see* Ch 7
22 John 19:15 (RSV)
23 Matthew 27:11; Mark 15:2; Luke 23:3

24 John 18:36–38 (ONT)
25 The Qur'an 10:32
26 Luke 23:25
27 John 18:40. The comment that Bar-Abbas is 'a robber' recalls Jesus' declaration 'All who came before me are thieves and robbers'. John 10:8
28 Ravindra, Ravi, *The Yoga of the Christ*, Element Books, Shaftesbury 1990, p 205
29 Matthew 16:21; Mark 8:31; Luke 9:22
30 Luke 9:23–25 (RSV)
31 Mark 8:37 (RSV)
32 Humphreys, Christmas, *The Buddhist Way of Life*, Unwin Paperback, London 1980, p 58
33 Mark 12:41–44; Luke 21:1–4. Author's adaptation
34 Matthew 6:19–21 (RSV)
35 John 19:23 (RSV)
36 Psalm 22:16–18 (RSV)
37 Luke 23:34 (ONT)
38 Matthew 27:51; Mark 15:38; Luke 23:45
39 Matthew 27:45–46; Mark 15:33–34; Luke 23:44; Psalm 22:1
40 Luke 23:46 (RSV). *See also* Psalm 31:5

Chapter 14

1 Numbers 21:4–9
2 2 Kings 18:4
3 Schonfield, Hugh, *The Passover Plot*, pp 12–13
4 Matthew 28:6–7; Mark 16:6–7 (RSV)
5 Luke 24:4, 10
6 John 20:1–17
7 Tolstoy, Leo, *Fables and Fairy Tales*, *trans* Ann Dunnigan, New American Library, New York, 1962, p 80
8 John 20:17 (RSV)
9 Mark 16:19 (RSV). Traditionally Mark ends at 16:8. The remaining verses are considered to be a later addition.
10 Luke 24:50–51 (RSV)
11 Acts 1:7–11 (RSV)
12 Acts 2:1–4 (RSV)
13 Acts 2:5–13
14 Acts 2:9–17 (RSV); *see* Joel 2:28
15 Acts 2:41
16 Mark 14:28 (RSV)

17 John 21:1–13. Author's adaptation
18 Luke 5:1–11
19 Matthew 13:47 (RSV)
20 Schonfield, Hugh, *The Original New Testament*, pp 531–2; Nicoll, Maurice, *The New Man*, p 79. *See* Ch 11
21 Matthew 16:17
22 John 21:15–19. Author's adaptation
23 Matthew 16:1–4
24 Matthew 12:38–40
25 Matthew 16:17
26 John 1:42
27 Watts, Alan, *Behold the Spirit*, Random House/Vintage Books, New York 1972, p 72

SELECT BIBLIOGRAPHY

As St Bernard of Chartres said: 'We are like dwarfs seated on the shoulders of giants; we see more things than the ancients and things more distant, but this is due neither to the sharpness of our own sight, nor to the greatness of our own stature, but because we are raised and borne aloft on that giant mass' of those who have travelled the same road before us. In choosing to confine this bibliography to those books that have had influence on the interpretation of the gospel story presented in the preceding pages, I acknowledge with gratitude the debt I owe the authors and translators of these works.

Anonymous, *The Cloud of Unknowing and Other Works*, *trans* Clifton Wolters, Penguin Books, Harmondsworth, 1978

Dating from the latter half of the fourteenth century, this collection of mystical writings on the path to realizing our inherent union with God is characterized by its simplicity and directness: 'At this stage you are to think of God in the same way that you think of yourself, and of yourself as you do of God, namely that he is as he is and you are as you are. In this way your thinking will not be dissipated or confused but unified in him who is all; never forgetting, of course, this difference: that he is your being, and not you his.' (From *The Epistle of Privy Counsel*, p 162.) Clifton Wolters' translation is both eloquent and highly readable. He also translated three further tracts by the author of *The Cloud of Unknowing*, which were published as *A Study of Wisdom* (SLG Press, Oxford, 1980).

de Caussade, Jean-Pierre, *The Sacrament of the Present Moment*, *trans* Kitty Muggeridge, Fount Paperbacks, London, 1981

Jean-Pierre de Caussade was spiritual director to the Nuns of the Visitation in Nancy from 1731 to 1740. Known in France as *L'Abandon à La Providence Divine*, this work was originally transcribed from de Caussade's notes in 1740, after he had left Nancy, by the secretary of the convent, Mère Thérèse de Rosen. Sharing the directness of *The Cloud of Unknowing*, its words of inspiration, consolation and practical advice likewise address themselves to those who choose to travel the path of self-abandonment: 'When souls discover the divine purpose, they put aside all pious works, systems, books, ideas, spiritual advisers, in order to be alone under the sole guidance of God and his purpose.' (p 97) Kitty Muggeridge translated a second volume of de Caussade's writings entitled *The Spiritual Letters of Jean-Pierre de Caussade* (Fount Paperbacks, London, 1986).

Huxley, Aldous, *The Perennial Philosophy*, Triad Grafton Books, London, 1985

First published in 1946 and defined by Huxley as 'an anthology of the Perennial Philosophy', this selection of writings from the spiritual traditions of East and West is arranged according to a number of themes relating to our direct experience of Reality. The writings are not only connected by Huxley's elucidating – and at times trenchant – commentary; they speak with one voice in their expression of that universal wisdom and understanding which is both the essence and hallmark of true religion.

Jaynes, Julian, *The Origin of Consciousness in the Breakdown of the Bicameral Mind*, Houghton Mifflin, Boston, 1990

As a psychological work Julian Jaynes' theory of the origin of consciousness may have its critics; but as a possible explanation for the origin of the gods – and their subsequent demise and rise in human consciousness – this is a thought-provoking book which offers an alternative perspective on the evolution of religion and religious experience.

Mack, Burton L, *The Lost Gospel*, Element Books, Shaftesbury, 1993

The 'lost gospel' at the centre of Professor Mack's compelling exploration of the origins of Christianity is the 'Book of Q'. Taking its name from the German word *Quelle*, meaning 'source', Q is a lost collection of the sayings of Jesus which biblical scholars have identified as the common source for material used by the authors of Matthew and Luke when writing their own, narrative gospels. In addition to providing the reader with a modern interpretation of the full text of Q, Professor Mack examines the beliefs held by the 'people of Q' and the making of the Christian myth.

Mâle, Emile, *The Gothic Image*, *trans* Dora Nussey, Collins/Fontana, London, 1961

Emile Mâle's classic was originally published in French in 1910, and in English in 1913 under the title *Religious Art in France: XIII Century – A Study in Medieval Iconography and its Sources of Inspiration*. I bought this book while studying painting at art school in the 60s, but only really began to appreciate its contents when working as a tour guide in France in the 70s, and again when teaching art history in the 80s. I rediscovered it, so to speak, while writing *The Elements of Christian Symbolism* in the early 90s. My copy is now rather battered as it has been with me through four decades – and four different careers – but Mâle's insights into the minds of those who conceived and built the great Gothic cathedrals of France reveal a unified breadth of knowledge and vision that is a constant source of inspiration.

Nicoll, Maurice, *The New Man*, Shambhala, Boulder & London, 1984

If I had to name just one book as the catalyst for my own interpretation of the gospel story, it would be this book by Maurice Nicoll. I first read it during a flight from England to the USA and although the author's emphasis on the psychological meaning of the gospels – which is perfectly natural as Nicoll was an eminent psychologist – now seems a bit exaggerated at times, I freely recommend it to any reader who wishes to explore the gospels further. I also recommend *The Mark* (Shambhala 1985), which the author was working on at the time of this death in 1953.

Pagels, Elaine, *The Gnostic Gospels*, Penguin Books, Harmondsworth, 1982

This stimulating and highly readable book interprets the 'gnostic' manuscripts found at Nag Hammadi in 1945 within the context of the controversies that preoccupied early Christianity. As Professor Pagels is careful to point out: 'The task of the historian . . . is not to advocate any side, but to explore the evidence – in this instance, to attempt to discover how Christianity originated.' But the author is no ordinary historian. She has a gift for bringing alive the past and relating it to the issues that concern us in our own time. I also recommend Professor Pagels' later book, *Adam, Eve, and the Serpent* (Penguin Books 1990).

Perry, Whitall N, *A Treasury of Traditional Wisdom*, Perennial Books, Bedfont, 1981

This 'Summa of the Philosophia Perennis' extends over 1,000 pages and takes the form of a spiritual journey 'towards recovery of the Primordial Self . . . which in essence "we" have never ceased to be'. Varying in length from a few words to a page or more, the thousands of quotations drawn from the world's diverse spiritual traditions are arranged in a thematic sequence that reflects the underlying unity of different spiritual perspectives and possible approaches to the Truth. Whether one chooses to read it through from beginning to end or dip into it at random, this book is a veritable mine of wisdom and inspiration.

Ross, Hugh McGregor, *The Gospel of Thomas*, William Sessions Ltd, The Ebor Press, York 1987

Hugh McGregor Ross has studied both the text and meaning of the Gospel of Thomas over many years. This little book presents a calligraphic rendering of the text, which serves to remind the reader of the hand-written original, and some helpful explanatory notes. I also recommend the author's *Thirty Essays on the Gospel of Thomas* (Element Books, Shaftesbury, 1990).

Watts, Alan, *Behold the Spirit*, Vintage Books, New York, 1972

Alan Watts is probably best known for his Buddhist writings such as *The Way of Zen* (1957) and the part he played in interpreting Eastern thought to a Western audience. One of his lesser known works, *Behold the Spirit* (1947) was first published during what Watts describes as 'the experiment' of trying to immerse himself in Christianity, to the extent of becoming a priest of the Anglican Communion. Subtitled 'A study in the necessity of mystical religion', *Behold the Spirit* is an impassioned plea for us to abandon our ego-centred dualism and realize our inherent union with God. Criticized at the time for its 'creeping pantheism', the essence of the book is summed up in Watts' preface to the new edition: 'The whole point of the Gospel is that everyone may experience union with God in the same way and to the same degree as Jesus himself.' I also recommend *Myth and Ritual in Christianity* (Beacon Press, Boston, 1968) by the same author.

INDEX

Sabbath law 150, 153
Sadducees 92, 146, 149, 152,
    168–9, 205
Salome 196
salvation, as meaning of 'Jesus' 110
Sanhedrin 68, 190–1
satan (original meaning) 188
Sayers, Dorothy L 37
Schonfeld, Hugh 70, 112, 195
scribes 92, 146, 150–1, 153,
    154–5, 156
Sea of Galilee 55, 57, 201, 203
    as metaphor 139, 142–3, 202
Seal of Solomon 98
Second Coming 50, 199
self and Self 172 *see also* will
self-image 32, 33–4
self-knowledge 66–8
separation 46, 47–9, 159, 168
Sermon on the Mount 45, 89,
    132, 165
Shavuot 199
Simeon 109–10
Similitudes of Enoch 70
Simon Bar-Jona (Simon Peter)
    see Peter
sin 159
    as 'missing the mark' 35, 42,
        130–1, 145
    'sinning' woman 143–4
    and suffering 52–3, 130
Solomon 101
'Son of Man' 70
sons/brothers analogy 119–23
sophia perennis xvi, 5, 13, 15,
    23, 72–3
Spirit, the
    born of xx, 68, 118–23, 131
    as breath 159
    as Breath of God 24, 69, 86, 87,
        118, 184
    as Bridegroom 41, 160, 164,
        166, 167
    community of xviii, 207
    as creative force 23, 25, 28
    dissemination of 199, 200
    as Divine Will/Will of God 63, 148
    as eternal life 53, 132
    as field of energy 53, 54
    as fire 200
    as God 195–6
    as gospel message and messenger
        128

as Jesus xviii, 50–1, 54, 58, 64,
    68–70, 108–9, 110–11, 112, 116,
    118, 122,
127–8, 136, 144, 149, 151, 154,
    164, 166, 167, 176, 178, 179,
    188, 192–3, 198
as life-force xvi, 32, 54, 81
as Light of the World 132
outpouring of 28, 134, 136–7, 138,
    149, 185, 200
personification of xviii, 50–1, 54,
    64, 164
Self-revelation of 65, 105, 108, 109,
    113, 115, 125, 127, 132, 133,
    138, 140, 166, 179–80, 184
as symbolic number 184, 186–7,
    200–1
as wind 68, 69, 128, 200
as Word 51, 103, 105, 107, 108,
    110, 112, 113, 115, 123, 200
spiritual blindness 62, 94, 131, 155
spiritual consciousness (new covenant)
    xvi, xx, 36, 85, 90–8, 107, 111,
    181, 196
    embodied by Jesus 94, 105, 106,
        109, 112, 114, 116–17, 134–5,
        142, 156, 188
    emergence at the Last Judgement
        85–7, 89–90
    emergence through last
        temptation 125
    established during Last Supper 178
    incompatibility with man-and-God
        128–9, 147, 148, 152
    and knowledge of God xvi, 85–6,
        93, 89, 93, 107, 123, 171, 176,
        194, 196, 197
    and obsolescence of Law 199–200
    proclaimed in Old Testament 26–7,
        85–6, 107, 115–16, 121,
        125, 171
    through resurrection 87, 170, 197
    symbolised by new garment 152
    symbolised by wine 152, 167
spiritual empowerment xix, xx,
    128–45
spiritual expansion and integration
    32, 172
spiritual food 42, 79, 124, 150–1,
    175–6, 202
    definition of 136–7
spiritual journey xviii, 32, 99, 101,
    139–40